MW01599173

THAT FINE INABILITY TO SPEAK

a novel by
Ed Herring

Copyright © 1997 by Ralph Edward Herring

All rights reserved

No part of this book may be reproduced without written permission from the publisher or copyright holder, except for a reviewer who may quote brief passages in a review; nor may any part of this book be transmitted in any form or by any means electronic, mechanical, photocopying, recording or other, without prior written permission from the publisher or copyright holder.

ISBN 1-885003-17-X

Robert D. Reed Publishers   San Francisco

With Thanks Respectively to W. Faulkner, T.S. Eliot, E.A. Robinson and T.H. Benton:

> THERE are some kinds of writing that you have to
> do very fast, like riding a bicycle on a tightrope...
> I listen to the voices,
> and when I put down what the voices say,
> it's right. Sometimes I don't like what
> they say, but I don't change it.
>
>   – William Faulkner
>   from <u>Faulkner-Cowley File</u>

> What does it mean, this barren age of ours?
> Here are the men, the women, and the flowers,
> The seasons, and the sunset, as before.
> What does it mean? Shall there not one arise
> To wrench one banner from the western skies,
> And mark it with his name forever?
>
>   – E.A. Robinson

> I have heard the mermaids singing, each to each
> I do not think that they will sing to me.
> I have seen them riding seaward on the waves
> Combing the white hair of the waves blown back
> When the wind blows the water white and black.
>
>   – T.S. Eliot

> and the wisdom of Thomas Hart Benton who said:
>
> What is called society is, of course, like the
> froth on a glass of beer, of no consequence.
>
>   – from <u>An Artist in America</u>

I dedicate this book to RAY BRADBURY
—he who is always there for me.

And to Special Friends Jack Haley, Bette Reese, John Powers and Ruby Herring.

All of the characters depicted in this book are ficticious and do not represent any actual persons, living or dead.

CONTENTS

1 NO LONGER ABOVE IT ALL

Ray Landre was positive that he had no electrodes attached to him yet there was a distinct pain in his groin, his chest and his temples. He had just made the ascent to Glacier Point and basked in a brief respite: he gazed across the chasm to peaks of snow and felt the cold gusts of wind stab at his burning esophagus and lungs. The pain in the calves felt good as though the pumping of the blood had invigorated all of his vital veins; the muscles were red from the torture. To be up in the white and green of the pines, to be surrounded by God's clouded breath proved exactly what he needed now that all was about to change. He had serious decisions to make and the drive from Long Beach, from the sad ocean with its refinery stench, seemed to regenerate him much like purchasing a redwood burl and getting loaded and spacing out and just imagining its growth.

Since his resignation from teaching, gardening's appeal as a new vocation grew upon him. The pain tugged again at his groin; he recalled driving home late last evening and viewing the raucousness in the backyard that presented a chiaroscuro silhouette of skunks mating on the concrete patio. He queried "Is this, too, what my love-life's future, a bleak outlook on emotional cement, is to be?"

He blinked his dark, long eyelashes as quivering tails of black and white stripes put a period at the end of his thoughts. He wished he could retreat into the lie of his gins; the fierce belief that we all must magnify time to defeat the lines of waiting for something to happen and the appearance of the enigmatic blue-black adversary to bear its ugly intention.

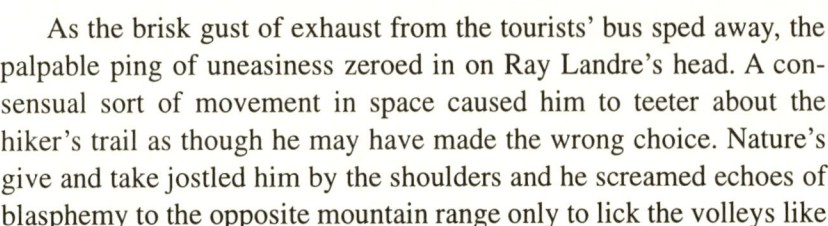

As the brisk gust of exhaust from the tourists' bus sped away, the palpable ping of uneasiness zeroed in on Ray Landre's head. A consensual sort of movement in space caused him to teeter about the hiker's trail as though he may have made the wrong choice. Nature's give and take jostled him by the shoulders and he screamed echoes of blasphemy to the opposite mountain range only to lick the volleys like a child at Halloween's front door.

Ray calmed himself as he prepared for the descent, some four and one-half miles of switchbacks among irritating flies and succumbed to the caution about the rattlesnakes or bears. His only companion was a memory from yesterday when he had helped a friend during a gardening job. The client's young son Jessie had pranced onto the front porch in his ghost's sheet so oblivious to the workaday world—that sort of nonchalance Ray now needed in his effort to leave behind the pose of responsibilities and cordiality required to stay on any job. Jessie was toting a cardboard box for taking animals to the veterinarian.

Ray, to make conversation, asked, "Hi, Jessie, are you going to the vet today?"

"Not me silly, the cat is going to the vet," he emphatically responded.

After a decade of teaching high school English, Ray had forgotten such innocence, such freshness. His trip to Yosemite had subconsciously been an attempt to rediscover such innocence or at least to feel reassured that it still existed. Making the descent, he imagined young Jessie tagging along behind him, occasionally stopping for a sip from the boy scout canteen. Friends were good and helpful. Ray felt the distinct presence of John Muir and wished they, too, could have been friends. Ray slipped through that Sierra granite where form overcomes one; El Capitan's nose peered down at his antlike being. Quaking birch leaves, nature's tiny earrings whispered long past secrets of his mother slipping down to the basement for an afternoon of ironing: the Merced streambed carried a family of deer to Ray's perimeter of breath—they would not allow him to pet them. He slithered through the valley floor back to camp.

Now that Ray was fortyorsomething, jobless and in the midst of bachelorhood he hefted an additional amount of tugging at his innards. His grandmother and father had made it uncomfortably clear that

2

unless he soon found his partner for life, the Landre line was doomed. The accusation was along the lines of self-chosen genocide. Ray held on to the inappropriate parallel to his distant uncle Arleigh who had found marital bliss at age 55. He had hoped that his decision, one summer vacation from teaching, to participate in a NASA co-experiment with Russia might satiate his family's desire for some sort of immortal recognition; however, their collective response had been one of disbelief and disgust. Since Ray was working out with weights at the time of volunteering, as the lady coordinator had looked at his biceps and ogled him upon the treadmill assured him he was just what they were looking for. He had completed numerous treks to the aviation facility and was near to signing away three precious months of his life to isolation one Saturday morning when the head nurse who had been assigned to draw more blood had done all the wrong procedures. She had blamed the low temperature of the lab for her inability to find his vein but since they were supposedly the experts, he was reluctant to follow through with the experiment. Incompetency abounded.

Ray's return drive to Long Beach refused all definition of trajectory: he blazed past vanilla pudding landscapes and masturbated past ice floes that didn't exist. He viewed shooting stars, meteor showers unpredicted on radio reports but nevertheless the moon-bathed terrain appeared promising. He understood how the heavens made love to the gently rolling hillsides and the stark crevices of cement. His mind became transfixed to childhood, sweeter than that of Jessie's. He rejoiced that he had met Christ and puberty simultaneously over his mother's ironing board in the basement surrounded with its mildew and poisoned mushrooms that smiled and grew in the cement walls caked with elm root and mice eyes — van Gogh pinheads of swirling matter. He recalled sensuously pressing his penis to the surfboard shaped board. He painfully reviewed the drowning minister during his baptismal and fought to live and suck breath from his ordained fingers, he rushed through the messy ordeal (wet gonads knocking as visions of his father shaving and a larger penis dangling at the basin. He painfully reviewed the drowning minister during his baptismal and fought to live and suck—Ray couldn't fathom why familial heads sent others to their various atoning hells while choosing to stay at home in fetal umbra.

3

A resentful, barely teen-age Ray coursed into his destiny, his pain, his torture: no matter, he began the mile walk, head held high in spite of dripping trail of holy water about his sweet white ass and ankles as the town queer pursued carside Ray's singular day of salvation, in powder blue pants and black and white oxfords: Ray acquiesced to his oddball haunting, "Want a ride home, free? Come on, get in, I know you wanna...."

There it was again, that give and take that Ray Landre had known all his life (appearance versus reality his sordid high school English instructor had pedantically pointed out as they matriculated through existentialism and Wordsworth and Tolstoy and Greek drama) The blushes, the reoccurring metaphor of his life, the archangel Michael seducing Ray into attending Hollywood Russian Orthodox Church services in his late teens; Ray had heard such moanings behind the altar, the icons—living in Los Angeles but wishing he were rolling in the autumn leaves of the ozarks—Ray remembered that son of his childhood minister that groped him at choir practice; was it a fantasy, a nightmare? It had happened and Ray had gone through forty years with similar guilt over incidents he had neither participated in nor pre-cipitated. Ray recalled his mother's rare occupation of stretching starched fine white curtains across the curtain stretchers positioned about the living room much like some Chinese dynasty must have dis-played folding artistic screens. That pain again attacked Ray's crotch as though curtain stretcher needles had taken pot shots at his penis...Father, Father, forgive....

Ray squeegeed through the Los Angeles silt; the moonlight creat-ed a filagree over the large open white space. Incense of the spent can-dle dropped by the fire hydrant's leak flooded the rearview mirror and he rolled up the car window to shut out the shoddy crucifix's crying into the night.

II

Ray's late night arrival into Long Beach caught him a bit groggy. As he complied with the stop and go of Long Beach Blvd.'s traffic lights, he could smell his past within the confines of his VW bug. He rolled down the car window. The Camel's smoke burned his tired, foolscap eyes; the smoke remained from his carpool colleague's cigarette that had permeated the freon-cooled air of the night. It was going to be another evening spent alone in front of the Marx Brothers spoof or a Ken Russell extravaganza'd flop like THE BOY FRIEND. The selection truly would make no difference. He would push past his thirsty hanging baskets of Wandering Jew and drooping coleus; he would retract each pinched-in calf and foot up the harsh incline to his rented flat where Samantha, his cat, would roll over, playing pussy-dead, at the turn of his key. The coffee table would still be dusty and riddled with butts overrunning his only two ashtrays: the ornate alabaster one, a gift from a Mexican weekend, and the other terribly gauche black plastic one stolen from Circus-Circus in Vegas some millenia ago.

The tv, the cat, the plants all went unfed. They could, respectively, he had found, survive. Even his prize oscar had once endured two weeks without gold fish because of some unknown disease; perhaps it was ich, white spot, fin and tail rot; a half dozen phone calls to tropical fish stores in the yellow pages had not resolved the inevitable. But that was some months ago, and he was again on some sort of feeding cycle. Gold dust expunged in wet bursts from either gill as the entrails were efficiently processed. Although Ray never minded this daily ritual, this necessity for survival, he often wondered what his students, now ex-students, the ones who "turned on" might have thought upon watching such a gluttonous and paganistic orgy. Eventually, the water returned to water much as two lovers, enraged at one another over some trifle difference, then the undulating emotions subsided into a kiss and a passive embrace.

Ray recalled the definition of a day that had gone well. He had successfully given two vocabulary quizzes; verbally assaulted two classes of sophomores for failing to appreciate the unique juxtaposition of the California-Caesar/Portia-Brutus love scenes in The Bard's play; and ultimately, he had made an ass of himself by walking, tippy-toe, with pursed lips, about the desks of some fifteen seniors in a dastardly effort to dramatize Robinson's superb diction in labeling Richard Cory as "imperially slim" as opposed to "just slim."

Many of Landre's colleagues had, when coffee-break allowed, accused him of being particularly prejudiced against one of his former Jewish students. The girl had been one of those tag-alongs, a pathetic, freckled child, rather buxom and shy. It had definitely been one of the classic hate-love relationships of all times. Ray had inventoried the student's abilities: it seemed that she was far better at conceptualizing plot and theme of challenging works like Guy de Maupassant's "A Coup d'Etat" or Tolstoy's "How Much Land Does a Man Need" by going to the chalk board and rendering a schematic drawing, respectively, of the statue's proximity to the townspeople in the town square as his schnozzle was blown off, or she could, after much deliberation and fidgeting (accompanied by whispering of her classmates behind her pigtailed back), draw a cemetery plot stenciled six by six by three. The only praise or condonation arose from the fact that Ray, as her instructor, couldn't draw a straight line if his tenure depended upon it.

Finally, the day for a parent conference had come. He was shocked when, in the course of admonishing their daughter for being the only child who refused to join the others on two "highly important field trips," the parents flippantly opposed him. The first had been a trek to a local zoo—the parents dismissed such exercise as time idly spent. The second had been a reluctance on the part of the darling to see the music center's revival of MAN OF LA MANCHA. The mother flicked her cigarette ash into her styrofoam cup at the very mention of the production, tilted her half-rimmed bifocal in a condescending manner, "After all, Mr. Landre, LA MANCHA is mediocre theatre." He had argued that they were discussing a mere sophomore in high school and perhaps something about the experience of traveling to the theatre with her peers might be rewarding; perhaps she would interact with her peers or hum the melody to "The Impossible Dream" while riding home on the school bus.

Dear Darling Helene, along with the alabaster ashtray and the oscar and Samantha—Helene, too, resided in Landre's flat. He could demand her presence in the bottom of his martini at the switch of a light. He could summon her threatening eyes to the swirling hand-pressed crystal he had bought in London. Stacks of unread essays sat about the living room and lined the walls of the toilet. He could categorize them by the various shades of yellowing due to age, due to punctuality and due dates. He used to fear that he might some-day be Graded himself for Negligence; but thus far, some ten years of moving through life a veritable Felix Krull conning his way as

6

Instructor, no one had inquired about the blasted sheets, not one parent or administrator, nor colleague, let alone the student who had submitted it for the master's perusal had challenged him. And now his resignation had nullified any such possibilities anyway. And to counter his family's peril of lineage, he merely needed such procreative thoughts of Helene.

The phone, although he initially had thought it Sam's tinker-bell, precluded his much needed piss. He had to send flying a set of "MacBeth's" to unleash the red cord and receiver. A wrong number: "Celia?" "Shit," he thought. "I wish some Celia were here instead of..." instead of a photo taken of himself and Brenda as they had lounged playfully on a misshapened juniper bough along the Big Sur coastline in a plasticized black and white photo taken by some bystander who obviously had had a palsied hand for snapping photographs. It wasn't a good photo, but then the memories weren't particularly good of the weekend, either. She had tired of horse-back riding. She had tired of the pool side. She hadn't seen "a single celebrity like Kim Novak," and Nepenthe's had definitely been a drag. In short, being with Brenda had proven to be much like spending the weekend with one of his students; the chronic complainer—even the mere mention of Brautigan would not have penetrated.

Brautigan reminded Landre of his army days. The pleasant times. Cleaning latrines, crawling beneath live fire, forging signatures on T.D.Y. ledgers for superiors because of the Inspector General's inevitable visit. Brautigan and his pussy-cat toughness reminded Landre of his old army buddie MAUER (or as he had said, "Landre ol' boy, you know what my name means: it's German and it means 'wall'; that's me, a wall" and he'd flex his bicep, implore Ray to feel it and then insist that Landre hop onto the recycled Harley for a spin. After all, Landre was the only individual on the Long Island post who had the guts, or lack of brains, to chance the risk of dying a misguided macho death nightly. Landre would find himself leaping over uprooted tree trunks and bits of two-by-fours in deserted housing tracts. The iron steed would race through the dark night. Landre would hold tightly to the wall before him. Landre looked at the walls in his pink-tiled bathroom. He wanted to retch. It was disgusting what his life of inactivity had become. He wished that that had been Mauer on the phone

7

once he thought about it. How could he take a shit in a pink bathroom when he had just experienced deja vu of returning a set of essays to puberty-puzzled prima donnas and studly football players and to the Helene's of the world—each of them had been disappointed in his own way that Mr. Landre "had failed to grasp the essence of their sensitivity to Lorraine Hansberry." They glared at him as though he were an invulnerable wall. He was not a wall. He, too, would like to take his class of thirty and perch them on some phallic black Harley Davidson about the size of the wooden horse of Troy, take them on a joy ride instead of subjecting them to the daily downer that he and they sensed but had never admitted.

What happened next stunned Ray Landre. He stripped the threads to his finger print on his left index finger as he opened Sam's can of cat food. Sam was a nose away and unknowingly licked Ray's wound. Ray knocked Sam across the kitchen with his other hand. He hadn't meant to but his wounds had always been personal...like guarding the stacks of unread papers...like the black and white photograph, like the phone call from Mauer that never materialized. Licking one's wound was something that Brenda would have prided herself in doing. He was sure that the lick of blood would make Sam sick but he had no idea what sort of remedy to administer. He thought the phone rang again. Perhaps a signal. But there was his wound to be attended. Sam kept moseying around the half-opened can and the possibility of cutting her nose disturbed Ray as he meandered to the medicine cabinet in the pink, slick-tiled room. The cat meowed several clouds away. Ray removed the iodine from the shelf. The cotton swab smarted. Smarted. God, he wished so. He hadn't seen a smart person in his classes since "the lazy-writer" Charlie Gerson had entered Harvard. And the rumor was that he had dropped out of Harvard—only to corroborate the English Department's concerted professional fears that the boy might have proven to have more potential than originally thought. At least Charles had been one of the students who could differentiate between illusion and allusion. He had understood metaphor. He, now that he was a young adult and out of high school, most likely understood that Ray's hurt did not hurt. It was all expected. The corn on his toe would brush against a stack of paper in the middle of the night and the paper-cut would cause him to stumble and he would utter foul words. The phone would ring at three am and it would neither be Brenda—nor Mauer! He would probably be billed, erroneously, for the call from some god-forsaken outpost like Leesville, Louisiana, where he had taken ten hellish weeks of basic training. He recalled that everything lethal milled around him in that red soil, ants and rattlers and poisonous spiders all slept with him in his sleeping bag. Ray would squint his eyes shut and say foolish prayers that he might escape Vietnam duty. Poison ivy was the land cover. It was his longest nightmare on record. About then Ray heard a gray rat as it was struggling in the trap which his landlord had set in the rafters of the broom closet. He would not check it until morning—which for Landre was a misnomer. He seldom slept therefore morning never came. He didn't empty the ashtrays often because their fullness reminded him of the times that friends had dropped by for casual conversation about Stanley Kunitz and Genet and other feasible miracles. If the oscar's aquarium light remained on overnight, Ray understood it might die— it needed its rest. Ray turned off the light for it and reclined in his stratolounger for the evening's treasures. Yosemite and its permanence in granite became such an ephemeral memory. Stacks of local newspapers and the want ad sections effaced layers of pine needles and student essays and successful relationships. He was so exhausted he even forgot Midnight's ritual. His newest hobby, the orchids, yawned in his direction.

III.

Ray Landre still had not come to terms with his resignation from teaching. As in so many nuances of his life, he had taken the coward's path: after ten years of coddling his pubescent dears, he had walked into a quiet, summer office to leave his brief note with his principal's temporary secretary. All seemed so simplistic, rather overlooking his anal-retentive personality, as though he had escaped restless nights of sour stomach and gargantuan guilt feelings to let-down so many parents and favorite pupils and friends. As cowardly an exit as the Oz's Lion might have chosen. His apologia omitted any referents like endless mornings of omelettes, coffee or gin fizzes with his ex-colleague and best friend Jon Cleveland. At least Cleveland had had courage to divorce his blonde angel of a decade, submit his resignation

9

mid-semester and fly off to Paris where he had worked the vineyards, built furniture for theatrical sets in Montmarte and willingly gone without the false luxuries of So. Cal.

Ray recalled that ancient job interview: when asked by the principal who he most related to he responded, "Stevens' man with the blue guitar." Ray Landre's secrets of existence, in fact, were most like a blue man with a guitar. He had given up hope of producing the great American novel in spite of very supportive critiques "You're a poet. You write well. Do you know this, or guess at the truth of your writing well?" Now his poetry calmed him; his on-going collection of verse resided under a catch-all title ranging from The Art of Embalming, To the City Rome, Room and Board to most recently Pruning to Shape. The evolution was endless and enhancing and necessary (and he was surprised to learn so late in life that other greats like the Sylvia Plathes had similarly nurtured and altered their titles).

IV.

"But there are just too many clocks here. Don't you understand? I just can't drop my dress and be comfortable and let you step into me and well, BE, I mean just Be and let you penetrate me and act like the ticking doesn't bother me because it does—it positively vernalizes me—can't you understand that?"

"Ya, heh yaya...but the beauty is you never know what time it is; never know what commitment you've just missed or must yet be fulfilled; for example, should one be at work, sleeping, grocery shopping, taking a piss or whatever. Now, take off your dress, PLEASE."

"Your please is an amendment I can do without. Besides, my answer is NO."

"But never knowing the time; isn't that fantastic? Doesn't that intrigue you? Surely, Sartre or Red Skelton had something to say about that, too. Did you ever read Faulkner? Certainly Quentin's mainstreet walks with the weight of time and death upon him is relative to our daily ennui; and certainly Dilsey's five o'clock solution was charming. I think that Lennie..."

"Who in the hell is Lennie?"

"Oh, now I see," as he zipped up his pants, "we're really communicating. I was going to say, Lennie was a faceless mechanism; a gut-

10

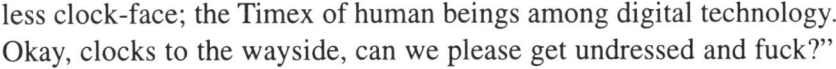

less clock-face; the Timex of human beings among digital technology. Okay, clocks to the wayside, can we please get undressed and fuck?"

The phone kept ringing and ringing: Ray dislodged himself from his recurring dream of clocks ticking and endless parade of gorgeous babes. He rolled over but the caller had disengaged himself: he punched the answering machine's guts and it spewed:

"But piles of it, Ray, dog shit all over the place—you have to do something about it; my neighbors are complaining, they're threatening law suits, the Humane Society will come down on me; they're talking quarantine for God's sake—I don't even live there, I just own the property and I've got my hands full here with crazy ol' Etta-Mary an t'other inmates..." Beep.

Beep, and the tirade was over. Ray tried to discern whether he was asleep or up taking his Pavlovian piss.

Since Ray was already awake he decided to establish his unemployed daily routine. He showered and dressed and fed his newly acquired nuisance of a Lab which answered to the name Midnight (or today "shithead"). He was coal black. Ray had also been warned that Midnight had bitten numerous people. He hadn't minded taking it on weekend drives to Dana Point or on the back roads to Lake Elsinore, drives where he had seen abandoned autos and runaway boats on trailers and an occasional shooting star. Midnight sat in the passenger's seat as attentive to it all as any human might have done.

Ray needed to drive his VW to the repair shop. Maybe escaping the confines of the apartment and its demands, like recent visits to the various nurseries, would immerse himself in his gardening. He thought how confining everything had become, the skunks mating on the concrete patio late last evening: his aorta kept syncopation to the spasmodic skunk tails and renewed anticipation, even romantically, popped to jolt his universe.

He might emerge from the trenches with parboiled opinions.

His teenage-self remembered being so angry at his father. The Santa Claus incident he had liked to call it. He had even versified a telling "self-portrait:"

> Nestled in all this suffering
> the most provoking, Father

11

how he drunkened his perplexed psyche
over birthing a fragile elf not mechanical.

I worked hours on a cardboard santa
in the musty basement of secrets
to erect on the front porch
only to have it burned in an oil barrel
singed the appletree limbs.

If only he could have praised
the caricature "not bad"
but how he looked me in the eye
and smirked to ma, "that one ain't mine."

" My Dad," Ray mused, "what a pain in the royal ass."

Now to add insult to injury, Ray had no idea, no sense of direction;
he had fairly decided upon becoming a gardener. That choice should
afford him opportunity to be his own boss, set his own hours and in
general be left alone. He had come to positively hate the masses. Their
incompetence, frivolity, shallowness greatly depressed him. But to set
out tender young shoots of lobilia or implant pregnant bulbs of daf-
fodil and tulip excited him. He had copious doubts as to whether he
could pull off this masquerade; however, pondering his past decade of
posing as an English instructor fairly convinced him he might also disguise his horticultural inadequacies.

Ray had tried his hand at other charades. That great New York
connoisseur Scott Meredith had praised his fiction as promising but
not yet publishable; "too episodic." Ray had tossed off such evaluation
as he recalled the careful structuring of Gatsby; "no true plot develop-
ment" as Ray recalled _To the Lighthouse_ or for that matter Garcia
Marquez. The writer's school had highly praised Ray's short fiction
but proceded to point out the imperative stylistic device of alternating
narration then dialog (Ray smiled at the lengthy page-paragraphs of
Faulkner and Marquez).

V.

Once Ray had dropped off the automobile, he chose to walk the
distance of ten blocks home. As he passed the New World Pharmacy,

12

he overheard two ladies as they craned their necks toward the second story across the street. It was an old red brick building with a store front below but lace curtains encased a silhouette of a lady as she gazed into the unique Long Beach mix of coastal fog and smoke.

"Is that a transvestite?"

"Where?"

"Up in that apartment window."

Ray silently recited, "to prepare a face to meet the faces that you meet...." as he eavesdropped on the two ladies.

"No, but it's rumored when she was young and married that she and her husband would swap clothes. Some felt she was more handsome than he as a mister. My son said there is a framed photograph of them on the television."

"Didn't the husband mind being thought of as lady-like?"

"Not really, but they didn't tell everyone. He was in banking you know. Once he died she actually began to take on masculine features—sort of let herself go. Old Rhino-snout the neighborhood kids call her. Cruel, positively cruel you know...."

The two women sauntered into the pharmacy with an air of perfume and chattering teeth behind them. Ray resented their lack of discretion. The word *cruel* gouged him. Yes, he recalled how cruel the children could be. Additionally, Ray knew who the lady was; he had seen her at the checkout in the pharmacy before. He noticed her obvious attempt in delicately arranging her hair, an upsweep, a lazy French knot. He had seen her camouflage of frayed cuffs on her dresses, too.

The lady in question was named Etta-Mary Fordyce. Ray knew this from greetings. To live alone and be in her late sixties she was preposterous to those in her building. A passer-by in seeing the silhouette was astounded that she would spend arduous hours posing before a mirror, adjusting some new shoulder bag strap and scrutinizing herself, her prepared image for the outside world. She seemed rather taken with her own image. Her handle of "Rhinocerous Lady" came from a peculiar hobby. She collected a diverse array of rhinoceroses: miniatures in soap stone, silver, wood, crystal; medium size ones in all media as well as precious stones; large ones in African as well as Italian bronzes. And this montage of rhinos, stampeding, in place, all over her habitat, were placed about her possessions, all odd

13

dust-gatherers in a multitude of poses; charging, heads down watering or feeding on imaginary grasses; gazing into the veldt distance or dreaming of prey; delicately poised on top of the soil of a potted dracena; some were stuffed toys and guarded an entrance to bath and bedroom; some were made in Taiwan by artisans who had never seen one yet made a stab at it in copper or some cheaper alloy and it looked like a cubistic rendering of a massive mouse or obese unicorn. She was considered an odd lady by what few visitors ever saw her home range.

"I've got me rhinies," she'd often quip and this possession made her feel unique. Her most treasured one was a sterling silver, signed miniature given her by an ex-lover. She was petrified to leave it setting out lest a burglar or unprincipled friend might cop it while she prepared chocolate dipped strawberries and demitasses of refrigerated Stolichnya.

Most people found it very odd, but after Mr. Fordyce passed away, all of Etta's friends referred to her as The Widow, i.e., Mrs. Willy Loman behind her back. As in the case of most widows, she found the continuance of life exasperating. Just to waste time perking a half pot of stale coffee; just to replace burned out light bulbs in silent hallways, hallways hung with once shared favorites of still lifes or seascapes from youthful holidays they had taken off the coast of Yugoslavia; and just to write insincere thank you notes about Arnie who no longer puttered around their dicondra backlawn as he had meticulously skittered along behind their pug Sapho as he tinkled his smelly decomposing yellow marks along the edge of the foundation or pooper-scoopering his "little turdies" into the dahlias which she had carefully arranged in a burst of purple and yellow rainbows.

There were the additional indignities surrounding death: sweet old Kubler-Ross didn't address herself to the finer moments of graveside visits; for example, back in 1976, in Etta's third visit to Arnie's grave within three days proved only one thing—don't leave your purse in the car. Some punks had obviously patrolled the cemetery and easily broken into and stolen her purse while she was foolishly crying and depositing fresh dahlias on the still soil that resembled the pungency of brown sugar granules spread across Arnie's non-breathing chest. The casket cost more than her fixed income allowed, but then that was to be expected, she supposed. She hated that he hadn't more thoughtfully taken care of such mundane matters. She missed him, that went unsaid; however, not so much out of romantic conceptualization as just mere routine of the mourning. He had made her life chaotic, yes, chaotic; there just wasn't a better word for it. If they were going on vacation he lost the railroad tickets (oh, not lost, misplaced as he would put it). He would have to return to the thrice-bolted door to see if the coffee machine was turned off or the trash carried out or the in-house burglar alarm was disengaged. It was a rare day when they didn't have to return for some petty purpose. She had loved Arnie: if anyone questioned that, they could read her diary or step into her subconscious attic. She must have written the phrase I LOVE HIM hundreds of times in the past forty years—who could question such devotion? On the other hand, who could have tolerated Arnie for one year let alone forty? He was the type who could saw, form, hand polish a pair of English walnut book ends or assemble an entire set of children's swings and teeter totter; he could knowledgeably discuss Joyce or Mann, and throughout all of the foregoing, he could convince any and all human beings, male or female, that he was the BEST around and yet his tragedy was he didn't really care for a solitary soul in the universe except himself. Etta-Mary began realizing this about Arnie in the third or fourth year of their marriage and why she had continued to look the other way baffled her and what few friends she confided in.

Snickering from outside her apartment, its abrasive entrance reminded Etta of her kindergarten days when she had made a movie picture of stick figures ice skating in a shoebox and she would twist the scroll for her classmates to unfold her creative story. This pleased her teacher which pleased her parents. She basked in that praise and the time, the years had passed too rapidly. Arnie, Arnie never had known her so youthful, she winced. The rhino released locomotive vapors and stamped nervously; his eyes jerked throughout the apartment. She felt small in the universe.

Etta pushed a button on the tv remote and a rhino godly galloped, head lowered, each shank and body portion a taut bag of brown leathery perfected jello male muscle, intent on galloping into the air, plunging all 6,000 pounds of determination to survive into the mud brown tarpits and gracefully exit to toss his riveted jaws about and then repeat his plunge only to emerge on the other side of the pool and charge at a concrete molded log and lazily scratch his back of his neck. He accomplished all of this, seemingly oblivious to the lady, no, to the contrary, to exhibit all of this maleness for the lady in his gaze.

The rhino disappeared behind a synthetic screen momentarily then he reappeared at the starting point again and looked poised and inscrutable. His eyes focused upon hers. As she came to an end to her calculations, amid jibberish and small droplets of moisture at her mouth, she turned off the tv, lowered her bosom again, and at this she appeared to be only half a woman or a gargantual blue skirt waiting for its other half to complete her. She sat to compose herself.

The stationary rhinos scarcely squeaked their leathery necks to acknowledge her. Their attentiveness played tricks on her, though; she could feel before hearing their swiveling massiveness, much like pushing over a row of rough-edged dominoes. Some sensor in their collective inanimate brain suggested, sleepily, that they cease communicating and eating and look around, to at least feign interest in their keeper's coming and going. She even imagined that someday she might need a walker or, god forbid, a wheelchair. The thought caused her to breathe a blush of cloud onto the chilly revealing windowpane.

"Hell, Harry," she greeted the crystal one. "Watch your weight," she grinned to the Philippine Wood one. She forced herself to look into the bedroom mirror, still bundled up like an English char woman. She loathed the widow she saw. She couldn't see her gender; she saw no "she", she saw no "he." She saw a wrinkled old mass of rhinocerotic bulges somehow asexually pieced together. Since Arnie's demise, she couldn't even own up to the expertise of screwing in a light bulb. She was content to spin onward into the vast universe, an amoebic sponge anchored to a green and brown sphere by her troop of impeccable masculine mascots.

"Little treasures, that's what ye 'rrrrr, all of ye," are the words that Ray Landre would swear he heard coming out the window as she disrobed to watch Johnny Carson reruns.

 INSIDE THE SHOP

THE NEXT MORNING Ray paid a pittance to pick up his VW. He didn't have time to fall in love; it was raining and the puffs of diesel exhaust from the idling rigs in the Winchell parking lot pulled at his lungs even before he left his double-parked VW. He loathed the crudity of every torsoed-trucker lined up before him: the flagrant red and blue tattoos of "Sal," "Mom," "Born to Lose," "Mean and Nasty;" the rusty brown rings of sweat beneath the armpits; the "God, was she great last night" syndrome of such a waiting line skeletonized Ray. With his filtered Kool slowly burning down, he reached the service window (the rainwater had collected overhead and playfully tapped the back of his hand as he thrust forth coins for a bearclaw and black coffee).

The first impression she made on Ray: she took a drag off her fag, whittled at a torn red nail and murmured some foul broken-nail bitterness, hoisted her left teat as though it were kicking inside. "Lucky me" Ray told himself, he could espy the rosy nipple peaked there for the trade, reminding him somewhat of Boucher's painting "The Bath of Diana" yet she had the potential of becoming Ivan Albright's warted "Soul Called Ida" all too soon. With such weathering complexions she might find then she wouldn't be able to sell stockings, cosmetics or donuts, let alone touch them publicly. The first words, "Emanuel, say, some help up here, get the lead out and shove that tray of apple fritters on the shelf before I shove you out in the rain." She had an unladylike way of baring her teeth as though she believed the recent unemployment figures on television.

RAIN. A phenomenon that Ray and nature could not reconcile in California. Rain arranging pigeon-shit stepping stones for the pigeon-toed truckdrivers as they queued up at the Bellflower donut shop like some caffeinic funereal procession awaiting orange and lavender puffs of confectionary nothing. The drivers kept fixed their stare upon her bulbous nipples that lounged over the counter whereas the humidity of the storm outlined them as well as liquefy her winks of iced-green mascara. She could have easily short-changed them and they might have thanked her; Ray would become one of her men in waiting or mistreat her but the dread that patters on his forehead resounds, "She'd love it, she'd love it," and the confusion continued.

The caesura didn't last long—Ray began humming an absurd melody, "Flight of the Bumblebee" as he often did while standing in lines. This curse of waiting in lines he had known in the army, the post office, pre-registration, Rams games. About that moment an earwig catapulted across the counter and his peripheral vision commingled vision and fantasies and caused him to drop his loose change that he had been rolling around inside his trouser pocket. He knew she had seen such foreplay before and he inwardly cursed the rain and insects. He felt that he was a near-native of California and therefore had a right and duty to curse the rain. Ray now stood eye-to-eye with his mistress of dough and circumscribed art (circumcised from penis to donut hole preoccupation) as she mentally took his fattening order of coconut-covered cakes. Ray felt extremely guilty for he was blowing all of Dr. Atkins' caloric counsel on one tart. He quickly remembered the self-addressed graffiti on his kitchen blackboard to "Lay Off the Pastry," but he rationalized that it was all in his trajectory: Work is at point C; Winchells lies along point B; he must commence at point A, and now he had the exposure to her juicy wares. Enough, he told himself, of my infirmities, Women, Winchells, Wet downpour. But this is the encounter that brought a lady named Ruby Frangible into Ray Landre's life.

* * *

Ray's next visit to Ruby Frangible's shop took a circuitous route. His VW had failed to start so he decided to thumb a ride. Within min-

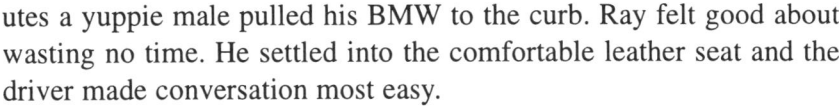

utes a yuppie male pulled his BMW to the curb. Ray felt good about wasting no time. He settled into the comfortable leather seat and the driver made conversation most easy.

"Are you married?"

"No, not yet." Visions of Ruby circled him and an erection tugged at the radio beat of M.C. Hammer.

"Well, I am. To the world's Beauty. Capital B."

"Where is she tonight?"

"Oh, she's in Paris: you'd know her if you saw her," he said with much enthusiasm; as if he had a secret he wanted to share with Ray and the world.

"What do you mean, I would know her?"

"Would you like to swing by my apartment for a while? I have loads of pictures of her. She's the gal you see on tv all the time, advertising the bras—the, you know, the cross my heart lady."

"That being so, did you say your name's John? Then why in the Sam HELL would you want to share her with me?"

"I'm just that kind of guy; I'm a very secure individual and she knows that. We could have a couple of drinks and you know, maybe just pull 'em out and unload all of that," he emphasized that as he glanced downward to Ray's unbuttoned levis.

"Thanks but no thanks; I'm on my way to a date myself tonight. If you could just let me off anywhere here on Long Beach Blvd. Thanks anyway and I'll be looking for that ad. I'll remember you when I see her. Adios." Ray felt real relief as he decided to walk the remainder of the distance.

****

This earliest sitting between Ray and Ruby aids in an apt description of a typical day for her. Heavy syrup, cherry syrup, and hot glaze seeped into the dimly-lit bedroom of Ruby Frangible. Like each evening of her existence, she awoke to the Jet-set orange beanbag chair that leaked its contents the same day she had brought it home from the Rose Bowl swap meet. The crazy glue and the clumsily placed black patch of decorator tape obtrusively made her day as she drew an analogy to her life, the stigma of perhaps her forehead being indelibly stamped with a skull and crossbones of a bottle of poison, or love and hate tattooed across her doughy smelling fingers. Her self-pity never ceased to whirl within her head like a tiny kitty's motor purring for love or attention. She, too, needed some preening, some brushing against to feel more than some goddamned wind-up, red-lipped, donut-window doll. Every morning she would toss off her gladiola yellow afghan and search for stretch marks in the giant haberdasher's mirror. She had read some article in a Lady's magazine, read that a woman ages each and every 24 hours and that she has a personal obligation to work on preventing that process from the first moment she arises in the morning. Baths. Salts. Creams. Exercises. She believed what she had read but never quite found the time to successfully combat the process. Instead, the same jolt of the smell of over-powering hot glaze being stirred by some new employee and that golden orange plastic pillion in the corner were what greeted her each day. She confessed that the yellow scheme was an attempt to hold in the sun—yet her lined drapes kept it out. She couldn't stand the sun blinding her, so the chair sufficed. After her usual allotment of draft beers, before Larry at the bar Viking Room would cut her off, mornings became more and more difficult, the stench of glaze more repugnant. The cherryooze filling was as pronounced as those mid-Missouri mornings when her grandmother used to put up her cherry preserves in huge kettles on their Tappan range. So long ago. Before all the cherries had, metaphorically, been picked.

Ruby Francis Frangible, nee Collingswood, ex-Felesky was born the only daughter to Sal and Emma Collingswood in Jefferson City, Missouri, on April 29, 1955. Her move to the golden west coast of So. Cal. had been well-conditioned by the sensual gyrations of one Elvis and a pinup of none other than Norma Jean Somebody, as well as centerfold upon centerfold falling out of school lockers and other family closets. Oh yes, her uncles had pinched her on the ass when they felt like it, and Sal and Emma had advised, "Just overlook it, darling, whenever you can." She had been told to accept monetary presents no matter what the circumstances because it didn't grow on trees nor would her happier days flourish. In short, to learn to fend for herself had been her father's sole advice. The tidbit had been ample to get her into her incessant matrimonial malaise. She had spent hours before her mother's vanity; it mirrored large feet for fifteen; thighs of promise, possibly pumped up by weekend hikes and carrying popcorn lard from behind the local movie screen, up the aisle and into her concession stand; a waist no bigger than her pet boxer's neck; and, speaking of necks, the slimsiest bit of muscle, like that of a fine thoroughbred filly. Her distinguishing mark was a strawberry birthmark on the calf of her right leg—and she would often stand on tiptoe, naked, pivot like a music box doll to indulge herself in what her father had often cuddled, "And she's got the prettiest legs in Cole County." Legs. Pshaw: foolish to digress to such nonsense she had thought. The only lingering trace of that young filly today was her birthmark (a far cry from Hawthorne's damsel, yet nice to perpetuate some element of beauty in Bellflower). Hearing such inventory, Ray briefly transposed her varied parts into an imaginary bra ad and pleasurable pain tugged again at his crotch.

Later in the interview Ruby snickered PRINCESS PAM and Ray quizzed her. The PRINCESS was a predominantly black night spot for dancing and drink-setups near the University of Missouri. While she was attending high school, she had managed to acquire a duplicate driver's license from one of her college friends and they would often make the thirty minute drive for-an evening of dancing.

As she described it, it was a marvelous world of showmanship. The premises had been an old converted theatre, floor gutted, and filled with starched white table clothes, anywhere from fifty to seventy-five tables somehow balanced on the inclined floor. There was hardly room to sidle through the narrow aisles that lead down front to a leveled floor section for dancing, and beyond that was a renovated stage for the smartly tuxedoed all-black band.

"I could easily visualize the chiaroscuro montage of electric organ and guitars and gyrating dancers and fresh white chrysanthemums in art deco black vases on each circular table."

Ruby caught herself in too much reverie and Ray shook her by the arm asking, "What are you thinking?"

"Oh, so ludicrous to say the stage held an all-black band; why more Fridays than not, the PAM featured Ike and Tina Turner and entourage. Guess you can say my formative years were weaned on The Best." She smiled knowingly.

Ruby Francis painted a picture of uninhibited blacks of all ages dancing in place by their tables while tipping strong drinks of Bourbon and water; or others on the dance floor precisely slithering among one another in perfect unison with their mad-cap costumes of the evening. Hair slicked back with a feather or strand of beads woven into the pomaded coif. Men in skin-tight black trousers and white silk shirts with wide ties of reds and yellows and greens pinched in with gold tie pins through the corners of their shirt collars.

Some audacious couples, as the evening wore on, would climb up on the stage to continue their symbolic dance of courtship and mating with fewer elbows in their faces and they just blended in with the band, no friction, no ugly scenes, as though they had, mysteriously, been invited by Tina to join her lovely lips and swaying pantheress gyrations. Or Ike might stop right in the middle of his song and join a couple in their dance, all so easy, all so natural. Still other couples, frustrated that they couldn't reach the dance floor instantaneously upon hearing their favorite tune of "Proud Mary" or "It's Gonna Work Out Fine" or "I Wanna Take You Higher" or "Save The Last Dance For Me" and would jump up on their table oblivious that buckets of ice and mixer would be thrown to the floor and afterwards the white table cloth would reveal their shoe shapes as though miles of Learn-to-Dance-the-Arthur-Murray way of instructional sheets were left behind (of course, for the Arthur Murray set all the untutored glyphs would be in some inscrutable, untranslatable language). The evening would seemingly suck all exuberance out of the participants; fortunately, the band breaks would allow the crowd to re-fuel and relieve their tired feet before moving into the next part of the bacchanalian enjoyment of hip movement and dashing eyes and flourishing of captured pelvic regions (although the outline was distinct). Only a handful of whites would show up out of false fear or inadequacy of dance or whatever, but Ruby said that she and her friends who went there to dance never minded. And another happening that never ceased to amaze her was that even at closing time the merry making seemed to overflow into the glistening macadam parking lots. Many a night she had been leaving and she would hear a parked car's radio blaring Wolfman Jack and his latest winner of a disc and the dancing would carry on into the rhymthical night, some sort of unspoken dance marathon that ultimately excluded the whites. She sensed some sort of secret yet in no way knew how to crack the formula. Oh, she had noticed some of the younger men eyeing her and a few stags had asked her to dance with them but her major hang-up in transcending this color-barrier had been her parents. She knew it might upset her mother, but her father would be irate should he ever hear of her interest in a black man.

Ray asked Ruby if her parents had ever found out about her evenings of dance at the Princess Pam. She remained in her orange beanbag seat but nodded her head very carefully up and down and a dark smile formed. Just as we all can have delightful secrets which we would want to share with others, she had often felt compelled to tell her mother of her curiosity and her seeming need to be among black people, to socialize...and oh, the sensation of life that Ike and Tina flushed into her youthful, hypersensitive system of blood and flesh. She had ached to tell her mom of the burning crush she had born for the high school football quarterback; how she had phoned him and met him, often, after school. But no one in her narrow-minded town or family would have understood. It was too soon in midwestern Americana pubescence. It was as though electrical wires were attached to her nipple and vagina and all lead from back in the seating area of the Pam and were wrapped around table legs and chair legs and sealed away under some of the black rubber runners in the aisles, but all lead to Ike's microphone stand or Tina's breasts; as though they belonged together. They were the black counterparts, the youthful counterparts to her wonderful parents—she genuinely related to the term of endearment Brothers, Sisters. But she knew that sort of confession would be out of the question. The truth would gnaw too deeply, too many past wounds and inadequacies and myths would be opened. She could witness a oneness in Ike and Tina on stage that was missing in her parents' relationship as she tolerated her parents' frequent violent arguments.

It didn't take too many visits, though, before she had run into a gossipy aunt of hers, a middle-aged couple who had also gone dancing. The aunt informed her mother. Her mother cried her shame and disappointment to the father. The father had beaten her severely, beaten her down in the cement basement where tree roots had cracked the walls, and black moisture marks dotted the cement, and potato bins unburdened grotesque runners from rotted and limed potatoes, and eyes of grey mice sat fearlessly by the coalbin room with its earthen floor. As his razor strap met her back and brassiere straps, she would glance to her mother's ceaselessly setup ironing board and manual washing machine wringer and tea-towels hanging from the clothesline. She wondered if he had ever beaten her mother for being herself. It wasn't a matter of contesting the strokes; she knew they were coming: it had been a matter of time. She didn't even mind the harshness, all the show, for, after all, the drinks, all the dancing and sneaking into the entrancing black world of the Princess Pam had been worth it. The wounds would heal; however, the longing for the contents of the black male silk bulging front pockets would not—she was sure of that as they walked back up the creaking, mildewed wooden steps to sob on the breast of a silent mother in the bathroom.

At this point Ray's alter ego kicked in. Intuitively, he knew that he had stumbled onto someone who held immense attraction for him; someone he might feel protective toward. Mocking harpies flew about the ceiling everywhere he went lately: overhead electrical fans, condor eyes bestially leering from among the sugar packages and creamers to uncannily accompany him in his search for some Beatrice who might await him. As Dante's Inferno had alerted him of "three hellish furies, stained with blood" might be the animation swirling above him; or L. Cohen secretly promised "Maria, I am 30, where are you?" Ray had become hopeless in his search to the extent that he locked himself away on Saturday evenings for fear of the low riders and hot teenyboppers and dual-carburetor cams that strutted up and down Long Beach Blvd. to peeling of rubber and motorcycle pandemonium of Hells-Angel-mutants gone haywire. He saw windows of autos advertising FOR SALE, grass and M.D.A. while turning over and over in his mind Bob Dylan's "Something's happening and you don't know what it is."

Ray tried desperately to console Ruby at this point; he genuinely wanted to exude sympathy, a sympathy that she could recognize. But she ignored him in a rush to complete her story.

"No need to feel sorry for me, Ray. You see, I had my fantasies, even then in my teens, to get me through the ordeal in the basement. I had my sleeping dreams and my awake dreams. Like the washing machine: each time dad would strike me I would mentally shove my budding teats into the cranking wringer, or plunge the agitator into my vagina. It wasn't so bad, some remote pleasure. You see, this was when I first noticed that I didn't mind the beatings. I had once seen my mother pull a butcher knife on my old man because of some petty argument after a night of drinking at the V.F.W. I tried to intercede but was ordered back to bed.

"Or, I had my recurring dream of the Marching Men."

"What's that?" Ray hastened.

"Well, I used to have these spectacular dreams of Black Men on Parade throughout my body. It was like my English instructor's description of Gulliver being tied down by the Lilliputians but I was a female Gulliver tied to the red earth in a Missouri cornfield and troops of black men and boys would walk on me and enter my ears and nose and mouth and vagina with bass drums and clarinets and clashing cymbals, and my shoulders and neck and arms would be laden with giant goose bumps that became hills and they would have to toil to climb over the bumps towards their various objectives.

"I would often awake in the evenings with a cold sweat from the marchings...."

"Why, you were a sort of marchioness, a grand lady, but one kept in bondage who was sought by all in the kingdom."

"Yes, yes, Ray."

"Were there never white men inside you, excuse the expression?"

"Well, sometimes, like old Al Glynne, or an occasional realization that they were all white men, but a group of Kiwanis men in black face. Strange. Or once it was Uncle Jack leading the procession, but mostly sleek, muscular, well-endowed black men. Once Ike Turner ran away from Tina and grabbed my vocal cords with one hand and my ovaries with the other from inside me and sang 'Young Blood' while holding his guitar in his mouth and stroking the strings with his tongue. And there were thousands of hands clapping throughout my circulatory system."

"And you had this dream over and over? Sounds as though your bedroom was often over-crowded."

"So, you see, I managed to have these suitors in my basement for that particular beating and in no way could father actually get to me.

25

He didn't hurt me, he wasn't even there. The bruises didn't last that long. And, of course, mom's gentle way with me afterwards pacified all. It's as though she untied my Lilliputian entrapment. And I could again be part of the mellow, sane family unit."

"Ruby," Ray had praised her honesty, "you are amazing. Some dream analysts would even go so far to state that you have suggested Jung's theory that universal symbols are ever-present in our continued ability to recreate age-old myths. For example, you felt thwarted in being your own personality and yet doubly sympathized with the Afro-American's plight. Just as Gulliver came up with variations on the diversions of the court of Lilliput, just as there were the rope dance and the stick leaping, etc., likewise, you found ways to divert your attention away from the pain of the moment. And as Gulliver, the braggadocio, claimed, 'And to confess the truth, my breeches were at that time in so ill a condition, that they afforded some opportunities for laughter and admiration.' You, Ruby, in going through puberty, budding all over I'm sure, probably felt you were being admired by the males of your community. Right?"

"Yes, yes," she told Ray. "But there is one other frightening aspect to this dream. It always ends with my being released and I'm standing on a corner in town, by a liquor store, and three black youths are coming out for a night on the town and they are snickering and opening beer cans, but, when they see me, they stop dead in their tracks. It's as though I never learn, or perhaps I want to be punished by my father or whatever he represents. Anyway, I invariably try to lure them to me, I don't want them to go elsewhere, to their dark secrets of manhood in automobile backseats, or drinking on a country road or stag to the Princess Pam. I want them, all three, with me, so I lift up my miniskirt to boast that I wear no underpants, for which I know Papa would kill me, but I do it and I mean their white eyeballs fall out on the pavement. It's as though their pupils are arrows zinging right to you know where and the goose bumps start all over again creating country stopping posts or crossroads for their carefree wanderings. I once wrote a note to the then-alive, world famous muralist Thomas Hart Benton in praise of his work in the Missouri State Capitol building and naively suggested that I could sit for him if he could capsulate my nature based upon my recurring dream. However, I never mailed it: Mother would

have killed me!"

"Well, I guess so; I guess so," Ray repeated his phrase of amazement to her. Ruby elaborated that her dreams had been so intense and taboo that she was never able to share them with even her mother or her diary. Ray understood. Ray hated all conquering armies after that sitting. He even dreamed of one that evening.

* * *

Ray's dream was one of wanderlust. He tied her to the Winchells' countertop but pulled down an awning that enveloped them and flicked on the CLOSED sign.

He was a midget in her fertile zone. He made a pilgrimage on foot. He lolled past the nape of her neck. He took a promenade down her cheekbone. He exhibited his fine horsemanship past her seductive eyes. He roamed and electrified her lips. He made the circuit of her cleavage and saluted her honey-bee tattoo (more tribute to her unbound nature). He was a vagabond in her navel. His itinerary was proving too exhausting. He bicycled up her left thigh of goose flesh. Soon, he was at anchor and immigrated nicely into port. He had reached the stopping place, a repast, an oasis; he cooled in the prepared foamy substance. There would be no returning from this land in the guidebook. It was a prophetic dream. He was travel-stained. All was now hopeless. She was an Amazon. Ray awoke screaming, and his scream sent Waldo into a sloshing fit so that sediment and motion created a brackish water in his aquarium. Some tenant overhead flushed his toilet and he noticed that the clock read four a.m. Like horticulturists who dream of discovering and naming after themselves a thing of beauty and rarity, he imagined his orchidaceous find, a pure white hybrid cattleya named Beatrice crossed with a smidgen of Thomas Hart Benton yellow or Persephone the seductress; thus his Ruby Francis would be known as c. Dante's Beatrice x c. Persephone Bentonia.

II.

In addition to her dream sequence, Ruby had wanted to apprise Ray regarding her early exposure to Southern California. As to ugli-

27

ness and malcontent, point in case, one Woody, Larry Woodruff, the last bastard she had tied the knot with before he finished shoving it to her and shoved on to Albuquerque. He had helped her out after locking horns with her at a local laundromat. She had been slowly wiping the laundromat sweat from beneath her bra-strap while writing a letter home to her folks during the rinse cycle and this creep in army fatigues butted in with a "Have change, lady, for a quarter?" She never finished the letter and change wasn't all she had for him. She pointed out that he shouldn't mix colored clothes with his whites and that an occasional shot of bleach could do wonders for his yellowed drawers.

To this day she didn't know if he was pulling her leg about his being wounded twice in Nam–he did show her some bluing of tissue on his left forearm and a bald spot about the size of a buffalo nickel right above the neckline in his otherwise thick head of brown mop. She had joked it could be leftover ring-worm tissue for all she knew. She hadn't minded petting his wounds, though. As he had said, Vegas was a 240Z-shot over the hills and a month of pounding the Hollywood pavement for a job (and unpaid bills) made marriage bells all the more sonorous to her. She hated the way clichés always filled her life, but love was blind and she neither saw daylight nor the Star Dust nor the MGM Grand casino nor the swimming pool nor shit: she saw the ceiling because it was there and continental-breakfast-included seemed as healthy as vitamin C or ham and eggs to their charge account beginnings.

Ruby told Ray that her only out-of-bed orally articulate moment had been the second morning when Harry had excused himself for some "important phone calls." He only absented himself some twenty minutes but that had been adequate for Ruby to get to know their room-service maid. She was fifty-five years old, originally from Paris and Ruby doted on such romantic notions. But it didn't take long to realize that Parée wasn't the city of lights to every native or visitor. She didn't know why but, for some uncanny reason, the term "sewers of Paris" always permeated film, documentaries, books, etc., about that infamous international city. Anyway, she, the maid, had been happily married for twenty-two years; she had met her ex-husband during the great war and he promised to bring her as his bride to America, and he ultimately did. They had owned a series of homes; first in Germany,

28

then on the large island of Hawaii, and finally on a cold December day, they had relocated in Missouri (coincidentally enough she knew Ruby's home town quite well and this helped create a quick-drying bond of temporary friendship in Harry's mysterious absence). The winter proved to be devastating. They had been short on cash due to the move from the islands and a TV set would even have been considered a luxury. She had spent long days alone in their dismal surroundings. She spoke no English at the time, therefore, mixing with potential neighbors had been out of the question. He would come dragging home late in the mornings, two and three a.m., from his job at the Harbison-Walker brick plant, and her frugal meals, fixed in the abysmal void of night, had been their only form of communication. The bed was kept even colder than the meals, according to her. Well, the twenty-odd years had been simply peachy until two short years ago. He had had the brilliant idea to move to Vegas and strike it rich.

The maid had lectured Ruby, "You Americans and your great myth of getting rich quick; I think movies and tv have so absolutely brainwashed you into believing this myth that for some weirdo like me to challenge it makes me the culprit, an unpatriotic alien. We moved and that was the beginning of our marital downfall. No matter where we would go, the supermarket, the liquor store, my god, even church, he was never 'with' me if you know what I mean: his faithful eyes had turned into leering, hungry, preying eyes, preying on any and all available ass around the Strip. We'd be walking down the grocery aisles and I'd considerately ask him if he preferred Delmonte or Iris pickled beets and BAMMO!, his radar would already be waddling in the pastry section for luxuries we couldn't afford; loganberry-lips and blueberry-breast, hips and loin of love, cream filled.

"He became a disgusting, ruminating animal and it didn't take long before our marriage was on the rocks, after nearly twenty-two years, mind you, and all because we moved to this perverse bedroom city where he would field-strip the young ass in public view." Ruby effectively had conveyed a sisterly revulsion to Ray on behalf of the maid.

Needless to say, Ruby queried to herself if this hotel, this bedroom was the appropriate beginning place for her recent marriage. Where was Harry right now, WAS he phoning, or was he shopping for pastries before he returned to momma? Was their marriage, in fact, doomed from the start? She could have gone on and on listening to this tortured, beaten woman but she had other things to attend; the cleaning lady could make her rounds again tomorrow, but Harry had best get his room in order. She felt sorry for the Parisian, though, after all, if it could happen after twenty years it could certainly happen to her and Harry. They had married without really getting to know one another AT ALL. They hadn't discussed sex, or religion, or children, for that matter, or brand name preferences like Delmonte or Iris or Trojan. And Harry certainly did not know of her secret desire to model ladies' lingerie in St. Louis. Oh yes, Ruby sure was something–the black sheep of her clan.

Ruby flew out of room 169 with her bruised breasts lightly flapping against her terrycloth robe. She would leave one bosom friend for another. It was only 7 a.m. and hardly any one was stirring at that time. A desk clerk yawned and rose to meet her harried demands.

"It is not customary for our customers to parade about in their robes, lady; however, if you mean that gentleman playing our special Holiday Package Giant Slot Pay-Off..."

Ruby reported that she ran to the giant slot machine some fifty paces away to join Harry and the swirling red lights. She had to clear her way through a handful of elderly Vegas regulars; whiskey emanating from the group like that of some Manhattan Beach singles bar that had been open all night. There was Harry with his back arched as if it hurt in the pit of his spine. She nudged him and he smelled her cheap perfume, or her jerky (freshly jerked meat) or whatever it was that he recognized about her. He pivoted and threw her up in the air towards the same daytime ceiling and bellowed, "Honey, we're rich, I tell you. I struck paydirt with a $500 jackpot. That's what all this excitement is and why I hadn't gotten back to you..." He set her down, she still was confused but soon an armed guard was standing there peeling off the twenty dollar bills. The wad of bills was enough temptation to set off a series of pathetic reactions in the early morning, smoke-filled lobby. Ruby felt somewhat relieved in that, compared to that other french-jerk's proclivity for women, apparently Harry's pitfall was gambling. Things could be worse she rationalized.

Her description of the old-timers' greed and dumbfoundment and transformation into some sort of panting animals reminded Ray of his visit to a neighborhood convalescent home at the sound of their lunch bell; the charging of callused hands as they propelled their wheelchairs and crutches and legs-in-casts into a small doorway that lead to the dining room. As a conglomerate, they were like the sands in an hour-glass cascading into the minuscule opening; a paradoxical rush for an impossible passing. Camel through a needle's eye was her comparison. That was the beauty of Ruby Francis; her story telling invariably triggered his childhood recollections (Wordsworth, Bradbury, Kosinski, all painful singular personal associations). Ray recalled the visit with Uncle Bob when he had miraculously reached the age of 104 and received the proverbial President's congratulatory birthday wish. Ray had written a dramatic monologue for a Los Angeles creative writing course, city college: "I was so shocked to see his two stubs for legs protruding from the lap, the red concealing afghan, but he had that twinkle to his milky eyes. Next thing I knew he was yelling 'FIRE, FIRE!!!' and I glanced for window exits as one might do on a commercial flight. Unlike me, no one else seemed to blink an eyelash. Momentarily, the orderly, a black robot appeared and lit ancient Bob's charred corn cob pipe and his fixed consternation puffed away without any thank yous. It was their system to guard against any potential fires."

This memory plunged Ray even further, back to his sixth year when he was a member of the circle around grandfather Joseph's deathbed. He looked at peace enough although everyone kept saying, "I hope he finds his Peace soon," and around midnight Papa Joseph summoned Ray's father and whispered his order "Go to the nightstand and fetch me those two two-bits." Ray recalled smelling the gallon paint buckets in the pantry with rusted lids that had been pounded in place by grandfather's sixty-four-year-old muscles. For Papa had been a house painter his entire life, and such is the respect and dignity of a hard-working man.

He smelled the familiar curtain-stretching starch and glanced around at the frilly unfinished curtains dropped by his neighbors for grandmother Myrtie to stretch for a pittance.

Grandmother had probably earned those quarters, too. Ray smelled the coffee can full of cherries cooking on the stove as grandma made preparations for her pies that would grace the church feed. Her perm stunk to high heaven from her plume of bluish grey hair but he knew her time was precious, a phrase she often quoted, but Ray kept thinking "What about old Papa's time, wasn't it precious? Wasn't that what sequestered-Faulkner kept insisting that Lennie and Quentin force upon others?" The confusion that seemed to be caused by the church's uncanny method of drifting in and out of his family's life tugged at him. He recalled burying his gold fish in the Blue Streak match box and that had ended that! Matter of fact, Papa's lying there had for the first time brought back to Ray the cold morning he had tugged at the frozen earth to lower their flopless bodies. Gram's perm was another step in her preparation for the inevitable at the funeral home vigil.

Jonathans and Pippins sweetened the room although he did notice one brown orb that was all mushy and sticking to the side of the wicker basket. The foulest was Papaw's chamber pot by the foot of the bed; Ray had nearly stepped into it when Joseph had winked and summoned him to his paint-encrusted fingertips. Ray noticed that grandma had tucked sprigs of crusted rose petals and cedar shavings everywhere even between the framed photographs and the peeling wallpapered walls as if she wanted him to know that Heaven would smell better than this horrid midwestern place. Her apron bulged with wads of Kleenex that she used to daub his mouth-corners, then she would disappear to the kitchen supposedly to check on the boiling cherries but young Ray noticed she'd use the same tissue to wipe her eyes so that steaks of red underscored her tired eyes like a Peruvian warrior who had forgotten to remove his berry stains before setting out as an expert fisherman who could easily spear two fish with one spear. She, too, was an incomparable human being capable of effecting the impossible. Prominent in Ray's memory was a fist of yellow roses that stood browning and rigid near Joseph's head, and the two quarters that proved less than a palpable inheritance.

The golden upsweep brought Ray back to his immediate senses. Ruby described the stampede in the Las Vegas casino as a cattle rushing towards Harry; it was devastating. The oldsters were around-the-clock boozers and had half-empty glasses of whiskey and ice cubes clanging and spilling on the cigarette-burned carpet.

One man, about sixty, in an olive, bleached-out sports shirt, threw his butt to the ground as he rushed up to the still-deafening siren and flashing red light. The excitement had proven too much for the old man, "I haven't seen this machine pay off, ever." He wheezed with what little breath he could find. The cigarette ash sent up a musty smelling odor from years of unvacuumed dirt tamped into the garish floral patterns of green and purple fuchsias.

"You dirty bastard, I just left that machine; that jackpot is rightfully mine. Mine, you hear!" shouted a lady with her cheap, yellow sun suit and varicose veins across her flabby knee caps. She had fluorescent green hair curlers that throbbed above her voracious eyes.

One old codger, with a bicentennial visor pulled over a thin patch of brownish-gray hair and splotches of vomit on the front of his shirt from earlier gambling hours, tore at Harry's arm that rested on the disengaged lever. He had a cigarette dangling from his lower lip and he kept mumbling, "Good for you, boy, good for you...," but his eyes were somewhere else, perhaps locked into some past lesser pot of his own, or glaring at stacks of chips that had grown at the dealer's tableside, had grown from his own nicotined fingers and headaches and too much drinking of cheap, watered down house booze, and from his sewn-up pockets that had known better nights of Black Jack hopes.

Other invalids of the crap tables and wheels of fortune embraced him and became over-solicitous. Ruby Francis said that she and Harry found it necessary, to survive, to band together and the siren wouldn't shut up and the light kept flashing in her eyes when she tried to look away from the old people, the prospectors gone dry. Eventually, when the crones realized that none of the spoils were to be shared, or that "dinner" was over, they picked their ways, singularly, back to the bar just on the other side of the wall in the hotel lobby. Many fell into some reverie, leaning their sunken, asthmatic chests on their bony elbows and sipped at the well-drinks (a liquefied euphemism). Some mustered up the strength to summon the Keno Girl and chance sixty-five cents on some whispered sure-combination. But most returned to their well-drinks and refocused their bloodshot eyes in the beveled mirror much like one would, after a night of dry heaves and carousing, stare into an inoperable television screen.

A bunny-clad photographer snapped their beaming mugs and it

33

was back to room 169 — $500.00 richer. That called for more release of tensions. He wanted to see more hickeys (as well as receive some hickeys) the size of silver dollars, now, strung across her breasts, and one silver dollar on each buttock. As he screwed his lever into her, he rallied and shouted, "JAK—JACK POT...JACK POT," at the top of his lungs.

"For Christ's sake, get it over will you? We're trying to sleep," rejoined someone in an adjacent room while pounding on the wall.

But, as Ruby F. concluded, nothing was to spoil! his special silver treasury of flesh and bruises that night. They were riding high and it had never been so good since their first time less than twenty-four hours earlier. Besides she eventually boasted after deliberating to choose the right words, "it was rather kinky."

Ray could easily visualize Ruby's trek through the gaudy lights and shine among the walking dead around her. But Ray was helplessly enmeshed in his own thoughts of the corpse of his grandfather. He was reminded of an indelible description in Gabriel Garcia Marquez' novella, _Leaf Storm_, wherein the narrator attends a funeral and says, "I thought that a dead man would look like somebody quiet and asleep and now I see that it's just the opposite. I can see that he looks like someone awake and in a rage after a fight." This was the silent shrieking face that death had created by placing small cavities of miniature zeroes for what once had been Grandfather's two eyes and mouth. The euphemism called a corpse that Ray remembered was not his grandfather but something, a prune screaming silent blasphemies to the heavens.

3 STILL LIFE: CAMELS FUCKING

THE LUCK OF SUCH SEMBLANCE of comraderie ran out within two weeks. Ruby had been open to relate all of these details to Ray; however, he eventually decided to make her privy of his recent hitch hike venture. She ignored his shock treatment and readily informed him that in her late teen years she, too, had modeled in her undies. All had been on the up and up but male relationships to include her first husband had greatly protested her exposure of flesh. Upon returning for a booth-wrapped-in-plastic sitting, Ruby commented upon his folded magazine in his hip pocket (usually he carried a paper-back-of-the-week which proved a conversational focus for them before leading into more provocative discourse). Ray explained that she had become his Bernice and that should she Be Nice to him he would do her no harm.

Ruby's HAVE A NICE DAY coffee mug always was at her side. Ray was made to feel ephemeral in that he was made to use a dispos-able paper cup. He would stare at her lacquered, white, cheesecloth uniform reflected in the formica surface. He allowed her to brew in his brown eyes. Ruby was amazed when he once announced that she had the prettiest legs in Bellflower, aside from those of Jerry Quarry. Ray compared Quarry to the notoriety of Mike Tyson before the fall. Ray bantered that none of the VIVA photographic "uncoverage" had revealed the slightest suggestion of a strawberry mark. He showed

Ruby Francis the issue that boldly displayed Quarry "The Fighter" while arm wrestling, while engaged in boxing, taking a shower, bicycling, seated nude in the mist and backdropped by the Statue of Liberty. Quarry roasting his weiner under a sunlamp. Quarry being massaged. Quarry violent. Quarry contemplative like a Rodin sculpture. Ruby wanted to keep the issue but he lied that he merely had it on loan from the Bellflower Library. He later gave her a gift subscription to which she feigned feminine blush...sure, sort of like a camel in heat.

Ruby's blushing triggered an unforgettable feigning for foreplay that Ray had witnessed some years back while at the Honolulu Zoo. It was April. He had been fortunate to be there at that time for it proved to be mating season in much of the animal kingdom. But it was the camels that dumbfounded Ray. He assured Ruby that if she should never see copulation again, she must see camels mate before the end of her days. The female prances about the enclosed area, head erect and prancing in circles, keeping distance from the male. She glances and lures with her black eyes, she wiggles her pelvic area with its ugly, dirt-worn haunches. Then she pretends not to notice him pursuing, hot and heavy at her haunches, but he does: and she starts a slow, low moaning, frightening guttural sound like 3,000 fog horns being set off simultaneously, like some coffin lid squealing open, like some automotive exhaust pipe backfiring; then just as he is about to penetrate she deftly spirals herself to a standing position and she quickly looks left and right as though she is not content with her audience or his style. She circles the ring a second and third time, and her barks and bellows grow in intensity. Ray could remember standing at the wooden railing and how his fingers had grasped the splintered wood because there must be an earthquake rumbling across the chain of evolutionary islands. Tears were seen to swell in Ray's unbelieving eyes. Ray positively knew, as he explained it to a lost-in-empathetic-thought Ruby, that during his second penetration (Ray expanded that he had nearly retched as the camel's hot, pepper-mill of a penis trotted past his hot brow) that she was in pain—the moans, the tossing of her giraffe-like neck back and forth, back and forth. She must be dying.

My god, she jumps from his forceps, his sweat-smeared haunches again, and she circles again as though she has other things on her virginal brown crew-cut mind, but none of the spectators can think of anything else. There is an elderly couple from Kansas holding on to one another out of fear that some sort of Disneyland robot animals have come to life and tricked them into witnessing copulation; there is a young mother covering her daughter's eyes and pleading, "Come away, come away," while both relentlessly look on.

There are others laughing and pointing to the pepper-mill, but Ray's fingernails dig deeper and he feels pain in his stomach as he explains matters to Ruby. He would like to have summoned the zoo-keeper or prodded himself to step in and come to her aid. Her moans droned on but he was upon her and suddenly there was a turn of her beautiful brown button, mucous-filled eyes to those of Ray as she allowed him to bring her to the ground and her neck flew loosely back and forth like a snapped guy wire, like a garden hose that has worked free of one's hands and it shoots every which way. And the sun overhead burned Ray's neck and forehead. Ray felt pulled to the earth and ducked his camel hair head to the dust as she gave in eternally. The male camel had known not to give up, yet he was never sure of himself; her moaning and philandering was merely part of *her* domi-nance in the total act.

Ruby had asked, "What did all of you do then?"

"We just walked away, just looked at one another with our empty, inadequate eyes, and feeling drained," Ray assured Ruby. "One man's eyes met mine as if to say 'So...so that is what it is really like...I never knew...I never knew.'

"Some small child came running to his parents yelling Momma, Momma, you should see the peacocks shimmering their fantail feath-ers, it's beautiful; may I take a picture?"

"Sh...shh," she reprimanded, as though he had tainted some silent atavistic prayer.

"One pre-teenager threw rocks at a turtle that was helplessly try-ing to mount another. Oh, it was in the air that day," Ray trumpeted to Ruby.

That was an explanation; Ruby blushed like a camel in April!

* * *

Ray wanted to pursue any possibilities for future conversations

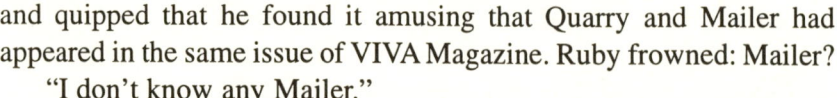

and quipped that he found it amusing that Quarry and Mailer had appeared in the same issue of VIVA Magazine. Ruby frowned: Mailer?

"I don't know any Mailer."

Ray verbally spread Marilyn Monroe and multiple marriages and "Prisoner of Love" across the formica like the cards he would long to play but she was befuddled and offered Perry Como hit list tunes and Ray withdrew his hand for the time being. She truly did not know who Mailer was and she probably wouldn't recognize Quarry except she did work and live in Bellflower; someone must have imagistically introduced her to this handsome, hometown aggressive form. It was during this early visit that Ray learned the preceding account of Woody and the Vegas honeymoon. She didn't mind letting it all dribble out. Ray could not suppress his curiosity—why hadn't she at least shared a Butterfly cinnamon roll with him? Did that ever prove to be the wrong question?

Her abhorrence for sweets fell into a particular category. She had a simplistic philosophy about likes and dislikes. She could explain it all; it had begun in her eleventh year of school (she was never to finish her year of graduation before Greyhounding it to Los Angeles). Her family had placed her in a nighttime job as concessionaire at the local theatre. Her monopoly-minded boss, Mr. X, picked up on her uncle's ass-pinching (while strictly enforcing his anal-retentiveness in the glass candy case and attempting to pry into other restricted areas). She would arrive as late as possible so as not to be left alone in the dark theatre before opening time. Out front, with the Hershey bars and the neatly stacked rows of chewing gum she felt extremely safe behind the illuminated glass case, rather like Tina Turner on stage in front of the lights where paradoxically she was less vulnerable. Whenever possible, Ruby would go without the popcorn lard that was stored, in weighty twenty-five pound metal pails, behind the movie screen (this did place her, at times, in a most vulnerable spot). His bald head and hen-pecked manner made her appreciate nothing about him except his weekly paychecks.

Long before pastry repugnance, she took something as delectable as her childish popcorn appetite and quickly puked at the slightest smell of the popper heating: something about word-association with chrome-dome and machine lid and lard ass and greasy, disgusting sea-

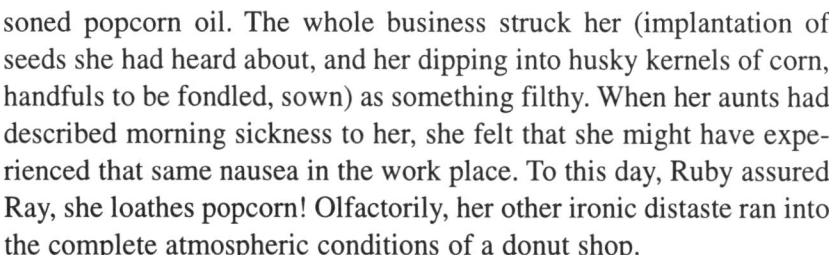

soned popcorn oil. The whole business struck her (implantation of seeds she had heard about, and her dipping into husky kernels of corn, handfuls to be fondled, sown) as something filthy. When her aunts had described morning sickness to her, she felt that she might have experienced that same nausea in the work place. To this day, Ruby assured Ray, she loathes popcorn! Olfactorily, her other ironic distaste ran into the complete atmospheric conditions of a donut shop.

Ruby explained that she got along famously with most of the clients, largely comprised of young adults from the neighboring co-ed college. She would even date a few university students merely for the adult-compliments tossed her way (her berry-mark, after all, and other pink budding berries) and for an occasional ride home after such frightful movies as The Creature from the Black Lagoon or The Thing. She would tell her new friends that, in fact, "the thing" lurked behind the screen and in the manager's office unaware to the paying public. They encouraged her to strike back, hit him, report him to the police, but as she reminded them, it was pretty difficult to fend off a gingerly goose when your hands are burdened with a metal pail of say thirty pounds of solidified popcorn oil. Easy enough. They had advised her to drop the pail on his toes—so, one night she did. It seems he had to be hospitalized and he had one hell of a time explaining it to his wife that he and Ruby had been behind the screen "procuring lard," while wifey had been policing the aisles with her ever-vigilant flashlight that locals remove their feet from the backs of seats in front of them. Messy situation. Her friends had found her outrageously entertaining. Little did they realize that they were saving her nightly from some paltry thing with a daughter-fixation and no daughter to fix it upon. They thought her some palterer, as they had been in their more affluent adolescent state. She could laugh about it all now with Ray as she reapplied her pink lightening lipstick, so vogue with the Art Deco resurgence.

Ray felt it good to see her laugh for a change. He treasured her laughter amidst baggies of donut holes suspended over the counter and little hand-printed posters of "Home Sweet Home" and barbs about baker's dozens bought from Ruby—while she wore his and hers throw-away barbs, small machine-punched paper doilies about her potential throat that temporarily concealed her basic religion from habit. Unabridged massage parlor laughter. She still felt sorry for the female camel, or feigned to, while Ray chased her around the interior of her sweet-shop more times than she would ever know. Her arms and fingers, bathed in flour, caused Ray to think of her as white statue, unlike other femme fatales. That was it—he saw her as a modern day statue, a Venus de Dali and he lined some verse on the Winchell's napkin:

> Pilgrim, pilgrim, wristwatch artist,
> drinking existential coffee;
> You are worthless 'til you learn to
> lotus sit and trim your goatee.
>
> Angel, angel, fancy hostess,
> serving hip swing (bosom bureau).
> You deceive with artful posing;
> masters see the harpy in you!

* * *

Ray most appreciated Ruby's older uniforms for one reason: the older ones were faded, not nearly as white, true; however, they were tighter. He had an easy mental inventory of precisely how many uniforms she owned, for he had closely observed each for distinct markings or runs in the material. On some she had clumsily embroidered the initials R.F.F. He once asked her why not RAF (thinking of flying) but she curtly informed him that her name was Ruby Francis not some fly by night advertiser. But returning to the tighter, more pleasing dresses. Only one dress, one that appeared to be at least two sizes too small for her, revealed an abundant travel-log of her rural cleavage. And, ever so scantily visible, there would appear a lone fuzzy outline of a black insect wing. One morning, while she wore this particular sheer-delight, Ray audaciously poked one of his index fingers to her bosom to peel back the white cloth. She mused that he might first ask permission...and coyly smiled, "You might just get stung."

Ruby lit into what seemed to be a well-rehearsed explanation of what was attached to the pneumatic slice of wing. She pulled the lapel back while removing his nervous hand. The smell and humidity in her shop caused sweat on Ray's brow and a dry, bitter taste in his eager mouth. She said that IF he were to be able to spy further down the mountain path he would see a series of bees, each alike, honeybees to be exact. The artist had promised her that her tattoo was to be one of a kind. He had shown her a picture in a tattoo-pattern manual as well as in *Man and His Symbols* by Jung, and each depicted various bees performing their tail-wagging dance to communicate to the entire hive the exact location of food.

Ray responded that he had studied this instinctual habit and kept searching his pocket, with his left hand, for coins, etc., for the text-book spread across her chest was proving too much and he imagined exploring for the nectar within.

She interrupted his image by glancing downward, saying, "That's nothing, though, Ray; beyond the dance, the ritual, the common bees, near the mountain peak (the uncapped nipple danced in Ray's head), you might see two drones vying for attention of the Queen Bee. She basks in her lonely splendor, waiting for a royal consort." Ray knew he was becoming her willful, self-destructing victim. He knew he might tailspin, at any moment into her bra, knowing that she was waiting for some false move on his part, some unallowable penetration.

Ray blinked his eyes. A gigantic billboard by the Hollywood Freeway flashed in his tortured mind. He saw her teats on an ad for Winchells' emerging from giant yellow pages. Two male fingers, Ray's, were treading a dotted line along the bees to the Queen Bee that overlapped the nipple and he was humming "Let your fingers do the walking..." Ray jumped when she again verbally interrupted his thoughts; he laughed at himself as some sort of media child lost in his freeway fantasy.

Ray threw his loose change on the counter and accused her of false advertising, of luring her customer to her hive and then turning him out unsatiated. She blushed that she didn't understand his words, that, after all, they were only discussing an inadvertent tattoo etched on her breast during one of her debauches in Long Beach.

4. UNDER THE COUNTER

RAY FELT THAT he was adequately dealing with the loss of his job; he began by filing for unemployment and plans of pursuing gardening as his own business. He was spending more time with Midnight, runs along the beach or drives at odd hours past Winchells. If anything he felt he might be developing a case of pooper-scooper elbow. But now that he had found his potential Bernice, his object d' amour, he felt inadequate considering the obvious competition. He did know one thing regarding Ruby though, he wanted to bring about a special, meaningful love relationship. He found her a beautiful human being. But she ejaculated such trite phrases as "right on, get it while you can, do it in the dirt, I'm a one-man woman, get the pigs, and that is a hot van (or "man", as the case happened to be)." The latter appeared to be bringing back the donut fanatics. They were returning to sample each and every variation on a circle and hole which the modern technology could create and this alarmed Ray.

Ruby Francis was proving to be a good business person: she featured "donut of the week;" she even did her form of library research by looking into the seasonal aspect. She told Ray during one of their sessions that if the mortuary business could predict what month(s) they could take vacation because they were short on stiffs, certainly she could similarly graph earnings. She did have difficulty accepting that each time a customer walked in, the mort's register rang-up thousands, hers thirty-five cents for selling their respective holes. "Inequity reigns," she said.

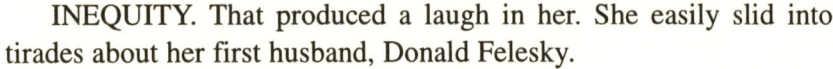

INEQUITY. That produced a laugh in her. She easily slid into tirades about her first husband, Donald Felesky.

"But I thought the Vegas dude was your first," Ray composed an unspoken accusation for response to her story.

"Well, to clarify, for thirty seven hours, until the rice had been thrown and I discovered in order to get in the sack with him I had to be a porno queen." She knew what anal retentive meant but he had read too much porno and they disagreed on definition.

Ray asked how she had met him.

"I picked him up in a discotheque along the Sunset Strip. During that phase when he looked better than the nude males performing on stage. After a few weeks we went there dancing again and he caught my eyes wandering. Donald, regulars called him Gringo, made the advances for me. The three of us headed home with several bottles of Mateus. The quantity of wine should have warned me he had insatiable appetites. The guys seemed to be getting along well so I wandered into the bedroom and was surprised to see a photograph of Gringo in a leather jacket, no clothes otherwise, with a chain wrapped around his balls."

"Didn't you say anything to him?" All was foreign to Ray.

"Not kosher with the other guy in the living room, oh and he by now had removed his tee shirt." Ruby embellished that she remembered a little foreplay but then she dropped out probably due to the quantity of wine. Someone had carried her onto the bed and fireplace light greeted her form as dear loving Gringo had thrown her down on all fours and he was encouraging their partner to join in.

Words that Ray didn't want to hear surrounded him: "I felt some hands exploring in and around then moving to gently massage my left nipple while a mouth was nibbling not so gently on the other. After about fifteen minutes of this petting I felt something nice and warm and yellow cascading over my horizontally positioned back; then Gringo joined in and I visualized that about two and one-third cups of come mixed with the urine on my back. This angered the other guy, Dino may have been his name, who proceeded to knock Gringo against the simulated fire (good old So. Cal. motorized gaseous flames out of fake ceramic logs). The stranger shouted that he would kill Gringo if he ever heard that I was treated that way again." This seemed

to turn on Gringo to become extremely violent with Ruby and their partner seemed to enjoy being ordered around. Ruby said she had heard of
such confusion of role playing on tv talk shows but to be experiencing
it first-handedly non-plussed her. It did enter Ray's mind that she might
have been making up all of this merely to see how worldly was he; however, such detail, shockingly, belied such innocence.

About then Ruby had to answer the hand-bell she kept at the
counter: a customer. Ray needed a breather anyway since he had only
known her approximately two weeks when she revealed the above.

When she returned to the stall, she attempted to explain the term
Golden Shower Queen. Ray's limited closet-information was her daily
bread, or it had been in the past. Ray tried to direct their conversation to
more pleasant experiences: "Didn't you know other gentlemen?" He
enunciated gentle as he gently placed his hand over hers.

Ruby said that in spite of Ray's possible facetiousness she felt it
important that they were honest with one another so the relationship
could grow. "Yes, I have known sweet men. When I first arrived in
Hollywood, I met Stan. His sole raison d'être was the search for the best
lid yet. We entered into an endless series of daylightless 'tripping' but I
could accept it all because he was 6'6", blonde, trim-waisted, an excellent fuck and he loved to subject me to 'suggestive bondage' while I was
tripping. He would make me wear earphones while he tongued me and
had me squealing for something more than the cat's swizzle stick that
he had hidden between the sofa cushions just for me ."

Ruby paused to recollect her emotions. She continued,
"Unfortunately, his mother died in between weekends when we would
be hopelessly and blissfully partying. The mother, besides me, was all
that Stan had in his life. So, as an aside, I took it upon myself to accompany Stan on a swing by the mother's boyfriend's apartment (they
appeared in their late 50's). Never having met him, we drove him to and
from the mortuary for his last respects (he reeked of Bourbon already),
plus I paid for a six-pack of beer in hopes it would see him through
another lonely evening. God, it's all coming back to me now; he had a
filthy cast on one of his legs, he was out of a job and was coughing up
some god-awful brown phlegm and crying all the way—I think her
name had been Viola. I just kept thinking I want something better than
this for me. It was sad, very sad; I just felt that Stan was part of that

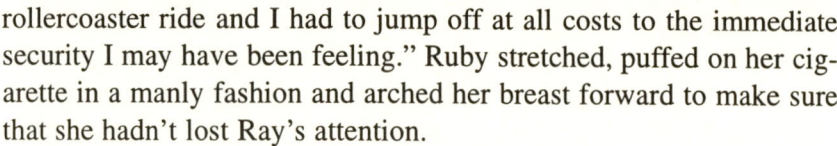

rollercoaster ride and I had to jump off at all costs to the immediate security I may have been feeling." Ruby stretched, puffed on her cigarette in a manly fashion and arched her breast forward to make sure that she hadn't lost Ray's attention.

Ray felt he should end this mental cruelty that she had chosen to share with him. He asked her to continue. She had had a crush on a Castillian named Garcia: she had met him once in New York City (some lover had paid her way for a whirl wind weekend). Garcia, chronologically, was at the age to be a father figure. He owned a fashionable Spanish restaurant along Lexington Ave. that courted lines of people each evening for the favor of the few available tables. He had done some modeling and his one claim to fame had been a cover shot on G.Q. and for the one evening Ruby entered his world, she saw the photo in a cheap dimestore frame that was on the bedroom bureau and he had angled a large mirror towards the bed to satiate his jerking off. Out of bed she had found him attractive and charming as he played flamenco guitar and sang lovingly towards her; in bed, kittycat tongues afforded more friction. (Ray, at that moment, imagined laving her breasts in pure religious worship).

*　　*　　*

At a later sitting, as if the previously related escapades weren't enough to challenge Ray's return, Ruby painted another venture. She labeled it THE GREAT ESCAPE. Frighteningly to Ray, this represented one of her most recent experiences since establishing herself in Bellflower. It/he was a thirty-year-old customer. He used to stop by enroute to his night job of chrome plating auto bumpers. On most evenings he would wear a suede lamb's-wool-lined, western-cut jacket, as well as cowboy boots and a Stetson (she had noticed him because her father had always worn a Stetson hat).

"So who put the make on who?" Ray felt that he was catching on to her audacious manner.

"Well, he kept telling me he didn't care for me in that way. I admit, I asked him to swing by later one night—I would be closed and he'd still be able to clock in at work on time."

"Why didn't he care for you?"

"Said I couldn't handle him, and he meant it. He might just prove too much man for me." Ruby assured Ray that there probably are such men out there but she felt compelled to meet his challenge.

They finally agreed to a rendezvous at his apartment. Ruby had noticed, as she entered the apartment complex, the neglected, dry pool, the dandelions, cigarette butts, dog turds, and abandoned pull-toys that bulged from the cracks in the 'run to hell' sidewalks that lead to his front door.

Ruby Francis assured Ray that she was not one to easily balk at threat of personal injury. She could handle herself.

"Then why degrade yourself to his level?" Ray implored.

"I was truly attracted to his Marlboro man image. I must admit though, I wasn't there a matter of seconds and clues to his bizarre nature surfaced. He snapped shut the bolt-lock and its echo of steel falling into place filled the living room, and to this day I still hear it. He commanded me to, before removing my coat, walk to the fridge and take the top ice cube tray from the freezer. I thought 'drinks' but soon noticed the cubes were bright yellow in color. He told me they were samples of his piss. He ordered me to place three in a tumbler and bring it to the coffee table where he was seated.

"I did so and started to seat myself when he barked that he had not given me permission to do so. I caught my submissive self and returned to a standing position, but in doing so, I noticed a half-dozen magazines strewn across the coffee table—all of the covers revealed strange scenes of women in bondage and belts and knives, and fake ketchup-like blood on bare breasts and buttocks. It shocked me, Ray; I had ideas that this went on but no idea that such blatant illustrations in magazines were available. I also noticed stacks of similar magazines underneath the table, as though some librarian had meticulously categorized them according to degrees of masochism.

"He next produced a single-edged razor blade and said that he was going to cut my underpants off my body. I diplomatically told him to cool it, that this was all new to me and I needed time to internalize his wishes. He reminded me that he had warned I would not be into his demands but that I had insisted..."

"But this, this is too much," Ray encouraged her to deny any further interest.

"But it was too late to bow out gracefully; when I made any move-

47

ment towards the door he assured me that I could try but would not be successful. He spoke with self-assurance that any political hopeful like Jesse Jackson or Gary Hart might gamefully employ–"

"I wish you had known me at the time, you might have called me to fight him off," Ray offered.

"No, no, out of the question. Besides I would never suck into my problematic life others who are outside all of this. Fairness comes into play, I feel. He soon slipped off his jeans but kept on his tee-shirt, his socks, and of all things, in place of undershorts he wore a jockey strap; it also was very yellow. I asked him What is that for? He threatened that I would not just automatically get his cock: he said that sooner or later I would beg for it—but first I must go for it via the strap. He had a routine: I must insert one of the melting ice cubes in my mouth and then lick his strap with my yellow saliva. I said I'm just not ready for the cubes, but I did willingly take the prone position, on my knees, and the jock smelled to high heaven. I suppose it was all part of his shock treatment, he never laundered it—said he even had ladies answer ads whereby he mailed them one for a charge, of course. He wore them when on the prowl; flaunted them once he lured his prey into his cave. He offered that I might peruse the magazines for ideas if I felt inclined. He said we would later watch movies on the bedroom wall."

He received a phone call, but his monosyllabic utterances into the mouth piece meant nothing to her. Men like him sometimes include a buddy on a night of drinking and if she proved good enough this time around, perhaps next time the buddy might be invited, too.

"How did you respond?" Ray was dumbfounded.

"I refrained from laughing nor did I say that would be fine. I just needed to survive the night. Next he threw me some rubber panties. I wondered where one found adult sizes. He told me to put them over my lavender ones. He next placed me over his lap and aggressively jerked his belt from the loops but surprisingly tapped it gently across my ass. He whispered some jibberish about 'I told you to be a good girl at the shop today...,' and 'Wait til your mommy gets home; she'd tan you even more if I didn't stand up for you. Now don't you love your daddy?'

"But for sanity's sake, I kept telling myself I am not his little girl; I'm twenty-five and he's about my age and I hadn't done anything bad. I just played along; after all, he wasn't hurting me like my real father's childhood strappings."

"Was that the end, I mean did you escape?" Ray made it sound like a simple solution. She said, undressed, he entered the dark bedroom, commanded she go down on the cock forced between solid stomach muscles and the smelly jock strap. At this point, she felt completely shut off from the outside world. She was his captive, much like an inmate doing time on Alcatraz who was shut up in solitary confinement and the light and sounds and warmth of life is taken from him. She still imagined the resounding jolt of the lock being brought down when she had entered. She didn't want to scream because she needed him. She winced when she confessed this.

She managed to get him off, where upon he immediately rolled her over on her side, insisted they cuddle, called her his good little girl, and said that if she continued being good to him, she'd have everything she ever desired. He would see to that. She could even close up shop and just be his lover. To think about it, and they would talk in the morning. He also, next time, wanted to stuff her groin and rear with miniature marshmallows, bing cherries, and hard boiled eggs only to eat them out of her. He had read about this, as well as once fished two hard boiled eggs out of a whore's vagina in Juarez.

Somehow, once he fell asleep, she eased from the bed, dressed in the living room and let herself out. She figured, by the fact that he didn't stir, that he probably knew she was leaving and it was part of his routine: how he treated his sex-kittens, sex-slaves. The good lil' girl gone bad, sneaking out by night; but he would adequately reprimand and physically punish the next surrogate child.

Ray secretly told himself 'I would flog her incorrigible breasts with my tongue, but sweetly.' Yes, Ruby Francis had known some sweet men in her coming out.

Ray asked her, "But how could you like such a bastard?"

Ruby paused for the correct words, knowing that any arbitrary syntax might offend him. "Well," she cajoled, "haven't you known, and tolerated someone you just couldn't believe—I mean believe a damned thing they said? Pump their stomach or pick their brain, but you don't find one ounce of truth? Like nothing? Where all is false?"

This stab at culpability caused Ray to flash upon such prominent figures as John Dean and John Mitchell. On the source of political enemies' lists. In fact, upon the alleged cover-up in the Kennedy assassination. Ray chose not to bring up the now public figure of Barbara Walters; he knew they could never agree how he felt she had weaseled into the network system. The possibility of ripe moments, Women's Lib, national insecurities. He thought of his secret stab at the writing of poetry, too.

"I remember a childhood sweetheart named Rose, sweet Rose, Rose Hathaway, and how we were once playing in the backyard and someone had carelessly left a rusted, old metal rake, prongs upward. She was barefoot and as we raced about, she stepped directly on it. I remember screaming yet feeling very excited at the sight of the blood. In later years I dated her and on an autumnal night, returning home, I pinned her against the freshly painted white boards of her frontdoor. We stood the entire time. I had just seen a shocking televised mastectomy and rebuilt breast operation. It all fused in my novitiate love making (and fused in Ray's wanting-to-please response to Ruby's dialog). Incision: dabbing of blood; wet red fingers sneaking up from either side of the patient's anatomy and inserting delicate rose-bush-pruning fingers of a Lawrence Olivier to sadistically snapon the flesh, his MARATHON MAN movie parting one red layer from the other layers, and the cold insertion of the cushiony surrogate teat. Miraculous that they can do it; but on tv? Simultaneously, my cold, slick hands were a dissembler; instead of the set of teenage, princely hands she had anticipated, they must have been more like surgeon hands needling under her teenage J.C. Penny blouse and slip and bra. They gyrated up, up to assault her newly found nipple-tissue and massage and pain and attend her." Ray sipped his coffee.

"How did she react?" asked Ruby. She studied his caffeinic trance.

"She was honest; said she never wanted to see me again. Besides feeling guilty and defensive all at once, I had to admit to myself that probably another boy or her father or a cat's tongue might have performed better for her needs. Her father had been a prominent doctor in our town for some twenty years. She was honest so I knew where I stood, out on some desert plateau, embalmed, prepared to fall into the common pit of adolescence. Moon-shadow on a lonely desert is reassuring; quiet, truthful in its way." In spite of the above sins of admission and chancing that Ruby would never again trust him for going public with his secrets, he now honestly had to admit his licentious nature would have him do it with Ruby in her cushiony orange plastic sphere bean bag chair.

5 THE DARKER SIDE

AGAIN THE RAIN. Ray Landre began an investigation of his possibilities to cinch the bonding with Ruby. His tales of confession left him, in his hindsight, a disgusting prospect for this premature desert prospector. He thought of suggesting that they someday travel to Europe: he had accompanied student groups before and the prospects lifted his spirit.

If rain was one of Ray's pet-peeves, certainly the desire to allude to her men in waiting as tenants of Dante's third circle with their lickerish gluttony was more magnetic in juggling his moods.

Upon proffering travel to her, Ruby trumpeted her unique travel log. "How about the Greek?! I was traveling alone so it was very easy to meet young lads. He was educated in Milan. He hated being in the U.S., but the money was better..."

"Wait Ruby, you said you had gone to Greece..."

"No, no. I meant that I've sampled various nationalities–it must be the same as going there if this guy was typical." She grinned from whitecap to whitecap. "I met him in a nightclub; he had sent me a drink and soon was lecturing me that I had screwed up my life by not finishing school. I felt flattered for he was the envy of all in the bar, male and female. I felt their eyes seeking him out. He flicked his pack of cigarettes just so and hosted my attention with wallet photos of his family and sister still in Athens (it all sounded good, anyway).

"He insisted on Arni Souvlakia and chilled Ouzo as a nightcap, before we had sex. He was the best maybe because he kept telling me he was the best! He had resorted to male prostitution before leaving Athens."

This all sounded marvelous to Ray who could now sit back and enjoy his cigarette and digest good black coffee.

Ruby continued, "He seemed to have a pattern. He insisted on meeting me at the bar, no mushy rendezvous at either apartment. He would invariably show up thirty minutes late which had allowed all eyes to have focused upon me. He liked for me to have purchased a couple packs of cigarettes for him and nefariously hinted that cigs by the carton would be worthy of his style of acquaintance. He had such a charming way."

"Yes, I understand that gigolos have outrageous natures," was Ray's response. Ruby shrugged that she agreed. By now Ray had forgotten their limitations.

As Ruby described it, they would ball and ball and ball. Their balling was no respecter of TIME. Ray recalled his Kafkaesque dream of clocks, the Hollywood pickup wherein he attempted to dissect <u>The Sound and the Fury</u> in exchange for sexual favors. Ray could now correlate Faulkner's definition of Time as a mathematical progression to 2+2+endless night hours meant an eternity of bliss; but how could Ruby so naively overlook that come 3 or 4 a.m. he would choose to kick her out of the hotel room that he, the gigolo paid for, yet ironically he would, in a fit of post-climax madness, insist on some grander sum of money for his stamina and handsomeness, the gimlet between his legs which even Ray could now visualize.

"Ray, charming or not, I was his. Petty revenges we are all capable of. Sufferings; humiliations. The first night he wanted only five U.S. dollars; the second, fifteen. The third and last he astounded me with a demand for two hundred dollars." She knew that others were overhearing her tears through the paper-thin walls. She blasted that she had no intention of paying him for sexual favors, that she sincerely had thought he loved her.

"What did he do next?" Ray could imagine himself in that cheap hotel room ready to defend her.

"I told him if I had that kind of money I might buy a train ticket to jump off the Golden Gate Bridge. He slapped me in the face, spat in my face, shouted some inane words 'I American, I see the sky, the clouds, the forest tops; I no step upon the ground,' added a few choice epithets about Ruby not being his choice of gems and threw me, clad in panties and half slip only, out into the hallway. Only one adjacent door was open, a fat lady withdrew as though she might have met Mr. Gigolo-witted before, but not before slowly lowering her Siamese from her terrycloth lap to the musty, worn beige carpet, shouting, 'Potty for mommy, go on now; it's cold out here."

Ruby embellished her story by describing his great Greek mop of rich, dark hair. She offered to go to the back of her shop and retrieve a photo to show Ray. Ray declined. Ruby showed Ray a pink camelia, most likely Tomorrow's Dawn, that was from their last night together. She kept it pressed in her Bible by the bed. She started to rise from the confining donut shop table but Ray assured her he could see that the Greek must have been exceptional; no reason to bother. He did request a refill, if it were free. Ruby smiled.

OPERATIONS: THE MESOMORPHIC ONES

Ruby F. ADMITTED that her feelings for Petri the Greek confused her, because, although she genuinely loved him and his thick and uncut masterful manipulation, she also thought of him as a brother. As a matter of fact, she recalled on more than one occasion having been confronted, by Petri and other male acquaintances who had wanted a long term relationship with her, with the cold, hard fact that she did not want a lover or a husband, only a strong relationship with a brother she had never known. She told Ray that she always denied the accusation to herself and disliked being labeled a prick-tease; however, when she reflected upon this idea, she might be somewhat guilty. She chose not to think about it.

Ray emplored Ruby to continue indulging him in his infatuation. He mumbled, "Brother, what a story."

"What do you mean 'brother'?"

"Just an expression, just a surprise, just Brother."

"Well, I'm sitting here telling you about my life, what about yours? Don't you have any favorites, any secret loves you choose to keep a photo of and use as a base of comparison of all others while making love to them? You're so quiet: your quiet way has been bothering me. You can open up, you aren't like these crude truckers who with me, nine out of ten times are cheating on their wives, and besides, I know they probably masturbated before they came here anyway.

That's one thing I'll never understand about you men—you beat the hell out of that thing and still you're on the make. As Petri once explained to me, the Greek men don't masturbate, they claim that such idle action causes the prick to go limp, and in order to bolster their manhood, they want to be ever-ready." Ruby snickered as she walked her playful fingers across the tabletop and hummed "Keep going, keep going" in a drummed cadence.

Ray complimented her coquettish tv ditty but reminded her that customers in the shop were looking their way. He fantasized about her silken ditty downstairs as he rubbed his knee against hers underneath the table. She lowered her voice.

"So, how do they manage to be ever-ready?" Ray asked.

"By fucking, of course. I think they have something there. If you're doing one of two things all the time, I mean doing it or thinking about doing it and none of that phoney, lame duck crap, then it's bound to be up and ready, perpetually, right?"

Ray responded, "Yeh, right, I suppose. Well, I can tell you a little bit about jacking-off. I hope this isn't offending you, is it?"

"I find it truly fascinating, Ray Landre!"

"Well, what brought all of this to mind was my inadvertently mentioning the word 'brother.' You see, that was the one thing my brother and I had in common when growing up. We did masturbate. I mean morning, noon, and night. He was older and quite naturally more ready, and larger. We might go days without even speaking to each other but, come the correct time in the evening before sleep, we would have some sort of unspoken understanding. You see, Ruby, our parents had bought a set of maple bunk beds for us and I usually had to sleep on the top because my brother would need an earlier start in the mornings. Also, he tended to walk in his sleep.

"It would all begin quite innocently on my part. He would whisper up into the wet, apple blossom night air, amidst the crickets' syncopation outside the open window and an occasional mosquito humming in between our two clicks, 'Ray, Ray, look down here, I've something to show you.' And he did all right, something like a muscular, crescent moon dipped in light yellow fuzz, as though it were lying in our sun-burned back lawn, a garden snake ready to shed its gorgeous skin. And he would stroke it slowly to encourage me to do likewise. But I had a special performance for mine, I would roll back the mattress and bed sheets and turn onto my belly so that my smaller erection could be inserted between the thin wires of the bedsprings."

"But Ray, didn't that hurt it?"

"No, there was something sensational about the feel of the blood-filled muscle against the cold, evening metal. And to alternate between that metal and my warm palm was not to be equalled for many years. I think now I am ready for you. Besides, no one was more special to me than my brother and to have him as my own special voyeur was perfect."

"Do you see him often now, Ray?"

"No, he's dead. But I would like to continue telling you about him before I chicken out. It's something that has needed to be said for some time. He just keeps waltzing around in my confused head, sometimes it's a cadaver, sometimes a whole brother that I see gracefully socking against the nerve endings in my scalp.

"Ruby, there's no sense in denying it; I've been progressively depressed lately over his death. This constant cyclorama of my brother, five years my senior, his excellence at sports and public speaking and way with the girls and affability with the guys, his being favored by the parents and the community and me swirl and swirl and the flame will not extinguish. I'm sure it had a great deal to do with my exodus from the Midwest, in search of something, someone; someone like you who will listen."

Ray munched on a cream-filled maple bar. "But there were such good times, such funny times. He humored me throughout my stay in the U.S. Army. I had been drafted while living in Los Angeles, and the Vietnam conflict was escalating. He visited and corresponded while I pulled duty in New York at a Nike-Zeus missile headquarters. My only salvation during that period was either escape to the theatre–I could easily receive free tickets to all Broadway productions through the U.S.O., or my sojourns on Fire Island during the summer months. I could coast along the Long Island landscape in the uppers and lowers of the Penn. R.R. and look around my compartment and see nothing but strange faces, no soldiers from my base, no sergeants or captains barking orders, no insane generals riding about the parade grounds on top of a fake missile to display their patriotic fervor for the post or their more active years in Korea and Vietnam. Those surrealistic moments of pagentry reminded me of reading of General Compson on parade through the town square; here in the twentieth century was a uniformed white crew-cut with puffy red nose, his too-large ears affixed to the crew-cut as though they were wings carrying him across the parade grounds—straddling a freshly painted shard of metal and displaying medals and a gold trident on stenciled letters of the head-quarters designation, a red shield."

Ruby Francis volunteered, "The picture I get is of an old, ancient man who should have been ousted, mounted atop a sleek robot, his woman, his sad, sad attrition."

"Exactly, Ruby, exactly.... To the best of my understanding, I was only eighteen years old, we had been placed there as figureheads of defense, but we were commanded by some sort of maniac who was deluded by some written orders, issued from deep within the Pentagon, that he was commanding men and artillery in a combat zone. Sad. The reality of the situation was that we merely pushed paper. My immediate supervisor used to reprimand me when I questioned the logic, the purpose of men asking to be returned to combat in Nam. 'Ray,' he would say, 'Just type the damned 1049, the orders on their request and remember, REMEMBER, the more of them that go increase the odds that we will stay. Type, lad, type.' I once wrote a war-poem based on these experiences; I could recite it for you." About then, Ruby hugged Ray and said she would truly want to hear it.

THE MESOMORPHIC ONES

I embalmed others without knowing–
I showed others without showing:
I typed 1049's* for those going
back to Vietnam in the rain.

Sergeant Mapez with seven kids growing
came to me penniless and glowing
red-nosed from boozing and balling:
I purchased his stripes with pain.

I queried my major why would Man
choose to leave wife and safe homeland

58

to witness such carnage and take stand?
he assured me in war all's insane.

I typed til my fingers turned blue
and followed his advice to accrue
a draw'rfull of forms, avoid miscue;
cowards like me stayed typing and sane.

Punishment came from the Moloch within me.
Each soldier, a shade cosmetic, returned
Bloodier, full of malaise, tagged,
Riddled with patriotic malarkey, no longer of
"Bacchic glee" and yes, the lovely misguided
Masochists, yes, the lovely mesomorphic ones!

*Military Special Request Form for Change of Duty

When Ray finished his recitation he amended, "By Ray Landre"
and smiled an embarrassed smile. He never shared his verse with anyone so unbeknownst as Ruby, this, in Ray's mind, had definitely
moved them closer in spirit.

Ruby playfully applauded which spurred Ray on. "I don't mind
admitting, Ruby-Dubbie, I was petrified that I might someday have to
go to Vietnam. The stories, the statistics, the shortage of equipment,
the rotting climate, the stench of corpses. I would toss in my lone room
at night, sweat pouring down my chest. My bed covers the next morning would look like a leaky water bed. Luckily, I could tuck away my
cowardice in that drab room of a lone bed and metal foot locker so no
one could see me. And each morning I would report for duty, I never
had to stand formation, and I would try to squeeze open my eyes and
get the coffee going when I would hear him, the Top Sergeant yelling
outside..."

"Him, who?" She tried to follow his war tale.

"I'll get to him in a moment. But let me continue about my brother; I've got to get him out of my system first.

"Upon my separation from the military, good ol' brother Aloysius
and his dear wife threw a party for me in their chic D.C. townhouse—
he worked for Naval Research. They had about ten couples, friends,
although I had never met any of them. Red, white and blue streamers

decorated the blazing, candle-lit rooms. All the couples were gayly alive, the majority in early marriage. I remember my sister-in-law toasting me, and her cheeky, 'O Dear, you are losing your hair like your brother, aren't you, hahaHahaHa—drink up everyone.' But I could easily overlook her bad taste, and drink her wine. They had thoughtfully purchased California wines of all varietals, Blanc de Blancs, Chianti, Rosé, Cabernet, and spaced them down a long table in the kitchen. The bottles of white and red were laced with plates of cheeses from all over the world. Scrumptious Camembert and Baby Swiss; Longhorns and Cheddars; Goudas and Muenster."

"It sounds simply lovely, Ray. I would very much like to have known your friends, and your brother, of course." Ruby wanted to say the correct thing for she saw how delicate a topic Ray's brother was to him.

"Well, Ruby, I must qualify, I'm just painting the initial picture for you. Lovely isn't quite the adjective for that party. The wine did it to me; the fact that they all knew one another, and I was the stranger, caused me to sip more wine while they conversed. It didn't take long before I was sailing into the realm of vaudevillian nightmare. It was my brother, though, who saved the evening, or set the unfortunate tenor of the remainder of the party. He proudly announced to his twenty-odd guests that I had been singled out by my commanding general, god love his image of a rocket shooting up the ass of a white crewcut. This captured on some slides that were shown to all.... I remember one spectator commenting that the old fart looked to enjoy his position at the beginning of the 4th of July parade, that he looked like something taken out of a wax museum and he wondered what sort of glue or guy wires had been used to poise the old fart atop the missile.

"Our post was warmly referred to by East Coast personnel as The Country Club. The buildings were two and three story red brick structures aligned beside curving cobblestoned roads that were dotted with giant elms. One could still get special permission to view the off-limits bunkers from Civil War days. The post itself had been designed by Robert E. Lee and harbored a top-secret tunnel, supposedly, under the East River. To enter the base was to enter another world and therefore, I suppose, the general had been sent to the correct place. I just never succeeded in understanding my fate in having been stationed there.

"At any rate, at the height of the party, my dear brother tapped his sweat-covered horned-rimmed glasses against his wine glass, and silence turned heads his way. One couple continued to make out beside the coffee table, and one young man had passed out in a seated position between the vise-like legs of his wife as she sat above him shaking her frowning face at my sister-in-law."

Ray concluded the verbatim account of the evening (wishing to be locked in her silken vise in rubric-ruby-fashion). She commented that she could easily see that I harbored a special place in my heart for my brother. I nodded yes, but added that I had always found it difficult to articulate that affection.

" 'Friends, friends, I propose a toast to my brother here. He is a War Hero. He has been awarded this medal and I'll circulate this photo of the actual presentation. As we all know, the death stats mount each day in Nam. Putting your All on the Line is as much as any individual can contribute to the safety and security of his country.' Al, the loyal sibling tipped a shot of Kentucky Tavern."

At that point, as Ray remembered it, a booming female voice resounded from a remote corner of the kitchen, "But what exactly did he do?"

"WHAT did he do? What did he do? Why, he fought and WON the Battle of Fort Totten...Bayside, Flushing, Long Island, New York."

"Fort w-h-a-t??" returned in unison.

"Fort T-O-T-T-E-N. He received the Army Commendation Medal, you know, the highest non-combat medal awarded."

Ray stared into Ruby's eyes to be assured he hadn't lost her. "A multiple of ahs and oohs filled the room. My inebriation was adequate to bring me to a state of melancholy. Separation from the Army was like anything else you can't abide; you hated it for the duration, yet, when the time comes, you nostalgically dote on it. I was caught between tears and laughter. I was caught between accepting my brother's well-intended compliments or acknowledging the facetiousness of his comments.

"Oh, yes, Ruby-my-sweet, I had a talented, beautiful brother. The merrymakers seemed to want some sort of entertainment from me, and my indiscriminate syphoning of the various red and white wines brought forth my latent theatrical talents."

"I didn't know you were latent or theatrical, Landre," Ruby was enjoying his story, after all. Ray gave her a warm hug and forgot they were in the smelly confines of the cherry-syrup sweet atmosphere of the shop.

"I borrowed the household dust mop and straddled the handle. I paddled my thigh as though I were galloping to combat on my missile-steed. 'Vel,' I began, 'my name is Genral Flise!' I paused with my right hand extended toward the swag lamp in the hallway as though some sort of mystical force guided my destiny."

"WHO?" came the resounding drunken responses of the merry-makers.

"Why, don't you recognize me, I am Flise. General Flise! FOX-TROT, LIMA, INDIO, SIERRA, EPSILON' How many times I had heard him, the real Flise, smugly and pathetically call out the military alphabet to communicate his unusual name whether over the telephone or to newly assigned officers—for no one upon first hearing the name could correctly understand it, so he rotely had taken to spelling it out, but that generally further confused the other party. But at my brother's party I had now become General Flise and I robustly exuded my new identity while scratching my balls with one hand and saluting to my audience with the other." Concurrently, Ray had chosen to re-enact the characterization for Ruby and she became rip-roarious at the chimpanzee-like goading of small donut-hole testicles.

Ray rushed on, "I yanked a cocktail napkin from the table and tied it around my arm like an S.S. insignia. I placed a ritz cracker over my right eye as a monocle. I placed a length of string cheese below my nose while wrinkling my upper lip to sustain the grey moustache.

"They were warming up a bit. My date for the evening had stood me up. She was a hot new addition to our post on Long Island and some family matters had precluded her joining me. I think, Ruby, that my clowning was a feeble attempt to cover up my disappointment. I had laid other ass in my private room at Headquarters but she had begun our relationship by cancelling. Anyway, I asked my sister-in-law to bring a roll of paper towels. I feigned a 'reading'."

Ray explained to Ruby that prior to this party his life had been one of retreat and inhibition. Once in college he had read an Allen Ginsberg poem, Howl; Ginsberg, a psuedo-beatnik in a happy coat, but he had been drunk then, too. She loved his caricature of the general and admitted it was a turn on for her that he could be so animated. Ray confessed that some self-chosen therapy had been high school and college stage productions but nevertheless he had never truly become any of the roles. His "Willy Loman" had just fallen flat on the college boards.

"I was merely blasé Ray X, enunciating pat phrases and all the time wondering what the audience thought. Anyway, on to my Washington, D.C., performance: I placed a bachelor button in my mouth and a decorative American flag from the flower arrangement behind an ear. The flower stem added to my feigned speech impediment. 'Specialist E-5 Ray Landre, of Headquarters Battery ARADCOM, on this day you qualify for the much coveted Army Commendation Medal and we extend our best wishes to you for your flawless devotion and attention to detail while stationed here. Furthermore, we would humbly ask that you reconsider termination of duty and extend your service to that of a career, whereupon we could duly promote you to the rank of Staff Sergeant...'" Ray had to admit to Ruby that at that moment it was like the parables of death he had privy to, as though one's life flashes before one's mental vision. It was sickening in that, at that moment of truth he was supposedly being discharged yet it was all being taken away from him. Appearance versus reality. He reported that he nearly panicked.

Ruby Frangible drilled, "What was your answer?"

"Well, let's not lose sight of who is who in the play!" Ray squeezed both legs about her locked knees to insure she was mentally with him. The unknown intimacy for him was overwhelming. He dribbled into his white jockey shorts. "I interrupted him by stating that I had seriously considered all vocational possibilities in my near future and that I had no desire to remain in the military but appreciated their martial kindness. About then, I think I passed out; the rush of the party-members looking down at my youthful, flushed face with the ritz cracker, the blue flower, the unglued mustache, the strip of paper towel across my bedecked chest like some sort of bib, all together must have presented a sort of collage to be trampled or spat upon. I think it was laughter that temporarily brought me back to consciousness, much to the dismay of my sister-in-law. My brother smiled and winked as though he had been insurpassably pleased with my performance, but the laughter and the wine served as a further catalyst to my latent histrionic nature. I became acutely melancholy. For the realization that this would be my final separation from those choice, carefree days with my military buddies closed in upon me. Only the silhouette of my deceased friend, a casualty of Nam, loomed over me. His freckles, his red hair, his quick wit swathed in his Tennesseean southern accent, and promenades in off-duty New York nights picked me up to the kitchen table again. My brother had warned his friends that he had a wino-poet for a brother, something his vanilla wife had never accepted, so I had one last buffoonish gesture to deliver. I reached into my breast pocket, a veritable Hal Holbrook, and began to read my Edgar Alan Poe, four-score-and-seven-years-ago proffering:

OPERATIONS (for Jim Miller)

don't fuck with me soldier about Vietnam,
and the cold wet nights and rotted leather of
your green boots
don't tell me about the girl back home
and the pink-assed baby you haven't seen
don't bore me with what a short-timer you
might be if the silent carpenter
doesn't tack the lid over your languid lips
I fished for causes and fell in love
I had more leisure time to touch
to smell the squirrels scurrying
across the dew laden parade quad
and hear the bass drum shaking the windows
or hear the barnacles at nightsneaking from the east
river up to
my lonely barracks and leaving me
and the boy down the hall played
with me and the captain tortured me
with his firm buttocks spread
with a skunk tattoo telling me
how good I was

well, fuck you, soldier, from Vietnam

for a Tennessee boy brighter than an Einstein
passed and touched me
he whispered Hesse into my brain
do you want me to bore you with
the time I flew back east three years
later and I cried everytime a
bootcamp shaved head in khaki uniform
came on board and I was the only
one that went insane
because when Hermes forces
his spurs into your heart at
two a.m. to tell you this redhead
from Tennessee had his left ear
and brain delicately removed from
his torso because he smoked too many
cigarettes and loved too much
and our mutual pre-Aids Cancer came
then don't fuck with me, soldier:

But I know, I've crawled across
the simulated velvet smuthole with promises
on the other side of barbed wire
(your smile is with me on lonely nights
when I can't sleep for your red hair
almost scraping my eyelids and
the soles of my teenage feet chaffed
red on the Greenwich Village walks you forced me
to take and I can only remember
the unfulfilled mutinies we parted on).

"After the reading, I became aware of the sarcastic comments
about my sentimentality, but I was weak from the experience, the
memory. My brother's wink stayed with me as he removed me to their
concrete womb-like basement to sleep it off on a cot by the mumbling
furnace. I had been shuffled beneath the clapboards out of embarrass-
ing eye and ear shot. It was that wink, Rube, that stays with me in the
hush of evening solitude. For I never saw Jim Miller again except in
the casket. And I recall having read a case history of a terminally ill

patient who had momentarily been declared dead, had had the last rites read to him, but who was revived. His account was that he had been lying in state in some mammoth domed building, lying on his back and face pointed upward. He had distinctly seen his deceased parents on the other side descending to reach him and a superimposed aura of a cross bound the three of them together as one entity. I remember that I cried upon reading that. Anyway, I think it is that wink and consoling face that will await me Over There. I certainly hope so."

Ray Landre hoped that all of this would satiate Ruby Francis' curiosity about his innermost thoughts and family. It was far more than he had confessed to others. It was more than his conscience had wanted to recall. It was not even a dream. It was an exercise in relinquishing what we are normally incapable of giving, this nocturnal, sibling, lustful role-playing.

"Some guests left my brother's house that evening having called it a party, Ruby-do. I knew better."

Ruby wanted to place a period at the end of Ray's military sentence. "What else did the Army impart to you?"

"Perhaps the only other significant outcome of my military career involved a renewed sense of maturation.... I was in the midst of basic training and knew nothing beyond calloused fingers, chaffed groin from strenuous physical exercise, blistered heels from daily five mile marches to the rifle range in too new boots; and that remotely, one day a radio in the barracks calmly announced that Nat King Cole had died. It was incomprehensible; it registered that I had been totally deprived of any knowledge of world happenings. It was this shock, that people were living and dying on the outside, that caused me to shake my shaven head and realize that soon I would become part of all that swift movement again. Vietnam, perhaps. Dinner at the Four Seasons. Subway rides. Coitus. Church. All perhaps. At least, though, Cole remains immortal to this day, a 'Gentleman in Satin.' No immortality for my Jim Miller, though...no gold records, just cold recordings of shadows."

Winks, parties, relating so much to Ruby F., a bit prematurely, Ray needed a drink. He needed it badly. IT was luscious Tankaray (Ray's mother was always generous when he would come home to the Midwest for a visit: he would remind her on the phone, "Now Mom, remember to have me a huge bottle of Tankeray." She could never remember or pronounce the word so she calls IT the Green Bottle. Similarly, maybe subconsciously, she did not want to openly admit to her consumption of alcohol so her habit, her wine coolers, had become "Honey, go to the kitchen and get me some of my stuff." Ray would playfully say, "Mother, you mean you would like some more of your wine cooler?"

"Yes, damn you, my Stuff."

It was a sort of game, a cat-and-mouse routine they played. And they, mother and son, held hands on the living room couch and some said, "You'll be a thought a sissy, a momma's boy," but Ray <u>never</u> cared one iota for she was his only sweetheart.

7 THE LIBERTY CAFE WALTZ

RAY DID NOT CONFIDE everything in Ruby. His journal entry, 3-21:

"I must have time to myself. In the beginning there had been rumors of DEMOLITION but I could hardly believe my ears. The long vigilant nights of wonderful prostitutes walking their highheeled clicks and tricks up the curlicue stairwells to their one-night profitable plays. The neon lights that seemed to dance with boundless fluid veins; the copcar cruisers that seemed to have to get out on the streets at least for a mental-joint, just breathe in the electric ping of Christmas lights and soot covered plastic greenery lining Long Beach Blvd. I think I had been part of that, too. But back to my disbelief -THE LIBERTY COFFEE SHOPPE. Months after the first shimmer of tearing it down, I chanced a stroll along its facade. I coughed and stopped the occasional oldster who also walked along murmuring to himself: 'Can this be? What will take its place? A sailor's bar? A tattoo parlor? Is there to be no liberty in this town of night-hawks?' There were no answers; barely a twisted, upturned, penciled eyebrow; one man pointed his cane up to a 45-degree-angled wooden plank that seemed to support nothing, no nails, no further support, as though those in charge of its demise merely wished to assure bypassers that it would come down, as though revenge would be had. I had to toss my frame past a young couple as they slithered out of Troy's Shang-Hi Inn's swinging doors; they hadn't known The Liberty in her heyday, so why not bump into a hanger-on like myself who had melancholically visited these premises on a belated lark in the first place?

"She threw up on his shoulder and he laughed and I searched my pockets for coffee change that I might escape into a neighboring coffee house with less class, less dignity.

"I drizzled into this nondescript coffee house, a veritable Prufrock, attracted to, yet repelled by, this world of embraces and laughter. The run-in with the heartless couple had beheaded me, degutted me; I knew that as a Lazarus I would not rise from this macadamized death—I was much like The Liberty skeleton up the block, it stood its ground for the time being, but it was only a matter of time before the bulldozers and the young blonde men with their tanned m. latissimus dorsi and m. pectoralis major in their shirtless, bermuda shorts style would heave their restless hammers and crowbars to the last throbbing inner core, hidden away in some leaning sections of antique wallpaper and corroded piping. The target is the architectural coeur where sarcoptic mange had set in and the 8" long gray rats set their incisors into one another's legs and tails, promiscuously passing on molecules of rodenticide like children tossing about volatile chemicals unaware. It would tumble as the better half of Queen's Park (the old Pike) had. I vaguely remembered now the last week of operation, the amusement park's Cyclone had hurled customers up to its shaky summit and plunged them to an almost sexual, breathtaking death at the bottom— the thrill of not knowing if, in fact, one might come out of the ordeal at all. I had stood in lines (and hummed *Sugar Time*, 'Honey in the morning, honey in the evening, honey at supper time; be my little sugar, and love me all the time,' all day, the day before its wooden stilts crashed to the ground like a creature that had outlived its promise, like the crackling body of primordial bones at the LaBrea Tar Pits. I felt silly as I watched couples, old and young, dip into the cool-excitement of their respective cars, silly when I positioned myself into the deep faded red-lined sarcophagus. I was happy for them, and felt a bit bitter that they did not seem to notice me, or if they did, I feared their sarcastic glances; they would most probably notice my bald spot hidden as best it could be. But how foolish...).''

In the diary, Ray had annotatively left his mark of graffito: an assault of stick figures covered the above writing: one with male appendage had an arrow labeled "Pru-Fuck" angled toward it; meandering another page was a childish roller coaster with a boy and girl standing, the arrow indicated "Me and Ruby/I wish I had known her then;" hashmarks with fleur de lis marked "Wallpaper covers cracks and mistakes;" crude sticks of some men, construction workers who coffee break at Winchells, some with arrows plunged through them.

The journal's next page began: "But how foolish; I'm currently in the coffee house and need to maintain a low profile. As when I had been entombed in the cyclone, I nestled into my Naugahyde seat. Upon placing my order, I had to shake my head because the image of a woman in her late sixties, with her hobble and her corrugated eye sockets, briefly realigned itself, as when you shake a kaleidoscope, and Ruby materialized beyond the counter top. I reached for her hand and the meringue on the lemon pie, so yellow next to me, shivered, and I had to withdraw my hand and grasp the dwarf stool's bottom and a net, one of those fishing nets, a 'pound net', flashed before my eyes, because everything, I should say, everyone was getting away too quickly. The girl who had vomited on the sailor's white uniform, the hobo sleeping it off in the shambles of The Liberty, the bobbing heads of youthful haired couples on the Cyclone, and this dear lady before me, all grew tails, all swam like spermatozoa down a channel in my mind with that snare at the far end, and the tramp kept banging his (or her?) head and fins against the interior of the net to get out, but they couldn't, and the rats had fins and gills and they multiplied, and I was on the surface of the Pacific with old liver spotted hands and wrinkles on my face and neck, yet my torso was youthful, I was chanting a sea song and gulls circled overhead and I tugged and pulled and laughed that my catch was good; but alas, when I pulled the net to the side of my skiff, the net was empty, and I retrieved a small multi-colored box and once I pried open the lid, canned laughter flew upon me and I knew, I knew....

"I had actually collapsed on the floor of the coffee shop and, upon being slapped to consciousness, she towered over me, the elderly lady in her yellowed waitress uniform, and in my vertigo I could see the distinct part in her head where a gaudy patch of mixed yellow and gray hair, a fall arched over a rat, met her sycosis infested scalp. Her lips had a 'sticky finger' cutout look as though she had dabbed on red maraschino juice with an eyebrow pencil. We cowered, perched on the brink of some past destiny as though we had known one another. We wanted to acknowledge our kinship—perhaps she was my decayed mother–but we fell from one another in due time. She was kind, but I refused her extended claw and quickly exited. I felt my way along the various properties and dreaded coming to the Liberty corner. There was a small flame smoldering about fifteen feet from the collapsed entrance way, small laughter from the spermophile was tucked neatly back in its shell, but I managed to climb into my dew-covered car and squeezed my way home."

Ray felt that there must be some viable kernels herein for either a poem or story not to mention the love letter that was roiling in his heart for Ruby.

8 "IN-RESIDENCY"

It was nearly 2 A.M. when Ray returned home. The time-lapse-effected blur of red and green and yellow traffic lights had etched an indelible blur of wandering up one-way streets that had intended to set him in the opposite direction. There had been a RADIO MYSTERY THEATRE segment on the car radio that had not frightened him nor made him laugh; it merely accompanied him through the various "warring sectors" of suburbia.

The radio episode dealt with the timely topic of the occult. A friend of Ray, a struggling Hollywood writer, told him that he used to write these and similar scripts for the Salvation Army broadcasts. He would churn out two or three a week for twenty-five to fifty dollars. Knowing such compromise, such prostitution disappointed Ray's faith in the man. Still, Ray's sense of expectation in others had seriously dwindled as he evolved. This had even created a rather "stand-offish" reputation for him. He hoped that this was not evident to Ruby Francis.

Over the VW bug's radio, Ray heard a tale of a farm couple in upper Idaho. The husband, in checking the barbed wire fence, had discovered two slaughtered cattle on the range and both had their genitalia mysteriously severed and the blood was completely drained from the two animals with no visual signs of needles or syringe. He had heard neighbors complaining of similar killings and felt a need to contact the state vet, who informed them that many such sightings were currently being investigated. Seemed that it involved some occult fertility rites throughout the entire northwest. No need for alarm. Needless to say, the farmer's wife went into convulsions when told. Luckily, a dog food commercial left Ray in a quizzical, suspended state of stupor.

Ray found himself pretending, wishing he were a dog who could so easily be placed on a cycle of foods for each stage of his life. Perhaps cream of banana in infancy, then chocolate grasshoppers, then raw hamburger, and, finally, cream of wheat for the gums of his senility. Maybe throw in a few day old donuts created by Ruby for dessert—and how he would lick her in appreciation. In his night-driving, the only activity he had seen was a group of teenage boys unmistakably pilfering a chain of roadway reflectors, like the old red kerosene lanterns that pockmarked the auto's route past soft shoulders and nowhere to go. They looked up at the passing headlamps like startled deer that momentarily checkout the interruption, then once again dip their long sleek necks to their mulching.

Seeing their boyish night-raiding bodies reminded Ray of a prank once pulled by three of his cohorts and himself. Hailing from a small town, one or two high school girls generally fell scapegoats, perhaps the same had been true of Ruby F. One girl, mischievously referred to as "Cherry Delight," was well-liked and came from one of the wealthier families. On one of the prowling nights, they had skidded their old Chevy to a halt at her front door, ran-the long distance from the street up her front lawn, deposited a stolen city street lantern, one of those red-glassed kerosene types, on her front door step. The wick bathed the front porch walls and ceiling with a warm red glow. When Ruby asked Ray for purpose and outcome he responded that they felt they had been particularly clever in their stealth but it was the matter of their collective conscience that started to tug at them.

"Why would such boys have guilt written all over them?" Ruby sincerely wondered.

"After all, some of us had dated, chummed around, laid, in fact, liked her more than most of the girls in our high school because she was, in some ways, one of the guys. We startled each other with accusations, each blaming the other. We also knew of her father's bad temper and realized he would more than likely drill her until the logical culprits' names surfaced." Jump cuts of the Long Beach boys scram-

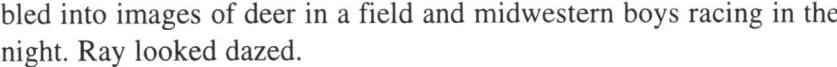

bled into images of deer in a field and midwestern boys racing in the night. Ray looked dazed.

"After much deliberation, we rushed to my parents who also had a reputation for listening to adolescents. The four of us confessed to my parents and at their encouragement we phoned an apology to Cherry's father over the phone. Luckily for us, her father threatened us, for he had already notified the police. He had seen our auto as it sped away. The only acceptable course of action was that we had to drive to her house, by now nearly 3 a.m., and stand in strict formation so that each might look her in the face and assure her that it in no way implied that she were a whore. It was a difficult lie to profess, but the threat of her father was breathing down our scared necks." Ray surmised that the boys he had seen on the streets of Bellflower could be as innocent as an imaginary Ray Landre he had summoned up that evening. The déja-vù disturbed his sleep for once he was ensconced in his apartment, seated at his kitchen table with his plant friends and Waldo, for two or three hours, for he vaguely remembered a spiral of fog letting in the weest bit of morning light. He found a handful of creased Winchell napkins tossed by the salt and pepper shakers, so he peeled off the top one and penciled the following:

> The arrogant chameleon
> polka dotted itself
> much to its lady's dislike.
> He, a sophisticate of sorts,
> and of stabie background,
> became Black Sheep.
> He glowed Red at Art
> objects and Greened
> at Nureyev's impeccable pirouettes.
> But still, he disliked
> Nureyev's street dancing
> and Yellowed so to bystanders.
> Shunned by his past admirers
> he Grayed away
> such a Blue daze
> for an incorrigible chameleon
> not able to set his
> koala, Kierkegaardian character.

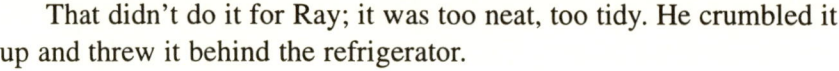

That didn't do it for Ray; it was too neat, too tidy. He crumbled it up and threw it behind the refrigerator.

Ray began again:

> "IN-RESIDENCY" (to Ruby Francis Frangible)
>
> You yelled at me last night
> (your mouth a persimmon canker)
> over my drunkedness
> I wandered through the
> wallpaper warehouse like
> some tarnished silverfish
> crippled beneath the
> loading dock entrance
> but I was plebeian enough
> to salivate over the patterns
> of pink cherubs floating
> amid avocado candy stripes
> and fleshy flocked morsels.
> Yet, we came to an agreement,
> we called it "a trifle; over-reaction"
> these adult threats; these teasers.
> It passed; I soon became pleased
> with your jellyfish gyrations
> upon my silver-string back
> scurrying in the dark
> down an endless aisle of cartons
> and toting wallpaper confetti
> stuck to my tarnished coat
> looking for my severed parts
> unbraided from the bolt,
> a phased-out defunct run
> of pulp ready for redyeing–
> a neat yellow roselet over
> pinstripe—conservative and
> stacked neatly in the warehouse
> domain: so much dyestuff.

As an artist might destroy his unsatisfactory canvas, Ray wadded up the poem and trashed it. He was perplexed why he had written such a travesty of their friendship; they had not known one another enough to yell and belittle one another. He climbed into bed. He missed her. He left the bed and shuffled to the kitchen waste paper basket. He sifted it out, flattened the paper. He retired again even though the heavy drapes could no longer keep out the sun. Waldo mocked Ray with his orange bug-eyes.

At a later date, upon showing her the poem, Ruby was a bit lost whereas the term "run" was meaningless to her. He explained that, among other jobs upon moving to the west coast, once when destitute, he had taken a job in a wallpaper warehouse. He attempted to explain:

"You know, dear, runs...r-u-n-s; it's a term for each printing of a given quantity of rolls of wallpaper. And each bolt of wallpaper is designated a certain run number. Well, if you purchase twenty bolts of Damask in January but fail to get around to the papering until, say, May, and you run short and need to repurchase, you run the risk of acquiring an entirely new run. Now what this means is that the red hues in the damask design may vary anywhere from light pink to dark purple although it's sold as the exact same paper. And once your hanger continues his job with the new run, he discovers that the papers do not match. This contiguity, or lack of, involves a theory that I've been attempting to apply to my writing—or for that matter the creativity of any artist.

"It is not enough to 'feel' such utterances as 'I'm in love, or I hate, or I lust after that luscious blonde across the room.' One must be able to convert that utterance to metaphor and still maintain the aesthetic quality of the experience. This universality will be inherent in the true artist, lacking in others. All of the honed skills of the paperhanger, all the quantity of superlative papers in the world will not bring together a work of art. Consider why today we merely paint over or repaper our tasteless walls; however, occasionally you read of French murals being meticulously removed, panel by panel, from some condemned building in Brooklyn Heights or Pasadena. The writer will likewise find need to gloss over, change, realign the seams or completely remove to begin again when he feels unsatisfied with the end-result. Often the consistency of the hanger's paste is too runny, yet the true hanger's work gels perfectly, automatically, each time. Likewise, the true writer pats together flawlessly his experience, aesthetic experience, metaphor and universality in one errorless product called a poem or a short story or a novel. Simply speaking, there are no gaps in the seams, no buckles in meaning or appearance and yet, due to subjectivity in creativity, the final effect will please some and not others. Unfortunately, some hangers will be called mediocre and some the best; some writers referred to as struggling artists and others having reached the mark. One may have had the profoundest of experiences, or totally absorbed the art of Cavafy or Nabokov; however, the experience and the art and the total product or job have little in common for the novice. There is the esoteric expression of this in Wallace Steven's ADAGIA, (aphorisms of an artist) or in the rather blatant experience of Auden's 'A Day for a Lay.' But I hasten to add each, more times than not, managed to blend each element. If they blend them, it works. Unfortunately, such celebrated artists as Poe or Ginsberg dwell in the land of one run or the other. Once the wallpapering job is completed, but in utilizing mixed or multiple runs, most viewers would not detect the difference as they walked from one area of wall coverage to the next, for they would overlook the discrepancies along the seams or might be deceived that the filtered sunlight coming in the heavily draped windows was casting shadows; and, of course, all of this to the already paid hanger's advantage, for a human being never cares to go back and re-do his work. Or, caught up in the newness and ultimate cost—the viewer and payee would not admit it. Likewise, the majority of readers, upon being introduced to new artists, would be incompetent to recognize talent. They would, out of habit, dwell on the past masters, depend on word-of-mouth via the critics or friends, or dabble in mass reproductions. Few could handle the daring of breaking with convention. The two realms would be applauded separately, but derided when found together. As you can see, this over-sight would create a complete perversity of the desired end result in art. I realize the importance of producing only the latter, yet the sad rejection that it can only result in."

Ruby F. had refrained from looking Ray in the eyes. She sipped her black coffee and muttered a "thank you" for the poem dedicated to her. She thought she was flattered.

TIGER, TIGER...
BLAKEIAN BRIGHT

Aᴌᴌ ᴏꜰ ᴛʜɪꜱ ᴅɪꜱᴄᴜꜱꜱɪᴏɴ drove Ray to make a lengthy application to his journal entry: he often recorded dreams for possible/fiction:

"Kiss me!" said the hunchback. "Trust me, I love thee. Kiss me here." And with the tip of his index finger, hand, arm, and little finger outspread, he pointed to his cheek, near the mouth. And Mario bent and kissed him.

Nightmare. Much good story-telling is dredged from our nightmares. Somehow the hunchback of Thomas Mann's "Mario and the Magician" always returned to haunt me. I had had an unsettling dream by the time I awoke the next afternoon. Apparently, the cadaverous hash-slinger from the night before had triggered a reenactment of that marvelous episode in Mann's CONFESSIONS OF FELIX KRULL when he is summoned to Madame Houpfle's suite to satisfy her longing for a youthful man. The same sleuthful foreplay occurred and I could see the makeup cracking from her wretched face as she desperately lay on her back and squinted her eyes so that he might "steal and plunder." ("Oh, how much more precious to me is the thief than what he took. Hermes. He does not know who it is, and it is he–Hermes. Hermes!") But, RUBY was in the dream, as was I. Our dear elevator protagonist of the moment had propositioned me for a ménage à trois and suddenly Ruby burst into Madame Houpfle's room. A horrendous argument ensued. Mme H. did her best to convince Ruby that she, too, should enter into our game. ("Perversion. Love is perversion through and through, it can't be anything else. Probe it where you will, you will find perversion.") Ruby presented a great deal of tears and threatened to never see me again should I consummate the Mme's obscene suggestions. Felix was beginning to make advances toward Ruby instead of the Mme. and I was becoming jealous and the bell-boy was pounding on the door that he might also be of service. I told Ruby that I had absolutely NO IDEA as to why I was in this chamber (as my conscience is still trying to figure out any plausible connection, since I had not known Ruby Francis intimately). I suppose it was some sort of wishful thinking and I had used Mme H. as a surrogate lover and mother. I snickered to myself that, when I next saw Ruby, I would tell her about my irrational thoughts. — End of journal entry.

Some days later, Ray visited the infamous donut haven. Upon entering the confined quarters he saw Ruby F. in the center of the outer room, in her neat white dress, wielding a crusty pastry gun in the air like Annie Oakley ordering around her circle of male aides and customers. The same poor Mexican boy nervously dropped a glazer rack that sent undulations of loud shock-waves throughout the petite shoppe.

She took her gun and figuratively yanked an up-yours motion that sent him scuttling to his knees to retrieve some of the defaced donuts.

"Would you squander the day's profits?" Ruby screamed at the lad.

Once she spied Ray enter, she cast a mischievous smile and nod of her head to him as though IS THERE NO END TO THIS INSUBORDINATION?!

It was truly good to see her again. Ray told her of his dream; consoled her in her "you can't get decent help these days;" and felt very much catered to once she pulled up a chair and they comforted one another. Ruby responded that she loved her part in the dream. Ray found himself being somewhat defensive as to her role. He called her "dear lamb," "mon petite poulet." The latter merely caused her to flutter her eyelids in blind acceptance as to what he might be calling her.

"Lamb" didn't even seem appropriate to her and he reminded her of
the biblical allusions of innocence and Christ at the well; he quoted a
bit of Blake's *Songs of Innocence*:

"For he calls Himself a Lamb, /He is meek, and He is mild;/
He became a little child./I am child, and thou a lamb,/
We are called by His name Little Lamb, God bless thee!
Little Lamb, God bless thee!"

(As Ray flagrantly cleaved her cleavage with his eyes; his temples
rushed) Her eyes looked way past his forehead as he quoted Blake
with his ministerial voice; she had to be daydreaming or thinking of
something, or someone of long ago. He didn't want to know. He just
wanted to yank her attention back to his world as one must often put
his foot down with an unruly child. She caught herself and giggled in
the childlike manner that he pretended suited her. He moved to the
details of his dream. Who Houpfle was; the complexity of the dou-
ble-narrator technique; (simultaneously, he extended his dream and
escorted her, in his mind, further down the passageway of the hotel
and whisked her into an isolated room, threw her down on the
starched, white bedsheets)...her undivided attention and glowing red
cheeks caused him to have an erection right there in broad daylight,
under her spotlessly clean formica tabletop. Ray wanted to ever so
gingerly insert his "donut stick" into her baker's dozen glazed hole.
(He imagined that he had no sooner twisted his ramrod into her
doughy chamber than a tintinnabulary explosion occurred and sperm
cakes and ovarian peapods vacillated, unnerving him like pubertal dis-
charge.) Ruby could easily see that Ray wasn't sharing all with her; he
could not help but think of the head of his penis, of his disgraceful fantasies in which he had taken liberties with her "lambian flesh." He was
repulsed by his own sexual proclivity. Would she see him as "a dirty
old man?" Were the truckers and hired help tittering in the back room;
did they think him a D.O.M.? Was he no better than they? If she were
the lamb he was most assuredly the tiger: "Tiger, tiger, burning
bright/In the forest of the night...!" And in fact, "Did He who made the
lamb make thee?" haunted him.

Ray lost his hard-on just thinking about the sylvan moment. He

81

stroked her hand for a moment and stood up to say good-bye. He paid her for his Danish and coffee with refill. He felt, upon walking out the front door, that she had earned her money and he pleaded with her that she not laugh at him. At least he had tried, even though he had little success. She seemed to understand Ray's intentions.

When Ray returned to his apartment, he felt it had been an up day. A bit of a headache from last night's Pinot noir, but nevertheless, the flirtatious fantasies of his ménage à trois in dreamland might prove sufficient to get him through the coming week. After napping, he awoke with a hard-on and gently squeezed the head while thinking of her leaning over dog-fashion. The telephone interrupted his lovemaking.

"Would you care to subscribe to Women's Daily...just seven dollars a...."

SLAM. Sometime, as with Jehovah Witnesses at his door right when Ray would be in the shower or taking a crap, he refuted their line of logic and always eneded cursing, but this time to slam down the receiver seemed adequate. Nothing much left to squeeze. He had to start the wheels whirling again.

Prelude for Variation on Dream to Sustain the Image (or as Kosinski universally expresses in his superb simile in describing an elderly man and a young sailor in a porno shop, peep show booth: "Like the quarter dropped into the slot, the other's mouth triggered a silent film inside him. In the darkness of the booth, he and his screen confronted each other."): introductions all around. Ray, this is Rena; Rena, Ray. Ya, hello, Rayie, I hear all about you and have been anxious to meet you. I must admit, I'm a bit nerrrrvous about this, but I love James so very much and he has a power over me, you know; I'll do anything he asks, and if he vents me to go to bed wiss you and him, zhen I have little shoice.

Yes, I understand. Ray's mind completed the imaginary.

James winks at Ray from the corner of his left eye so Rena cannot see.

Rena continues. "You know, Ray, James simply has not been able to get you out of his mind since you two mets over drinkz resantly. Why ziss morning, at eight a.m., he rolled over in bed after cuming in me z' second time and saids Rna, we've got to make a rendezvous with

Rayie. So here ve are. Ve didn't have much trouble finding your place, but parking is a bitch around here. My knees felt veak in valking up here."

Ray could commiserate for, in his mind, this too was his first three way. Besides, women like Brenda had proven such bores. They were either ripping him off or calling in the middle of the night wanting money, or...

James' bold voice cut an image into Ray's fantastical dialogue: I'm so horny, you'll have to excuse me but I'm very straightforward. Perhaps this James was the man he wished he could be. Now Rena, Ray and I are going in on the bed. You can stand in the doorway and watch, you can stay dressed or get undressed and join us. You may even leave if you choose. But we are going to get it on. This is how Ray imagined he might handle a similar situation with Ruby. James seemed sensitive to the feelings of both his male and female partners.

Ya, I vatch for now (Rena sheepishly drooped her blonde head of hair until her chin nearly touched her French bra cupped about her petite teats and exposed nipples).

Ray knew she wanted to join. The two men undressed only after Ray went around and shut all the windows to control and lock in the moans and shouts. Selfish. Careful. All started floating. The huge four-poster started gyrating (like a water bed, but not a water bed) like a merry-go-round in slow motion and Rena kept standing in the door-way feeling her breasts and lifting her skirt. James kept enticing her by grabbing Ray's cock and saying Look at this, Rena, don't you want it? Won't this feel good inside you? It does in me. Then the dream comes in a jump cut for Ray: James goes down on Ray; he eats her; he fucks her; he pinches her right nipple hard, into the air and guides Ray's mouth to it; he inserts one finger, then two into Ray's anus; it stirs him, Ray in the dream-self, and Ray grabs for one of the posts or her small pink foot or James' cock, anything. Somewhat miraculous how all three work and come together. James pulls out and winks undercover again. James pushes her to the headboard and holds Ray's buttocks in his firm boxer-trained fists; he forces his juicy smelly cock into Ray's mouth and shoots while looking at the collective profile in the mirror. He boasts of the quantity of his load and whispers, as Rena dejected-ly shuffles down the hallway to the john, Man, coming in your mouth

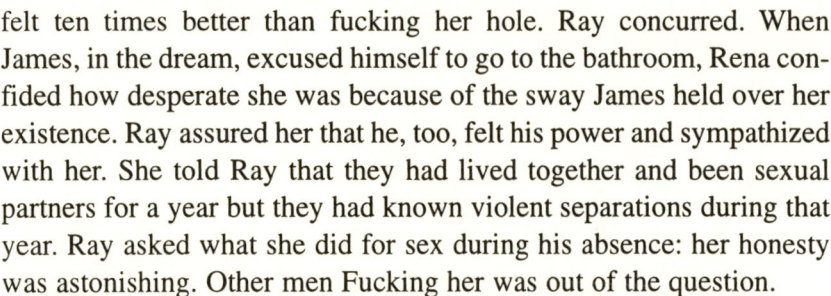

felt ten times better than fucking her hole. Ray concurred. When James, in the dream, excused himself to go to the bathroom, Rena confided how desperate she was because of the sway James held over her existence. Ray assured her that he, too, felt his power and sympathized with her. She told Ray that they had lived together and been sexual partners for a year but they had known violent separations during that year. Ray asked what she did for sex during his absence: her honesty was astonishing. Other men Fucking her was out of the question.

She asked Ray if he knew of the eau de cologne 4711. Yes, he said he often bought it for his lady friends. She continued that Glockengasse No. 4711 also made a second product called 4711 ICE. It seemed that she, on lonely nights, would lie nude in the darkness of her room, after the three children had gone to bed, and stimulate herself by rubbing the ICE on her nipples and massaging it into her vagina. She confessed this a sort of self-inflicted pleasure for the ICE caused a rushing, burning sensation whenever it touched the skin. Later, Ray vaguely remembered seeing a gigantic bottle of 4711 on Ruby's chest of drawers. It all fit together eventually. The telephone rang and that's all he could remember. His stomach and head were upset for hours after the dream. He felt as though he were still on the swirling bed of concentric circles. He looked in the medicine cabinet for some Dramamine. Anything to bring him back down. The only good dream, Ray told himself, is a wet dream. And Rena was unmistakably Ruby Francis.

10 ✪ OSCAR AND VENUS-FLYTRAPS: BIBLE AND OBITS

Rᴀʏ Lᴀɴᴅʀᴇ ꜰᴇʟᴛ he could discern between being intoxicated and alcoholic; he was not an alcoholic. However, his derision of the previous day had served as an adequate catalyst to make him drink himself blind. Additionally, he felt that he never bothered anyone when he did drink; the most harm might be that he neglected to feed his oscar Waldo, or "starve" his kentias and dracaenas and his prize Dionaea muscipula. As a last and self-destructive measure, he might fail to feed his orchids–they were in a class unto themselves and he had once begun a thesis paper entitled LES ORCHIDÉES. His greatest pleasure was knowing he had never completed the paper whereas with each new acquisition, his mind became bombarded with new theories and favorites. He had become addicted to procuring the exotics, long since coveting phalaenopsis, cattleya, vanda and an array of paphs (paphiopedilum). He had made special trips to Hawaii and South America for his curiosity. Any stranger to his apartment might think him some scientist in residence, what with his platters of deceased flies and matted gnats and four inch tweezers lying about (as to strangers, though, he would only now consider Ruby Francis). He had a dwarf atomizer and eye-dropper for measuring the exact amount of moisture; the humidity trays, the giant egg-carton shaped box with

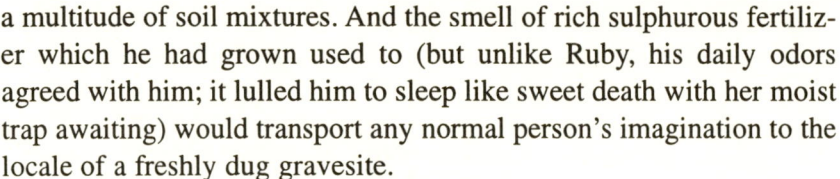

a multitude of soil mixtures. And the smell of rich sulphurous fertilizer which he had grown used to (but unlike Ruby, his daily odors agreed with him; it lulled him to sleep like sweet death with her moist trap awaiting) would transport any normal person's imagination to the locale of a freshly dug gravesite.

Ray showered and shaved. He abated his offensive breath of Bourbon by brushing and gargling with Listerine. He splashed a bit of English Leather (flashed on 4711) on his cheeks and headed for Winchells. Ray wished to try another sitting since he had cleared away so much stale air. He also decided to keep all future dreams to himself, and as to the subject of sexual arousal, that was definitely out. As Ray parted the Pier One import brass bells on Ruby's screendoor, he found her scanning a local newspaper. Ray was pleased to see that she took an avid interest in the world since they had never discussed current events.

Like a dodo bird (he wasn't sure if it was because of his hang-over or fear of erection or the crustiness of the clientele) Ray bumped against the table leg and her paper fell to her lap (lap, lick, lunge, love; lemming, limmer). Laughter. She grinned and asked Ray to join her.

"What's happening out there in that great big world, Rube?"

She grinned sheepishly and held up the section that had intensely occupied her search. Ironically, it was the obituary section. Ray had been so enamored with her live parts on prior visits, he had failed to notice that the obits were the only part of the paper she ever consulted and she did this daily.

"Of course, Ruby, that, you arouse my...curiosity...."

"Once I deviated from the obits; I answered a PERSONALS item in the L.A. Times. Mistake! I had just arrived on the Golden Shores of SO.CAL., via the Greyhound terminal waiting room, claimed my sole trunk of clothing, lugged it about and plopped my can on it—I had heard the ominous stories of becoming local prey. The ad ran:

> WANTED-female roommate. Must be serious and
> good-looker. Apply in person, 5432 Olivia St
> (in the rear).

I took another bus to said location; was greeted at the screendoor of a garage apartment; he seemed most pleasant, said his name was

Gerry and once I handed him fifteen dollars, he greeted I was IN and could pay him more later. It was my first experience with a 'straight roommate.' He cautioned me that he wanted no hassles. He was twenty-three, wore only tee-shirts and Levis. I was not to touch his valuables which turned out to be his bacon and tomatoes or milk in the fridge (that's all I ever saw him eat in the three months I lived there). Bathroom privileges meant who was in there at the time. Lights were to be out by 11:30 p.m. I liked him, first impressions and all, so I accepted."

Ray soon figured out that Ruby meant platonic relationship when she had labeled Gerry as a straight roommate.

"He never seemed to have time to talk once I was settled; besides I was out pounding the streets for a job. I remember once feeling particularly depressed and my ankles had swollen from the bus rides and flights of jobless stairs. Gerry must have heard me crying and knocked on my side of the room wall. We spent most of that evening philosophizing about drinking, politics, god, family and finally he turned about and cast his problems upon me. He probably thought it all might make me feel better.

"It was all very involved. Many things he said made no sense to me. He kept mentioning SDS this and SDS that. At age eighteen, he had become affiliated with a handful of first year college students because he felt he loved one of the girls, Allison, and idolized their leader Hank. One night they had accepted the challenge of a neighboring college's SDS group leader's plans and sneaked onto campus at LACC with some homemade explosives. He had been guaranteed that no one would be hurt, that their only intention was to shake up the officials a little; no one would be around at such an ungodly hour.

"What ensued was more than any of their smug group was willing to take credit for. He had told Ruby that at his naive age, he might qualify to be a sneak thief, but he was certainly not of criminal fiber. They followed their penciled map and found their way to the Admissions Building basement (or so they had thought). The leader and a second member planted their deed while Gerry and his girlfriend Allison kept watch should anyone show up. Overlooked was the nightwatchman who made his rounds about that time. A door rattled, they set the explosive and ran. They returned to the point of origin and

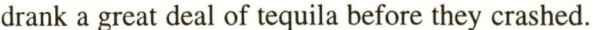

drank a great deal of tequila before they crashed.

"However, the next morning, the newspapers carried bold head-lines of 'One Killed and Two Injured; LACC Blast.' Gerry claimed that he had nothing to do with the incident; he deserted the other parties and took an assumed name. It had been difficult to locate a job and acquire a driver's license without all the proper I.D., but slowly things were taking shape. He told her that her share of the rent would help and he trusted that she had listened to all of his 'confession' with absolute confidence. Soon, though, he had to move on."

"Do you hear from him?" Ray allowed his sheltered background to show.

"Not really; I've lost touch with him. But I still harbor great compassion for him. I don't feel that any human being should have to live in constant fear of being apprehended by the authorities."

"We all have to pay our dues at one time or another. After all, you don't even know his true identity let alone where he might have traveled to by now." Ray wanted to father her.

"So far I haven't seen anything about him," she jostled the obits up and down with both hands in front of her like Ray might separate seeds on a level piece of cardboard. "I spend a great deal of time worrying about him."

Ray noticed that she never clipped out the obits, just kept piling the spent pages in her back room or tucked under her bed. "They could create a fire hazard, you know."

She responded Not Likely. She was a vigilant saint; rather the Cattleya 'Lovely Beauty' all white blushed with a hint of yellow.

As an aside, though, to Ruby's tale of SDS, and subsequent to Ray's leaving teaching, he often noticed in the news magazines lengthy essays upon the new political correct stance on campuses throughout the land. He felt this wave of righteousness versus Right versus free speech might well have stemmed from such tunnel vision advocates as those in SDS or the Black Panther movement. He could envision going back in time and effectively using the material as supplementary reading in his impeccable lesson plans, say for the teachings of George Orwell's *1984*, or Martin Buber's *Fundamental Relations: I-Thou versus I-It*, or Reinhold Niebuhr's *Thoughts on Christian Commitment*. These were topics that Ray hoped to broach with Ruby in the future. As to considering lesson plans and their contents, Ray truly needed to transcend such mind-sets; that was ancient history.

Ray mentally composed a ditty after one of his newly found gardening accounts:

> The flower felt petulant today
> normally a gem of disposition
> but being asked to clean gutters
> of guana and rust chips, decomposed
> leaves, he mentally turned up
> his nose at the turd-infested lawn:
> Cursed her wealthy soul, forgot
> his precious investiture,
> his vigilance over snaps and petunias,
> pansies and perfectly weeping
> wisteria.
> His motto, "I'm out making
> the world a little greener, today."
> And my little helper Randy
> always quoting "The Color Green
> is from the Heart"
> to his self-made tune.

Ray smiled smugly at himself, seeing them as two small boys with an agrarian secret others could in no way comprehend.

II.

Ray rather appreciated this weird interest of Ruby's, though, this keeping abreast of the daily obits. Admirable and understandable when one thinks about it.

"Yes, yes," Ray told her, "I think everyone has some person from his or her past who he would like to spy on, keep tabs on, hear from or be able to anonymously peek at from the woodwork and say 'Yes, there he is, a bit altered, but safe and healthy and the same ol' Joe Schmoe I use to enjoy.' It's a sense of permanence. I remember once, upon moving into the Bellflower area some years ago, the phone would awake me in the middle of the night, sometimes two, three, or four a.m., oh, about once a month. An aged, wheezing female voice would quiz, 'Ray? Ray Landry? Is it really you, dear?' And I would, time and again, try to explain that I was a Ray Landre, but obviously not the one she had known. Once established that she had known her Ray over forty years, I explained that I wasn't even near that age at that time. She refused to accept the reality, the impossibility, the disappointment. She wanted to believe that I was hers. There was invariably the gamut of resulting confusion, the silence on the line, my short temper at being aroused at such an ungodly hour; I would become curt, curse, call her a crazy old lady who should be locked up once I set the police on her. I felt very sorry for her and, you know, to this day, although I move from one community, one location to another in this vast southland, I still hear from her even though I carefully change my phone number, she somehow comes across my name, Ray Landre, and tried one more desperate time to reestablish a connection with the one she loved and yet I rebuke her."

Ruby asked, "Did you ever meet her?"

"No, although I could somehow envision this faceless being on the other end of the phone wires as a mental patient who is mercilessly condemned to being enveloped in layers of restraining jackets and adequately gagged. Then on hostile nights she, in Houdini fashion, escaped by weaseling her corpse-grown finger nails between the straps and stealing down an unguarded corridor to a pay phone booth where she easily dials information for a new listing for Ray Landre. No one stops her in the hallway because no one recognizes her without the straight jacket and muslin gag. Her legs are hairy and she limps from lava beds of sanguine bed sores."

"God, Ray, you paint such a gross picture...."

"Her pleading reminds me of Ingrid Bergman's role in *Goodbye Again* as she yells to her fleeing youthful lover, 'Please understand; I'm old, I'm old,' and she forfeits her passion for him for the tragic security of the older bastard she has lived with for five years. The old hag is pleading 'I'm old but, Ray, if you'll just take me back one last time. Just acknowledge that I exist.' The only space of enamel in her otherwise algaecovered dentures is where the gag has rubbed and it is this space that emits her sparse questions that end up in my bedroom receiver. She is disgusting and I would like to kill her. I've never killed anyone other than in my poetry. I once killed a cat, it took three poems, three variations, three killings; but all are the same cat and what Pandora the cat symbolized in my life at that time became effaced. The other death I planned was an obscene phone caller, so although this elderly mad woman is beyond knowing the danger, she might be my next victim...and I nearly forgot...I also killed my father and only brother, but that was metaphorically speaking." Ray gave Ruby one of his sinister smiles.

Ray could see that he had frightened Ruby. What he had hoped to be a bit entertaining for her had flip-flopped and besides, he could see that Ruby's search for Gerry was more admirable; she felt love and compassion for her past friend. And, when all is considered, for Ray the only true sections in today's news are the obits and the comic strips.

III.

Once home, Ray began an unfinished journal entry poem: title?

Party Line

> a journal of things to say to the bitch
> who awakens me, middle of the night,
> with her obscene calls
> first, the smack, smack double-bubble
> a wild woman, frizzy spaghetti hair
> her cherry throat once whizzened
> a guttural, monosyllabic beauty
> I think I'll dial O
> and punch her right in the kisser
> I'll rip the damn thing out
> before baring my balls
> to any saliva smacking jerk out there
> like her

Ray attacked the page with scribbles; he focused his thoughts on the beauty of Ruby and tried again; softer strokes, fluid lines:

LES ORCHIDÉES
(for lea-carol fordyce)

Like the orchid's placement throughout the salon
you are lovely everywhere
enhancing the gardener's eccentricities
and opening, time capsule fashion, secrets
she's lovely in Paris, too, but cinched in
with babe and repetitious schedules
by someone's foreign-languages and formulas:
she's no fear of life's echoes just as
the Princess Mikasa doesn't tremble
with each settlement of the house's foundation
or a babe's crying away the pregnant night
The orchids are gentle and lovely and kind.

A treasure from the orchid society's sale
out of its snug forest of fellow seedlings
prepared to begin Death in its bloom
she too at her period of ovulation
plucked from ageless African soil
then it's back to Ouagadougou, girl.
Orchids ride well if packed well
in shredded newsprint from Nairobi
and don't intellectualize their uprooting
they just pose, to test the loyalty
of the inevitable, not needing the humiliation
of reminder of the complete needling absence ahead.

At a spurt of so-so motherhood
barren now her years do grow:
the orchids are gentle and lovely and kind
and oh so expensively enslaved.

When Ray died, the obituary could say anything they chose to
include Donations to Charity of Choice: he just hoped his friends
would send orchids, fields of exotics to surround him.

11 "TOUCH YOUR SOLITUDE TO MINE"

THE PHONE WAS RINGING OFF THE HOOK. It was Tuesday, about noon, and Ray awoke to the gin-stench boomeranging from his pillowcase. The dryness of the night-before's booze sucked in his cheeks and lips; his teeth seemed coated with garlic and tunafish salad. He took just enough measured time crossing the sunless-parquet (he gave daily thanks for dual-strength drapes) to ensure that the party on the other end would, hopefully, give up, but his stride was too turtlish. He yawned his pointed, toothless, horny beak from his gillaceous shell; the caller was Ray's Girl, Ruby Francis. She had located him through a gracious operator (Ray could never discern what an unlisted number meant).

"Why, Ruby-duby, I'm flattered." Both Ruby and Ray knew what he meant for he had never given her his phone number. He had reason, he wanted to maintain certain boundaries. He had not wanted to go too far in the relationship, too prematurely. He had always been the aggressor and sought her out. He had bought her pastries and went to her window selling nothing except himself. It was too like an overly excited bidder at an antique auction: the reluctant eyebrow darts, the timid fingers rise, the precarious hand and wrist quiver; the auctioneer barking "going once, twice, SOLD to the buffoon in the corner–one genuine used rubber worn by the Marquis de Sade while engaged...; $3,000." All of this went through Ray's mind before he effected his newly found phone voice for her, "What exactly is wrong, my dear?"

"Wrong? Oh nothing like that. I am depressed somewhat. Nothing I can't get over. But I've thought a lot about things you and I've discussed. I even look forward to your visits. Perhaps you've noticed the last couple times how I reserved our table" (she did this by not cleaning it off until Ray arrived; Ray told himself a wee bit lazy but nevertheless he appreciated the sentiment).

"Ray, do you think we have a chance?..."

"Well, I have been speaking to you..."

"And I to you..."

"But a chance about what...," he stared at Waldo who was making menacing circles in his cramped quarters of algal laced glass. "As I told you, I am excited that I'm going to start my own gardening service..."

"But I suppose you know that I could never abandon my donut venture...It's my livelihood." Ray could hear long clear inhalations of her cigarette in the background.

"Well, as you say, Rube, we have been speaking, but maybe that's part of the problem." He, too, puffed.

"Oh, do we have a problem? Or is there a chance? You do feel there is a chance, don't you?"

Ray continued to respond to the tenuous: oh, he knew what she was driving at and, if there was anyone he did not want to cause to squirm, it was Ruby. "In part, it's the men who line up for you and their comments, they are disgusting to me. I see no kindness in their faces."

"I know that, Ray; it's just good business—it's been paying the bills. And they bicker over the petty rising costs. I can't please them no matter what I do. My glazed and coconut holes are no longer delectable, they aren't movers the way they used to be. Why, used to be I could sell five, maybe six dozen holes by eleven a.m. Now they just sit in the case. My god, they get stale, hard. They mold by the second day. But you, Ray, my sweet, you are different. You take time. You compliment me on my fresh-perked coffee; you flick glaze particles into your hand and throw them into the trash. You never leave a mess. You don't complain, that means so much. Your mouth waters at my dimpled cheese blintzes."

Ray's imagination heard "blitzes" and he fantasied holding his machine gun to her vagina; his entire body vibrated an intense secret campaign in between her mellow soft-perfumed breath.

"...and Emanuel adores you. He says he never has to wipe up after you...."

Ray's word association reminded him Dribbles at home in jockey shorts only; not in public.

"What I'm getting at, Ray...."

"Ruby-cube, I appreciate your phoning. I was sleeping, though, and have a few matters that need attending to this morning. Waldo and Pretoria, my Venus' flytrap, are about ready to devour me if I don't nourish them." Ray could see his roguish tongue completing a thorough lap lavation into Ruby Francis. "You understand?" Ray changed his tone and enunciated:

> Deftly sing it, lady, praise
> How I love me in your maze,
> Gladly lost there, never found,
> In your honeyed underground.

"What was that you said, Ray?"

"Oh, no-thing, no-thing, my dear," he couldn't resist a little mid-morning W.C. Fields phone-play, a fancy phrasing fore-play. "I'm merely quoting a little Bradbury-versification...."

"But I thought he was a science fiction writer?"

"He is, but much more. He can lasso stars and populate new worlds; he can breathe life into a salamander or create love in male and female robots—" Ray then whispered, "—h-e i-s," long panting breath, "G-o-d-d-d-d-d! I think he had you in mind when he continued his 'Touch Your Solitude to Mine':

> O. men by thousands, such as I
> Would gladly 'neath your sweet grass lie
> To claim what's tucked beneath your lawn
> Will rise as fresh and young as dawn.

"And that, my dear, is precisely what I am doing, rising, and intend to do, rise. You must know I care. I get ever the tiniest tinge of

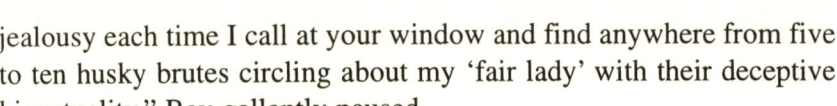

jealousy each time I call at your window and find anywhere from five to ten husky brutes circling about my 'fair lady' with their deceptive biceptuality." Ray gallantly paused.

"Oh pshaw, Ray. But I would really like to know more about this writer Bradbury, or at least what you think and know of him."

"Ruby, the way I feel is that he is absolutely optimistic regarding the human race. I mean, we could have, could read, as the object of literary criticism and interest, an author who is so negative that we would be constantly exposed to down-ideas and adverse consequences—a purge of mankind, if you will; however, Ray Bradbury dwells on the beauty of human relationships, the love that exists in the universe. He brings about the death of machines when not seen in the control and light of human qualities. He has a story, I wish it were required reading, called 'And the Rock Cried Out.' There's an American couple traveling in Uruguay. They are out of touch with the civilized world, some time in the future, but unfortunately, in traveling through small, impoverished villages, they are associated with the white travelers who have gone before them, travelers who have been supremely guilty of being in too much of a capitalistic rush and leaving behind only cigarette-burned hotel furniture and the flash of the dollar bill. They are now in the minority. Significantly, although they appear to be doomed at the conclusion of the story, they remain loyal to one another. They must keep their personal pride, their love, their humanity about them.

"My favorite character, though, the one I identify with, was old Garcia tooling along in his 1929 Ford. He gives the stranded American couple a ride. He reads week-old News for a more objective perspective of his out-of-the-way world. All slows down; headlines are nothing—sly deception. He philosophizes 'Why you can spit on it (newspaper) if you wish. It is like a woman you once loved, but a few days later she's not quite what you thought.' Ah, Ruby, the superb simile. The need to slow down before it's too late.

"I will read it to you some evening over coffee. You're much stronger than the wife in the story, but you'll love it. He, Bradbury, is a supreme optimist and we all could benefit from his wisdom and his hope. He won't always be around but he will always be around. You'll see. He once autographed a paperback for me, _Something Wicked This_

Way Comes, my fav. I felt stupid, childish to ask for it. But I'm glad that I did. It's something personal, sort of like owning your own author, see, and possessing the knowledge 'this guy is a swell friend, he writes for me.' He's burning, exhausting all avenues in his writing, right now, somewhere. I'd offer anything just to buy one of his dreams. I wager they are sensational—a mixture of Woody Allen, Spike Jones and Andy Warhol with a touch of _Fellini_ and _Mahler_ orchestration. He's positive. Keep that in mind, Ruby. There's too much of this negativism shit around us and he's out to exorcise it from the human race. He even interprets The _Exorcist_ as a pure illustration of motherly love. Regan's mother will go to any extreme to help her possessed daughter. Instead of dwelling on the ugly side of life, he extracts the beauty. Any true artist does the same, Poe, Polansky, Jesse Allen, Updike, Dylan." Ray retired from the receiver.

"You are a charmer, no doubt, Ray. You, you don't mind that I phoned, though. Please say you don't."

Ray lied, "Everything is fine. I'll be in touch soon. Please be patient. My flesh, my body is sorting out what my mind debates. Keep the ovens hot. Let the glaze flow! Bye."

* * *

The phone conversation triggered within Ray one of their previous sittings. Long after their original introduction and hedging formality, Ruby confessed that she was most curious about Ray's other-life, his private or secret or sexual proclivities. He assured her that there was little to tell.

He did proffer a recollection from an early age when a neighbor boy would command he and his younger sister to undress and lie on the bedroom floor while he carefully tossed metal-tipped darts into the air and let them fall where they may. Once one of the darts pierced his sister's thigh and it took several minutes to stop the bleeding. "I do remember getting an erection, though, so I hastily replaced my underwear. I also can still see 'Crazy Mary' who lived behind the city dump. She would come loping to town with her gargantuan, unshaved legs and we, as kids, used to jeer obscenities at her from our neighbor's rose bush and tiger lily fence. Early on, I had asked my mom one summer evening why Mary's boobs bulged so and hung so unattended like

97

two oblong plump watermelons inserted in her moth-eaten sweater.

"My mother said 'The young lady is filthy, deranged, and only escaped incarceration in the local state hospital because of her sad story and sympathetic local officials.'

"In her early teens, Mary had been made pregnant and jilted by some college boy. He had left no address or intentions of helping her. She had, as the expression goes, 'Gone off the deep end' and everyone just left her alone to walk to town every other day for a six pack and her self-inflicted badgering from the respectable people on their rotting front porches. I wondered what it might be like to envelope such bulbous rinds in my young mouth, but never confessed this to my concerned mother's watchful ears." Ray had drawn a parallel for Ruby regarding her confession of man-lust for her black football star.

Ray continued, "Actually, a stranger relationship intrigued me the most. A boy two years my senior, named Klancy, was most cruel to his playmates. He was a short fart who ruled the neighborhood with an iron fist. Many an afternoon I would see him hold a kid to the ground in the adjacent garbage strewn lot and force him to say nasty words or Klancy would spit in his face. He loved to tie up the playmates and leave them howling to the rusted idle Studebakers and Fords strewn about the dirt. Or, he would blow up prophylactics and force them to open their mouths that he might taunt them. Uncannily, he was always good to me. He seemed to go out of his way to assure me that I needn't expect any such roughhouse from him. Deep within, I wanted to admit that it might be more desirable than he could possibly know, but I never made known these unthinkable feelings. I do remember one summer evening when his parents were away and he asked my parents if I might stay with him, that we would sleep on their huge, battleship gray front porch. It was well-surrounded with wooden shingle railings and no one could see our pallet or our young forms in jockey shorts."

Ray had paused, not sure if his refinement might offend. He surmised that Klancy had fantasized throughout the week what games they might play to pass the hot night. One hour he would be Gene Autry twirling an imaginary lasso from one side of the porch to where Ray was anchored on his bare knees. He would feign to pull Ray to him and go through tedious efforts of untying him. He might softly swat Ray across the butt or pull the back of the shorts down a quarter

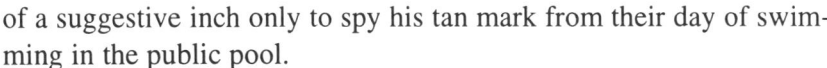

of a suggestive inch only to spy his tan mark from their day of swimming in the public pool.

"Another game of role playing, Rube, was one of Pirates and their violence and captures. I think Disneyland's Pirates of the Caribbean has supplanted such fantasies for today's children, but this was real. He held an invisible sword tip, which he carefully described for me, to my navel, after boarding my ship, and commanded that I drop my frilly shirt and drawers for him. My mind raced with rumors and incidents of what he had done to others at recess; he had often been known to hold down his playmates, ruminate a plug of fresh chewing tobacco, and then carefully drop and spit squirts of it into their eyes. I turned my back to him and did as he asked.

"About that time I heard a chuckle from behind one of the living room windows and saw a shade flash shut inside the open window. Klancy and I simultaneously realized that his kid sister had been watching much of our play all along. It was childish games and childish embarrassment, but as I'm sure you see, a night I have never forgotten. He chased her to her own room and rejoined me, whereupon we climbed up some trelliswork to the roof atop the two-story house. The sky was one of stars and a full moon. This was pre-television-antennae invasion of the village sky and an occasional mocking bird would woo us to sleep. Klancy lay back exhausted and my heart throbbed that our secret might be found out. Nothing much was ever said again and we continued being friends throughout high school."

Ruby seemed most startled by Ray's report of the last incident. She said she had never been exposed to such unusual circumstances, such cruel individuals. This caused Ray to raise an eyebrow as he thought of some of her escapades, but he decided to leave well enough alone. If she wanted to live in her half-believed piety, he didn't want to be the one to upset her. This particular conversation, though, had forced Ray to come to terms with his loss of job, lack of girlfriend, and forced him to more clearly see that his sought-after goal was simplicity. He could see that her exposure to SDS and lustful relationships that she had labeled as loving, that she had dumped a great deal upon his shoulders and he needed to concentrate upon his gardening. His inner voice kept him in line.

12 THE CROSSROADS OF EPHESUS

CHRIST AND SDS: Christ for SDS? Christ in SDS? Sad Decadent Society? Ray had no explanation for his rudeness regarding Ruby's phone call. He felt flattered yet he chose to reject her. He found himself a turbulent adolescent in an ancient carcass. He was reminded of fair Lois in his college days. She had sketched him nude : she wasn't afraid, it was he who balked at her offer. Although her face was pock-marked and her hair unmanageable, she was warm. Like himself now with Ruby, she had wanted to be wanted. Lois had stalked the student union for companionship. She was a bottomless thermos waiting for scalding emotional warm-ups. She sponged, scavengered for friends in every nook and cranny of her limited exposure to academia. Like a teenage boy who needed the money and scraped barnacles from ship frames for nickels and pennies, Lois prostituted herself. Ray had seen her in mutual Victorian novel and Art history classes. Then no Lois. Dr. Fairey-Rose had even thought of reporting her as missing to the campus police. But word eventually reached the classes: Lois had joined SDS—Oh happy day! She now belonged.

To compartmentalize, a liberal democrat (not that she would know the difference). She might fulfill Norman Mailer's description of one who suffers from a 20th Century "chronic disease," that of needing an object for her novitiate hero worship. He goes on, in his *Cannibals and Christians* to place his finger on her (and SDS's) inherent problem:

101

> The art is to practice duplicity and double-dealing
> with a sense of moderation, taste, and personal style;
> the secret is to remain alert to the subtler shifting
> realities of mass communication: what sort of news
> in this season is likely to become national, which
> oratory will happily or unhappily remain local.

Acceptance where possible. Lois' tragedy was that she was being used. She was a victim of duplicity, double-dealing. Those huddled masses of weaklings or hecklers that congregated to listen to their amplified, angry, destructive voices in the mid sixties were victims, but those like Lois had been given a double dose of "students for a democratic society" sort of brainwashing. Acceptance, rejection. She ultimately left SDS's failing fold, and later word indicated that she had committed suicide, OD'd. She apparently never found what she had been looking for because it didn't exist. It had all been disguised in a young, articulate man's ego who had more than dirty politics in his mind. Various news agencies would, weekly, uncover plots to completely disrupt classes and blow up key buildings on such prestigious campuses as UCLA or USC. Blind, obedient sheep like Lois and her ilk were infuriating Ray.

Being particularly critical of others, Ray had to ponder that he was now categorizing Ruby in such leagues as street walkers, brainless whores, yes a harlot...but he knew he was daily growing to love her. Ray often scribbled scriptural nonsense throughout his journal, a sort of self-inflicted sermon to pump him up emotionally. Like Matthew 21:1-46, wherein Ray could espy Jesus' triumphant entry into Jerusalem, his toppling the tables of the money changers in the temple; his healing the blind and the lame. His parable of the Vineyard.

To differentiate between those who "profess" and those who "act." His sermonizing clarified that "actions speak louder than words; repent and ye shall be saved." To quote: "Jesus saith unto them (the chief priests), Verily I say unto you, That the publicans and the harlots go into the kingdom of God before you." Jesus' performing of miracles did sorely present a threat to the financial and spiritual security of these men. When they had looked upon his acts and saw the dazzlement and awe of the onlooking children, they became most defensive.

Christ reminded them, "Out of the mouth of babes and sucklings thou hast perfected praise." Such biblical assurance gave succor to Ray's misgivings when he considered Ruby's past. She was not, after all, the disgusting Pious of the priests' personality nor the Pious of Graham Greene's fictional antagonists. Ruby Francis Frangible is merely herself, no more, no less. And lastly, Christ's denunciation of the priests and his prophetic rejection, "Therefore say I unto you, The kingdom of God shall be taken from you, and given to a nation bringing forth the fruits thereof," more easily allowed Ray to construe (or misconstrue at will) the favoring eye of Him cast her fruit-bearing, compassionate way (Ray again cast himself among the men-in-waiting at her window).

To further explore Ray's passionate paranoia regarding his wishes to consummate their relationship, he considered his conservative bit of traveling across the Continent. One of his fondest memories involved a pilgrimage to the last known residence of the Virgin Mary (though he is not Catholic) and that same day scuttling across the Marble Street of Ephesus, that 3,000 B.C. creation of the Delphic Oracle. He scaled the hillside of the Cave of The Seven Sleepers—this myth seemed to reinforce Jesus' promise that God will protect the believers who earnestly try to stay on the straight and narrow. He could smell a cool, verdant breeze cascading down the parched hillside. He staggered to dip his white hands in the same sacred water that Mary had drunk during her last days.

Ray next washed his dusty face of its shame and guardedness. Then he staggered into the reconstructed last residence. He grasped a lone white candle to complete the inexplicable urgency that tugged at his chest and his groin. He stood before the makeshift altar so a-golden with myriads of lit candles and long-eroded rock above and around and beneath him. Her statue, dark and somber, cast its eyes down into his, but he blasphemously could not help seeing his earthly mother, his woman of known-Sacrifice and Good and Sorrow. Ironically, he directed his prayer to his Earthly Mother after gasping those many thousand miles of pilgrimage and falling at the near-toes of a non-entity in the form of a hologram. He fled from the sanctuary with sweat ringing his shirt collar; he bumped into an octogenarian who picked up her three-legged aluminum walker, inch by inch, to coerce her black shawled head and elephantiasis legs to the same altar. Ray wanted to wait and see, and know that she would kneel; it might take 24 hours to get the courage and correct state of martyrdom, in complete submission to her Lady's sorrowful unction, but he needed air, the cool refreshing isolation of this mountain top, the shade of the olive trees, to once again partake of the spring water, sacred water, holy moisture of Christ's suffering agony (he remembered his youthful mother drooping forward to insert her nice breasts into her cross-my-heart-bra). A gigantic blimp of siamese twins emerged in levitation above the olive trees: Mother and Madonna joined at breast and hip—they looked sweetly to one another. This apparition was probably the most significant dream of his life up to that point.

Ray often annotated, by use of an overly large capital D in his journal entries. He thumbed back to the pages that readily reproduced the Dream:

"It seemed that I had returned to my birthplace. Both parents were still alive. Mother, mind you, not father, had supervised and constructed an entire upper level to the existing house. She had converted the attic to a series of box-like rooms. I entered through a hole in the living room ceiling via a shoddy ladder. Father was unable to climb the ladder because of his failing health. In the upper region mother was green of flesh and she walked about with a carpenter's apron and penny nails in her mouth and she flourished a hammer. The floor and walls and ceiling were of newly cut pine and all smelled fresh as if a busy lumberyard. I could see dark black dotted lines along these surfaces as though she had meticulously created all of this from a sort of pattern. She had a check list in her hand and she was so proud that she had done it all by herself. Everyone seemed complimentary including my dream-self. I was, in short, amazed at the industriousness and professional workmanship.

"An aunt and uncle of mine were having an argument about their wayward children, how rotten they had turned out and why had it happened to them. Another uncle, in real time deceased, was present in mom's upper region; he kept disturbing the domestic harmony by insisting that he needed to walk to town for a drink. The bar he mentioned caused some concern but I could not convince him to heed. He left. I soon begged leave, too, and enroute noticed a sleek red Corvette

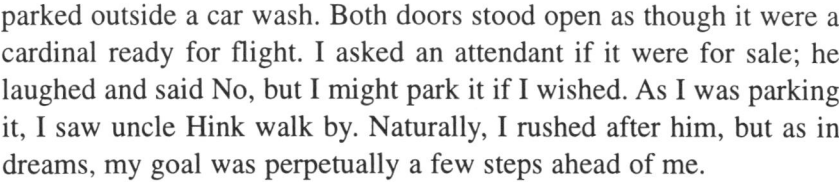

parked outside a car wash. Both doors stood open as though it were a cardinal ready for flight. I asked an attendant if it were for sale; he laughed and said No, but I might park it if I wished. As I was parking it, I saw uncle Hink walk by. Naturally, I rushed after him, but as in dreams, my goal was perpetually a few steps ahead of me.

"He and my father, father on his crutches, walked in the door of the Falcon's Nest Bar—they were swallowed by hordes of people drinking ale and laughing and swearing. I could smell amyl nitrite; I could see yellow puffs of poppers seeping through the cracks in the wallboards. I could smell grass, too.

"I suppose the anxiousness to detour them from this bar was my realization that they could never understand the difference in the generations, could never understand just how decadent we had all become without meaning to (certainly a tinge of guilt on my part). For my father to experience a disco while comparing it to his younger days would, I suppose, be as traumatic as Solzhenitzyn's account of his portrait of the Easter Procession at the patriarchal church of Peredelkino. We, the Youth of the World, had progressed to a new low in our adoption of dope, amorality, sexual promiscuity, spaciness and our new luscious vices.

"And I heard funereal music: 'Love Hurts' and 'These Boots Were Made for Walking' and as usual the participants. Some thirty female groupies with pigtails and Alice Cooper eyes undulated across the dance floor in Hustle-fashion and I blinked to see them as thirty Louise Lassers and Roseanne Barrs snorting coke. Father wasn't totally there, in my dream. No, I was too late. I could see father across the crowded room holding to his crutches with one hand and holding his other to a mouth and a breast and a limb of various strangers in an attempt to record and understand; but he kept shaking his head No, No. He finally became drunken and fell to the floor where no one noticed or reached to help. His end was horrendous. I saw two splintered crutches covered with blood embedded with roaches and bits of glass from the amyl capsules. His scalp was really all that remained. It looked like a deteriorated mouse left too long in a mouse trap. They swept him up the next morning along with the rest of the sawdust. Meanwhile, mother was sweeping her immaculate new upstairs oblivious to her husband's demise the night before. It wasn't that she didn't care or love him, he just didn't exist anymore because, after all, he had been unable to reach her plateau, her rooms. Everything in her world was officiously handled. She would continue serving her borscht and sauerbraten and Mogen David wine on her green settee and reading her son's journals. Next Christmas she might splurge and duplicate Luchow's towering old-world tree by poking it through the attic hole and fill the downstairs with truck loads of gifts, thus sealing off, further, the outside. She would endure. The dream ended and all the major objects and actions are understandable in Jungian terminology. The upper room, the list, the fights, the red car, the bar, the sweepings. All an inescapable part of the dreamer. All hermetically sealed away." Ray closed the sleek black book of entries for a breather, for a smoke.

* * * * *

II.

Again the July heat of unchanged Turkey closed in. The sense of chronology tried to nestle into Ray's lap much like an ancient cat from childhood memories continues to lounge about or influence one's frame of mind. It was 1976, a bicentennial attempting to enact itself elsewhere. He rejoined the blistering bus seat of his tourist group and no one would sit next to him; he must have looked half-crazed and his armpits and shirt collar and forehead were drenched. He fanned himself with the fifty cents postcard he had somehow purchased from a youth of dashing black fingers before leaving the grounds. He had fallen victim to the children who were always there ready to pounce; it seemed the universal plight for the lone, vulnerable traveler. He pinched the crown of his nose, right between his aching eyes, as he rethought his prayer to the lady. Ray had belabored his "lain to the side crutches" that only he could see. He found himself thankful, loving. His mother had served him well. His only atonement involved something that Priapus (that incomprehensible statue of Bes seemed ever-present, played in his head like a Punch and Judy show character, bright orange replica of a man's head with protruding nose and ears, a boy's squat body, no arms, and a swelling cure-all for mankind's ills;

106

his testicles sucked into his abdomen as though he had just discharged his essence, yet an absurdity to think that Priapus ever erupts, for that implies an absence of white mass, it is inherently ever-churning in his petrified form we call Priapus for he most surely lodges in each of us, we only have to accept his residency) could understand. Mary and Mary's painting cries because she had to cope with His now Crucifix-ebony reminder in the hallowed place instead of his manhood and equally as all-encompassing Love has to be experienced through metaphor, through symbolic climaxes; an epiphanic moment for the masses who no longer appreciate such ritual.

Such thoughts brought Ray, in his past time-travels, to the great Marble Street of Ephesus. Ephesus, the original cradle of culture and enlightenment. The Bath of Scolastica with caldarium (hot section) and frigidarium (cold section); the Arcadian Avenue with gutters atop buildings and beneath streets, the Gymnasium, the various Agorae, the pleasure of the ruins of the Library of Celsus—and the double excitement of seeing it "rebuilt" yet his visit too early to see its completion. He realized that the invention of parchment (over papyrus papers) stems from this cradle; the fountains, the Temple of Hadrian all flooded his vision. Ray wondered whether the all-knowing articulate guide might well have removed himself each morning from the relief of Hermes strolling along the street. All preceding the Roman empires. All preceding modern mankind.

Ray didn't have to consult his journal of those past days. The serpentine map that he had drawn in the pages raised itself in his mind now. Tucked along his promenade was the center of town, the crossroads of sailors and merchants alike. The advantageous corner, adjacent to the library, hosted the Brothel. The Brothel, what a wonder! The guide amused Ray with the idea that, pointing down to his toe ever so authoritatively, here most probably existed western man's first attempt at mass media, his first attempt to advertise a certain commodity that was in great demand:

> I tell you wayward visitor to our fine Ephesus, this
> is a vortex of activity that though the winds of time
> have erased, nevertheless, straighten your back, inhale,
> close your eyes and imagine the four damsels in

colorful gowns, representing the four seasons,
lounging about the confines of this foundation, and,
yes, waiting for you to come—tired and sensing the
stable soil beneath you; before bobbling waves of
the Aegean to their arms. You see, here on the
marble square four etchings: in the center
is the form of a human foot with an "+" to the top
of the toes; in the upper left of our foot is a
pouch-shaped object with dots across its shape;
to the lower right of the foot is the bust of a
woman, hair piled high on her head; and beneath
her is a rectangular shape. Our sign, our billboard
if you will, indicates the following (although
rest assured that those ancestors of mine, filing
willy-nilly ashore here would have had no need for
explanation, just the mere appearance of this "sign"
at their feet would have been enough. Anyway, what
it means, this forerunner of your Marshall McLuhan
psychology is: the foot is "your" pathway, walk
straight ahead, the cross indicates the next
intersection or cross-roads:

...(as the guide's spiel revisited Ray, he could only consider as he
walked along, this veritable sailor of vision that he had become—this
sign of foot and the body of knowledge that it connoted would thus
begin his erection)...

the pouch would be your coin-purse and the dots
inside the shape would be your money;

...(Ray noticed the guide wink in his direction; he was reminded of
James' wink in his recent sexual fantasy: he could only wonder now,
would she be fair, would she be a blonde or brunette, to his liking or
an old hag, would she be young, say twenty, or has she taken the job
because her husband is a lecher, or has he run off and she desperately
needs to take on the role of prostitute to bring bread to her baby; would
she cost five dollars or twenty; would she, as Tennessee William's El
Camino Real U.S. stud and whore, whisper to him, "I'm sincere, I'm
sincere...?")

The bust of woman is indicative that one might well
find what he is looking for at this intersection, a
woman to accept his money and tender love;

...(certainly if these four beauties had had their eye on Priapus'
statue and had knelt in admiration, it would be an evening of humiliation and unfulfilled fantasies)

and lastly, the rectangle was indicative of the library,
the edifice of man's mind in sweet repose across from
the Brothel, standing as a testimony to the blending
of the physical and intellectual.

Ray returned to present time: he was comforted as he sipped his
gin and tonic and basked in the realization of the residency of Mary's
close proximity to the cat house of Ephesus. For surely Ruby was no
worse nor no better than any of these women. She had loved and been
loved, she had had a compassionate heart, she had tried to understand
Ray during his unpredictable house-calls to her establishment. She
might in fact replace his visitations of far-off lands and a need for such
spiritual stimulation via vicarious experience. It was all very refreshing. He decided he would see her this same night. Her phone call had
proven a catalyst. At first he had resented her abruptness in seeking
out his unlisted number, but it all now seemed acceptable. He felt
expended; he vaguely remembered masturbating. A specter of a caryatid stood sentinel, served as his voyeur. This all felt good to Ray
Landre; he would see Ruby tonight. So much had been resolved.
However, would she like him? Or had she, in fact, seen Priapus' form
already. Had spoliation set in? Would she take him in, like a helpless
minnow, and expunge his pilgrimage to her altar like so many scores
of wornout sponge, ready to return to the Adriatic Sea. He would see
her tonight.

III.

Before leaving to see Ruby Francis, Ray briefly recalled her
Lilliputian dream and his earlier dream of tramping about her
Gulliverian prostrated form. Whenever Ray dreamed of Ruby, he was
inescapably reminded of, linked to, his dreams of his earthly mother.

As of late, this figure was decoupaged with layers of religious ladies and crumbling caryatids. The upper room of his dream might become Ruby's domain. Ray was always nonplussed by friends who told him they never dreamed. Most REM scientists now agree, no dreaming, no long-term memory. Ray felt that his dreams were as exciting a part of his psyche as were his vitally physical moments. Ray felt that when he had difficulty coping with his life style, or with the horrendous stories of Ruby's sexual appetite, or the loss of loved ones, or his personal inadequacies, he found release of these daily tensions in his REM sleep. When Ray had once suggested that his dream-content was more complex than hers, she quickly claimed that she was less inhibited because she was more actively involved in meeting others. Thus she had less need to dream or in any way be concerned with remembering them. Ray told her she was missing the point; that Rapid Eye Movement probably occurred several times in one night of sleep, although the individual may well not recall the context of these dreams in the waking hours.

Ray had elaborated that he kept a journal at his bedside and upon waking from sleep he would record as many details as possible so he could more easily recall his dreams. She was surprised when he told her that many writers do this whereas dreams play an important role in their creative outlet. He tantalized her that some of her dream-telling had served as a catalyst in his own dreams and/or writings. At that moment, he had let his mind wander to a new, though related, acronym: R.T.D. (rapid tongue delving). After all, in casual conversation one tended to pronounce REM as rim. Oftentimes, Ray realized he was dealing with her on two levels of comprehension. Discussing rimming or rim sleeping and vicariously entering her secret world excited him. Her men, her sleep, her dreams, her family, her future.

IV.

That night, as Ray was accompanied into the donut shop with his dreams, his fantasies of virgins and caryatids and exotic prostitutes, he was seated and related his thoughts of travel and dreams with her.

Ruby humored him by relating one of her stories. One night she had exited a local laundromat and found a flier on the windshield of her car.

MADAM ADRIENNE

Psychic Reader
Born with strange wisdom and mystic powers
Advice given in all matters

I can help you in Love, Marriage or Health

INTERNATIONALLY FAMOUS DREAM ANALYST
(every dream has a message or warning)

Call for appointment today

* CH3-7225 *

"Did you go?" Ray took the bait.

"Did I have any choice?" had been her response.

Turned out that the madam used this as a front for a call service. She even invited Ruby to join her ranks, but Ruby told Madam Andrienne that she had sincerely hoped for some sort of insight into her dreams and problems. She wasn't naive to her 900 options, she added. They ended up sharing a bottle of Chianti and did the town. Ruby told Ray that she vaguely remembered Adrienne drunkenly wandering off with some sailor who was stationed in San Diego but had found his way to a Bellflower tavern after a brawl with his in-laws. Adrienne's advice had been to reject all men. Stay with her donut shop and remember that her two well-formed jugs were about the only two reliable things in this world.

Ruby wanted Ray to top her story. She pleaded with him. "Well, thinking about Priapus earlier and seeing your fine clientele here, I do have a couple of stories for you. My first vignette took place in the wallpaper warehouse, remember? The characters were classic to include a pompous ass of an owner with an affected French name and accent–something like Remy Courvoisier. They could have peopled a novel. One of my fellow workers, though, was an escaped convict and was hiding out from Eastern authorities. He kept us so entertained with his stories of violence and homosexuality that no one would have finked on him. But my favorite was an older manager who confided in me that should I want to do something rather unusual some lunch hour, I might take a dental appointment with his dentist. I told him he was off the wall, that I seldom needed dental work. But he opened his lunch box and I nearly fell over. Inside, taking up the entire area was a plaster cast of a penis and balls. I simply didn't understand; Bill explained He's a damned good dentist, he just has a fixation on penises. After he works on your mouth he propositions you to cast a plaster mold of your cock. You don't have to do it and he pays you. As a matter of fact, your dental bill usually totals out zero.

"What the hell," Ray announced to Ruby. "I went. He was a kindly, distinguished chap. His degrees of dentistry lined the Los Angeles office wall in the Bradbury Building and the majority of his equipment appeared up-to-date. Since it was the lunch hour, I supposed his assistant had gone out. The fact that I had been referred by Bill seemed adequate to put him at ease in asking if I would consent to the casting. Everything went easily and painlessly. My penis had remained limp until the moist white solution surrounded it, then it stood erect for the duration. When I laughed about the rigidity, the doctor commented that in his years of casting he had never seen one flounder."

Ruby asked Ray what he did with the thing.

"He did give it to me but lectured that I must not take it out or move it about for some hours lest the plaster not set. Naturally, as Bill had guessed, the dentist kept a second molded form in his back workshop. That was his preoccupation, that was his intent. He hadn't tried anything strange with me, as I had feared and no one entered the office during my appointment. I left with quite a smile and a tubular brown lunch bag under my arm. I exited the elevator onto the Wilshire flow of nooners.

"My second vignette for you, Ruby, took place some years later in a downtown L.A. reputable oil firm. I had been asked to work overtime one Saturday and since I needed the money I accepted. I had gone to the restroom when I heard the fire alarm on our office floor. I vague-

112

ly remembered that some of my fellow workers had been sitting at their respective desks when I left, so I rushed back to my floor to ensure that all were out safely. As I surveyed the forty some desks, I could see no one and had almost run out of the room when I heard a click in the corner that housed our ultra-modern Xerox #3100 Large Document Copier. A buddy of mine, bathed in a green glow, was crouched over the duplicating plate of the machine. I hollered his name but he didn't turn around.

"He had obviously heard the warning siren, so I realized that he was desperately trying to finish a rush job, something he felt top priority. I tapped him on his shoulder as I glanced over to see what he was copying: it was his member massaged and rushing with blood. He had it squeezed tightly in his fist and pressed to the green-tinted glass plate. I noticed that the copy indicator was set for twenty copies."

"Quite an ego," Ruby mustered. "Go on, go on!"

"Well, when he noticed I was standing there he finally looked embarrassed and stuttered an explanation. I merely advised him that soon there would be firemen rushing into the room with water hoses and axes and there might be electrical fires at any time; that for his safety, for our safety, we needed to expedite matters and rush to safety below.

"He confessed sheepishly that he had personally set off the alarm, that for some time now he had been obsessed with the idea of Xeroxing his penis. He theorized that if he were climaxing while duplicating multiples of twenty then he would be effecting super-orgasms, and he might even send out chain letters for some sort of response from men and women. I told him that I had no intent of turning him in, and that he should have the freedom to do what he wanted with his cock; however, on the job was no time for such frivolity. He eventually cooled down and felt confident that I would keep his erotic secret. I never saw any of the copies; I think there was one that came out half-assed blurred and he had unthinkingly wadded it up and thrown it in the trash can. Maybe some night cleaning lady had happily found it and kept it locked in her cleaning room. Or more than likely it had been discarded. But it just seems to me," Ray preached to Ruby, "that when it comes to sexuality, nothing has changed since the days of Ephesus." Ruby agreed without truly comprehending. She liked his two stories, though.

On later occasions Ruby would ask Ray, "Tell me the one again about the Xerox machine," or "Now, how did that one about the dentist go again?"

Ray felt she probably never really believed that the incidents had happened. He told her that the first was a parable on reproduction, and that the latter served as a lesson that although we grow old, our manhood, our sexuality would be forever youthful. They were both parables of immortality.

13 CHANCE MEETING

THE NEXT TIME that Ray Landre saw Etta-Mary, the local crone, was again outside the New World Pharmacy. She feigned high fashion by wearing a candy red likeness of a cardinal upon her frilly hat. As he cruised past, he noticed she was engaged in conversation with a younger lady. Easing past, he wanted to deny what he saw: it was Ruby Francis. He allowed the traffic light to change to red, then he stealthily slipped into a green parking zone. Failing to get Ruby's attention, he eventually honked his bug. He saw her slip Etta, the Widow, a piece of paper and then run to his car.

"Get in; how could you know that person?" The two units of thought jelled.

"How? She used to frequent my shop, but as I told her, it must have been years since I last saw her." Ruby smelled nice as though she may have sampled the perfume counter. Wisteria?

Ray queried, "But what could you two possibly find to talk about?"

"Loads," Ruby countered. "For example, after telling about her deceased husband, which she always does, she affects her gossipy voice (Ruby fidgeted in her tight skirt and blouse which sent wafts of wisteria suckers to wrap about him; his white knuckles froze to the steering wheel; he forgot if the bug was in first or reverse): ISN'T IT JUST TRAGIC ABOUT THAT YOLANDER GIRL DOWN THE STREET? An orphan you know, abused they say by an ex-marine for a father. Well, no ordinary abuse." Etta-Mary, according to Ruby, had wrinkled her rhino snout just imagining the worst. Most likely not the pure abuse reported in tabloids of abusive parents who sell into slavery their offspring or those who lock them away in closets for inordinate amounts of years, no something more subtle. "Subtle, sophisticated, he was schooled in Shakespeare, a scholar of Yeats and G.M. Hopkins; especially sadistic, they say, even his own colleagues at the college campus. And the wife in her choker of a black leather dress serving frozen peas for faculty dinners and not one hair out of place— that expensive pearl necklace just to serve tv dinners. Sad, yes very sad. And they say he badgered many of his colleagues, too."

"Honestly, Ruby, how could you pander to such filth. How could that recluse of a woman possibly know any of that on good authority?" Ray let his eyes direct a dotted bee-hive line of vision from his driver's seat into the interior rearview mirror to Ruby's heaving cleavage. The giant v was a palpable line of attack. "Anyway, I just happen to be going your way, my Beautiful Flower of same city. I'll drop you off." He didn't want to divulge Ruby his true thoughts, how the sight of Etta-Mary pained him—she was a rubber stamp of that same caryatid that stalks the wasteland between Long Beach and Bellflower, the crone in the Liberty Cafe before its demise. He felt faint. "Rube, stay away from her, for me, ok?"

14. DESERT FLOWER

THE WILD, WILD WEST. Ruby emphasized that the most exciting portion of her life, according to recent recollection, had been a series of spontaneous treks to Death Valley, U.S.A. Ray admitted that he had never gone there; she suggested that the ominous name had caused her to put off the initial trip time and again. It was a passionate affair with Hans that had precipitated their decision to pack the Mercedes and six month old Dalmatian (couch dog) Trixie along with iced-down Camembert and Pouilly-Fuisse and barrel on to the lodgings that he had arranged at the Death Valley Ranch. They occupied one of the quaint cottages near poolside. She confessed to Ray that she had bitched the entire drive because the land had been nearly void of wildlife or vegetation.

"Oh, I saw marvelous purple-cast sunsets and sand dunes and gigantic cacti like multitudinous erections dotting the desert on postcards sent to distant relatives but such scenes have been touched up and do not reveal the hue-truth. Abysmally void, with bleached dribbles of sand that only reflected other pock marked grains of bleached sand. And it got in my drawers and my nostrils."

Ray had been asked in for a nightcap before turning around in his VW back to point A. "What are you talking about" (for it was he who wanted in her drawers).

"The sand, dummy." As Ruby continued her plight, she held forward her white hands. "And it edged its way into my fingernails and scalp. I had to constantly scratch my seat and my scalp.

117

"Hans didn't believe me; he was so cruel at times. The sand even penetrated my ears and I kept secreting yellow wax that had caught flying sand as the car blazed over the 300 miles. Hans would brag about how the Mercedes tore up the road and left those other sons-abitches behind, eating his dust, inhaling his sand! He kept me busy pouring wine. He would fart as the auto took hairpin curves. Once I saw a wild mustang kicking up its heels, oblivious to the motorized horse parallel to it. I really liked the idea that there was no fence to contain his running."

"So, it seems like you had the perfect setup," Ray set her up.

"That's what you think! Besides the fact he never wanted to have sex, he didn't know the meaning of slow down, of planning ahead to avoid lost time later. He wouldn't allow me time to set up any road-side camp, to lay out the clothes and neatly arrange the toiletries. Ladies like that sort of stuff, you know. I love to tear off the paper indi-cators of sanitation on the toilet seats, to rip off the glass covers and smell the sweet soap that advertised other places that I wouldn't want to visit with him. It was always Hurry Up this and Come On, we'll miss the horse riding sign-ups for the next morning." Ruby frowned.

"Well, hopefully you saw some of those famous formations I've read about, I can't remember their names, but..."

"Oh, sure; I'd just begin to digest the Devil's Golf Course milling around as my shoetip touched some geological freak of corrugated igneous rock when he would want to rush back to the swimming pool in order to cool off. That was a riot, too..."

"What's that, desert flower?"

"Justifiably, on our first visit, he was not allowed by the manager to enter the pool proper because his hair was too long and such hair styles required a bathing cap or Forget It! He never forgot any trans-gressions: to Hans, a grudge was a grudge. He habitually picked fights...and paranoid? The part-time life guard/stable hand's repri-mand was almost cause for fisticuffs. So, on that particular evening, with no pool, no acquaintances, no formal dinner attire to dine in the more desireable restaurant at the Inn, it was, Ray, 'a real bummer for me.'

"On another day we took a drive through the gap to Dante's View—that caused the 'Benz to overheat. Some asshole in the car in front of us decided to stop and the oneway was narrow enough to only allow one car at a time. He was just on the verge of leaving the car to pick a fight when I decided to use my head; I worked up his cock by rubbing it manually then sliding my head between his abdomen and the steering wheel and giving some fine head. Naturally, this pleased him and the car had long since pulled away. Hans did become a bit edgy when a helicopter, probably that of a ranger, buzzed overhead because he felt they could see down through the open sunroof. He couldn't zip up his fly fast enough." Ruby had boisterously laughed as she beamed into her coffee mug. If Bette Davis had "those eyes," Ruby had her laugh; you never forgot that Ruby laugh.

"But the best was Telescope Peak at 11,000 feet. Once we had ascended from the dust and barrenness of the 282 feet below sea-level plain, once I spotted the moisture on the macadam, then splotches of snow, then I could forget all of the hourly humiliation that I had been subjected to. I enjoyed the absolute stranger in the saloon as he cruised me, more so than Hans undressing me in the dirty little cabin the night before. Also, for the record, I objected, loathed the Dalmatian's watching from his corner rug where he was tied with his peachy pink hard-on standing out in the night light. Hans had insisted that Trixie stay in the room, and watch us if that's what dogs do. But as I say, Ray, the elevation, the snowdrifts, accompanied by a score of wild burros standing about the road uncertain whether to go about their business of feeding, afraid to take their eyes off our purring maroon coach, all make it worthwhile."

"Yes," Ray encouraged, "I've read about the burros. How exciting that must have been; I can just see your hair flying at that altitude and the crisp moisture on your face."

"Apparently, these fine brown braying anachronisms are being protected up in this land of forgotten years and someone watered them and handcarried their semen to insure procreation, but it is all so bleak up there near the timber line. Another startling sight, if you persevere, is the stand, the row of Indian-Beehive kilns for charcoal manufacturing. I had gathered all sorts of brochures on these features, I didn't want to miss out.

"Hans simply had wanted to park the car and continue walking upward to the summit. He shouldered a Browning .22 semi-automatic

119

that he had bought especially for this trip. I couldn't understand his insistence on taking it along because by the time we would reach the summit it would be dark and he would be unable to see anything at which to shoot, save the Valley lights like miniature traintrack lights far below. I insisted upon walking into the giant rock Beehives before continuing our climb. The first one smelled damp and musky. Hans seemed afraid and waited in the safe light of the entrance way. I walked the entire perimeter of the first one and placed my nose close to the algal surface. I even pocketed a small chip of the brick."

Ray flashed on that same chip of brick which he had noticed on her kitchen table in the window by her Hills Brother's coffee canned wandering jew. It wasn't a healthy specimen. Ruby was always aghast when she saw the healthier cuttings that Ray had raised and brought to her as presents.

"I tried my voice in this huge cavity, Ray. I whispered his name, I shouted my own. The thick brick caught both and nullified both. I liked the way the external light formed a white ring about his silhouette in the kiln doorway. I pretended that I was zinging arrows about his torso with my make believe bow as I had seen men do to their carnival women when I was a child. Hans didn't like my game; he called me childish and ordered me out of that stupid place. He said that the hives, all seven of them, should be flattened." Knowing him as she did, she feared he meant it and urged that they continue their walk.

"Trixie loved sporting past the fallen limbs, and he slipped up steep, ice packed ravines. We passed a sign posting that the park could take no responsibility for persons going beyond that point in the months of heavy snowfall. This was such a month, late March as I recall, Ray."

"I can just see you two gingerbread figures scaling some mammoth Christmas tree, your diminutive forms circling the 11,000 foot elevation and the moonbeams occasionally lighting an exposed rock or ice floe." Ray helped Ruby sketch her canvas.

"I saw a gray bunny scurry from beneath a leaning log. Its mate was left behind, beneath the log, dead. There was a trace of red beneath its mouth that was opened to the white snow. There were bright round droppings to its hind. We threw snowballs, maybe six each, at one another. Hans paused to rest, in a suspended, crouched position, his muscular calves bulging from the weight of him upon their support. He cradled the rifle across his knees and Trixie stood with her head near its barrel." Ruby said she was silent as she coaxed Trixie away with a stick to be fetched. "I felt that if I couldn't save myself I would attempt to protect Trixie. I tried to kiss Hans but he moved away from my lips, fell over backwards and the gun discharged. The bullet lodged itself some twenty yards away, in a dead tree stump, and the bark splintered into the night air. The moon helped our eyes make sure that that was all the trajectory allowed. I helped him up. He wanted to build a fire. I objected, but as always, he won out. It felt good to hold our hands up to the warmth. I had clumsily left my gloves in the Beehive structure.

"The next morning, when we appeared for the horseback riding sign-ups, he threw a scene. Hans was on time but when they told him that he would be accompanied by a walker, the program was not for independent riding, he blew his stack. I was sympathetic to their demands whereas I was ready to celebrate in favor of the horse's good fortune. On the other hand, out of a sense of survival, I respected He Who Held Grudges. There were some ugly words, the people in line cast curious eyebrows our way and he left by threatening not to pay for our room if they didn't apologize and allow him to ride his horse his way. I knew we could anticipate, at the least, a later encounter with the desk clerk at check-out time.

"Every trip should have some crowning moment: mine did, rest assured. Our day at Scotty's Castle was worth all the august moments I had to spend in and out of the sack. As usual, he drove and I read aloud the throwaway brochures." Ruby was never sure if that was their arrangement because he couldn't read or because he was too nervous to merely be a passenger. Even while driving his thumbs would go pitter-patter across the rim of the steering wheel. Some men jostle their legs by rocking them on the balls of the feet while otherwise sitting completely still, and some men just couldn't keep their hands motionless, even while steering a car at 100 miles per hour. Hans' ceaselessly went pitter-pat, pitter-pat.

Ruby parodied the tour guide's history, "This is Scotty's Castle. In nineteen..., Walter E. Scott, or Death Valley Scotty,... One-time prospector built this palatial desert mansion...at a cost of... In this, his

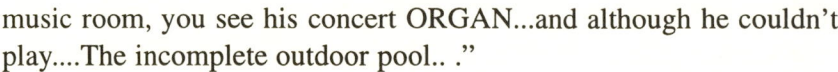

music room, you see his concert ORGAN...and although he couldn't play....The incomplete outdoor pool.. ."

When Ray asked Ruby what most impressed her about the castle, she could only refer to the size of his organ in the music room and the peculiar swimming pool outside the entrance. It bothered her that the tile work had not been completed, and the fact that this huge hole in the desert that had been intended to hold water, yet had never known water. While on the tour, she imagined that she had squatted and pissed from the walkway mid-pool while a shocked tour guide rushed several tourists past. She had also insisted on climbing the extra yardage to pay respects to Scotty and his wife's resting place on the hill behind the house. Ruby exhibited a strange appreciation for those that she came in contact with, first-handedly or spiritually. Ruby reminded Ray of her intentions someday to create a scrapbook collection of obituaries of famous people like Jane Mansfield and JFK. "I felt that if I was allowed to walk through his corridors and gawk at the bedcovers of this once-prospector Scotty, then I could at least make a few extra steps to say farewell to him." She meant this and such sincerity is what endeared her to Ray Landre.

Ruby had been dismayed that Hans' sole interest and comment since the approach to the property was "Gold this and Gold that." For, as the story goes, to this day Scotty's strike goes unfound. That he had so carefully concealed it that no one had been able to find it irked Hans and elated Ruby Francis. The only real evidence of its existence had been his ability to spend great amounts of money during his visits to Chicago and San Francisco.

Hans had visually ransacked the twenty-odd rooms so greedily that Ruby could barely see one room to his every five. So, finally, she had just sat down in a guest's bedroom. She motioned him ahead and suggested that they meet at the end of their tour (out by the car). She knew he had been deaf to all she had said since mentioning the assets of the estate while driving up to the castle. "I just needed a real rest from his hairy arms and nervous thumbs. Away from the steering wheel, you see, Ray, he was ten times the worse.

"But all wasn't to naught: during my break from Hans I managed to meet a young man. I had noticed him by the turquoise tiled swimming pool. He had been alone and sunning by the waterless pool in the desert. I guess he was eighteen, max. but obviously worked out with weights or played football. Now in the confines of the castle, he bought me a Coke and showed me photos of his family. He confirmed that he would be coaching underprivileged kids at a summer camp at Big Bear. I had to bite my tongue not to tell him I thought so. I let my eyes nod yes as they passed from his biceps to his levis with one unbuttoned-button. The bulge had to be what I hoped for—a crowd pleaser. I racked my brain as to how we might rendezvous. I thought about Trixie's feeding time, or possibly when Hans might be showering." Having established they were at the same Inn, Ruby inquired as to his room number. He acted surprised, according to Ruby.

"Some friends are also staying at the ranch, but not in my room," Carlos began.

"We agreed upon a time, or at least that it would happen that same day. I told him I liked the number thirteen patch sewn on his left rear pocket. I also told him not to worry if he didn't have a rolled joint with him for I would be concentrating on his main joint—Priorities, sure I had them during the duress of time. I guaranteed him that I would teach him all about that mysterious phrase and cinema-phenomenon that boys his age had heard about—Deep Throat, deep touch, deep liquid, deep, deep, I pondered what depth he would require (just as I wonder that about you, Raymond). I wondered what special techniques I or he might need to apply. It really didn't matter, though; anything would be better than making love in front of someone's goddamned daffy Dalmatian. But that settled it. Scotty's Castle proved to be the high point to my vacation. I will, of course, explain.

"That evening Hans and I decided to hit the sack for a long nap before cleaning up and dining. Hans had no sooner begun his series of snore-cycles, that graduated from an indiscernible squeak to that of a Friday morning Civil Defense Alert blast, than I set in motion my plan. Trixie had adjusted to the noise. Trix could snore right through it all, too. I still had on my halter and shorts from the afternoon drive, so I left the room and found Carlos' number 24. He had left the door ajar. I peeked in and saw him lying on his back; he was lying there with a white terrycloth towel draped over him and his cock that never seemed to soften. I rejoiced that I had foregone slumber.

"Carlos appeared to be asleep, until I tiptoed into the room and slowly closed the door. I had just grabbed the chain lock, heard a movement on the bed behind me when I turned and saw one eye still closed, but the other one wide open and it winked several times. His tongue protruded from his pink lips as the tip touched his nosetip. He had a grin across his whisker-shadowed face. Do I embarrass you, Ray?"

"Yes, and No. Your detailed account tends to make me realize the necessity to listen further. We owe that much to one another." Ray lightly rubbed his crotch and shrugged a little boy's shoulder coyness. Ray thought of the teenagers at the Queen's Park in Long Beach and their sneering at his loneliness. Perhaps some had already been with men like himself and had a reason to sneer. Ray also thought how fortunate would these same teenagers have been if Ruby-Sweetheart had been their teacher.

"Then I jumped on top of him and threw the towel into the corner. I barked a Bow-wow which totally non-plussed Carlos. I found minor triumphs in the fact that I came to his room. I took the head of his cock into my mouth after treating it to a Butterfly-flicker; this head that was already as swollen and large as Hans' entire shaft and head. I reached for his glass of iced-lemonade on the bedstand. I sipped a melted ice cube into my mouth and playfully sculptured it about the honored head again. I was teasing and saving the balls and shaft for better things. I had estimated Hans' sleeping time and would make the cock want me to return perhaps the next day before checking out and returning to Bellflower. I have to admit, from that time on, I find love-making with young boys to be far superior the second and third times. The first climax is too excited and pre-mature but subsequent foreplay and orgasms might last hours. I carressed my teats around his balls as I held the cock to my red lipstick lips. I massaged his anus with my pinky: he refused this at first, but ten seconds later he gladly opened up to me. I flipped my hair across his chest, I darted my tongue to his taut navel; I reared and spat a huge globule of spittle into it. I first laughed, then Bow-wowed."

Ray asked, "What was his reaction to all of this?"

"Are you kidding; I didn't open my eyes once! I could hear other clients walk past the window and all were talking about the brawls in the Saloon, or the weird man who had made a poolside scene the previous day; the man who slept with his dog. Et cetera."

Ray envisioned all of this amidst Ruby's "braying." He comforted her that it must have been nice to be "staying" in a different room so she was able to, momentarily, disassociate herself from Hans' humiliating bondage.

"I finally created Carlos' eruption by yanking his trembling hands to my over-sized nipples—I whispered 'Follow the bee's path to momma's hive.'"

Ray was in synch with her tale for truly Ruby's breasts were extremely unique in form; instead of being full 360 degree cups, they were uniquely pointed forms like crescent moons that drooped forward with over-sized nipples. He had never seen anything like them in anatomical books, porno films or in spying upon his neighbors while nude sunbathing.

"What proved my ace in the hole that there would be a repeat?" Ruby quizzed Ray. "I promised that it would be better next time, tomorrow, if he promised not to jerk off that night. What could he say? He delivered me a thousand mumbled, submissive Yes's. I reared back, for a last time, slapped his cock of steel and molten lava across my face, hard, whack, and quintessentially rammed my throat down to envelope all. I psychologically took it all away from him, drained him of his youthhood-head, only to jump up from him and straddle him and feel it still there."

"I can assure you, as we've mentioned before, Priapus is doing his work everywhere, always." Ruby laughed good-heartedly at Ray's reminder. Her igneous story-telling donut bulbs inflamed Ray's crisp cloven legs. He, too, felt young and rejuvenated, and drained for a moment. "Did you know the lad a next time?"

"No, alas; upon my return to the room, Hans was awake and beating off. I swear he timed his ejaculation to the turning of the door knob merely to spite me. I could not have cared less but, like your dear, coy lady-camel, pretended to be extremely irritated at his distrust and Circuitous Machinations. Never fear, Ray; I, too, can be empowered with words."

"What did he say to you?"

"He got right down: 'Where have you been, Slut of the Valley?' Slut? Get you, you dog-lover. 'If it's any of your business, I've been to the saloon and picked up this six-pack so you could have something nice and cool upon waking.' I threw the package on the wet sheet beside his now limp penis. I had had enough foresight to buy a quick alibi. I don't think he ever found me out; however, he did insist on packing and we left within the hour.

"Of course, that certainly wasn't meant to go smoothly either. With his knack for pissing off the public, he bitched at the cleaning lady—not enough towels, the bed never made, no hot water when he needed it. He told the desk clerk that the fucking cardboard shacks they called living quarters ought to be shipped back to Tijuana and doused with kerosene and set afire. He swore that the pool was an oversized toilet bowl; and, if they were to advertise horse-riding in the future, they should, by law, be required to alter the text to include 'Bring your own horse.' Hans stormed out the wooden floored office with threats that he might stop payment on the bill as he pocketed his over-drawn Master Charge card. Furthermore, as to their food service during our stay, they must have served Sizzler-rejects to the tune of Statler prices.

"I swear to God, dust flew from his too-large $200 black cowboy boots with ornate paisley tooled patterns as he walked Trixie to do her business by the hitching post at the entrance to the office. I noticed, for the first time, that his walk was a bit too effeminate. He clinched his fist and raised his forearm and shook it defiantly towards the confused, frightened desk clerk who stood gazing out a picture window at this mad couple loading into our maroon, electric piece of German machinery.

"The frosted lettering DEATH VALLEY RANCH seemed to dance across the clerk's face as an extension to his handlebar mustache so he became a disproportioned billboard tacked down in a remote part of the desert. He was chewing on a #2 yellow pencil and shaking his head left and right as his raised eyebrows watched Hans throw Trix into the back seat. I swear, Hans didn't even check to see if I had adequately drawn in my feet or closed the door. Eventually, the glass-faced man laughed because he observed that Hans was jabbing at the electric window switch but it would not respond. His temper caused him to smash the window with his fist and it formed a rather large crack. He cursed and the old timers on the wooden porch turned their heads away. Little interrupted their whittlin'. All of these color-ful desert gentlemen, too, just shook their heads as they collectively watched the ugly American tourist exit their domain to take his railing onward across the mapland U.S.A. to act offensively for others!"

In blatant mimickry, Ruby concluded her tale of her past lover, "Hans opened his door as he was accelerating in reverse, 'Now, ya all come again, he-are.' With his forced southern accent he continued to offend, 'Why s-h-i-t, you idiots couldn't run a hotel let alone a jackass stall in the boondocks!' He thrust us into forward and barreled onto the desert road near one hundred miles per hour. There was no time for sightseeing and he fussed at the wheel for the return trip while I sat silently cross-legged thinking of my afternoon soiree with no guilt, and I silently cursed the desert for its joke played on me. During our one pull to the roadside, I squatted and made yellow steam. I recalled the inexplicable adage 'You must have pissed in the middle of the road' and genuinely felt a sty commencing to form on my left eyelash.

"And, Ray, what pleasures did I know on the return home? Hans shot six cartridges at Joshua trees and missed mostly. He did fall one elongated limb to which I jeered what a big man that made him, for killing that awful desperado. 'Why Look at the Weakling of an Amputated Varmint Standing There in the Fucking Hot Sun.' He belched, and shouted that I should get in the car, pronto. And he added a threat that I might be his next target. I must say, in conclusion, I found him little and disgusting ever-after that day. I may be a sexpot but I know Hans was the worst sexist I've ever known. Also, I never had a desire to vacation in Death Valley National Monument, U.S.A. again." Ruby's facetious tongue found it a lovely wasteland where Americans took advantage of their decadent ways. They left open their motel doors for flies and air conditioners to flush out the noon-heat; they insisted on dripping water taps and unattended radios and TV sets to entertain the shallow night desert horizon and occasional raven sta-tioned atop a phone pole.

Ruby's story, her travelogue, brought to mind for Ray his own tour guide at Ephesus; the mere juxtaposition amused him. He felt confi-dent it could supply him with many suggestive doodles for his friend, his journal in sleek black leather dressing.

15 REPRISE: HASHSLINGER WALKS INTERSECTION

RAY WAS IN HIS APARTMENT when he felt an enormous explosion. In the southland of California, one must be prepared to ride out the land-storms, the Big Ones, the mass movements, the rock and roll measured in intensity from 0 to 10. The miniature tea-cup planted with a hopeless spider plant that usually idled away its time in his kitchen window rocked back and forth from the after-shock. In today's precarious life-style of sonic booms, air force maneuvers off shore; daily automobile collisions at the neighborhood corner; earthquakes that register 6.3 on the Richter scale at the drop of a hat; newlyweds throwing electric irons and other assorted time-bought appliances at one another, in this sort of defensive living, Ray had no idea of what direction to look for the source of the explosion or if rigor mortis might have prematurely set in his middle-aged bones. It might be any of these, or the rumblings of Bellflower teenagers gone wild with some sort of Cinco de Mayo zany motorcade. But soon Ray identified firetruck screams and police-car sirens rushing into his second story window. A black mushroom cloud seemed to be billowing above the block where Ruby's house might be located so he let drop his kelly green bathrobe, dressed, combed his hair-piece into its counterpart, strands of leftover shadows of his once self, and he ran the length of two blocks before realizing it, turned around and started his car. During the short distance, Ray felt a throbbing headache which caused a flashback to that of his peter throbbing beneath her wiped-clean tables in her clean establishment some weeks ago, and the near explosion that he, and ultimately she might have experienced had he not contained his ever-growing faith and feelings for Ruby Francis.

Ruby's recent tale of Death Valley had forced Ray to read some of his old text books, Turn to the Masters of such problems in relationships he had told himself. He mulled over the classic findings of the revered Masters and Johnson team, looking for some possible answers to the seeming dysfunction of their sexual union. He toyed with the idea that her tale of Hans and Death Valley could easily become a classic chapter in one of their research books. He thought of showing Ruby the chapters on sexual hang-ups as orgasmic disfunction, impotence and premature ejaculation but concluded that she might well write her own chapters and teach them a thing or two. Dr. Ruby Francis Frangible, Sexologist: Ray laughed to himself as he tooled towards her shop.

Demolition and shimmering confusion of Ruby and a dreamed inter-corpse, and the coffee-shop cadaver who might be to any observant lover the most intact Caryatid anchored in the rain and destroying smog that daily envelopes the Erechtheum atop the Acropolis; these three white eroded complexions of womanhood chasing Ray Landre down Bellflower Blvd., chasing him with no mercy except to tighten their grasp of his balls, and the fire, cannon or laundry out-of-control smoke. Ray saw Ruby Hashslinger Caryatid standing before him about his second block of running from his parking space. He waited for the traffic signal to permit his crossing the intersection, and She hopped a few steps further in front of him, the rivulets of hair and neatly folded cloth sticking to her thighs, her left arm broken at the forearm, no nose, breasts nice and firm, eyes mascared with rain marks, her crown a marble crescent of Ionic capital holding up his sanity, holding up her vagina for his reach. He paused. He struck out with his fist to knock her from his path. Motorists honked and shouted obscenities. One five-year-old hanging from a car window shouted "Daddy" to Ray.

Ray bolted into Winchell's to find an excruciatingly humorous profile lying parallel to the floor. Her white dress and shoes and complexion created a sense of suicide, whereas there was a faint similarity in her prone position and that of a chalk drawing by a homicide inspector to trace the mortal remains of a murder victim at some scene of crime. But there the comparison ended, it was simply ludicrous. The humor overwhelmed Ray. Ruby's dress, upon closer scrutiny, her hair and eyebrows were coated in a harsh black soot obviously from the explosion.

"My God, Ray, one of my blasted ovens exploded." She had once told Ray that she still utilized the antiquated gas ovens out of frugality. Ray feared for her life for she looked to be in great pain and her four limbs jutted in four opposite directions much like a pin wheel caught in mid-air, made motionless by a reversal of winds. Her head was cocked or twisted as though it had snapped behind her ears. Her right calf was upturned to reveal her choice berry birthmark and his cheeks turned equally as red in eye-tracing his imaginative penis to every open port available. Her rather large rump seemed flat on one side and perfectly round on the other cheek. She had been crying a bit and her mascara had run. She appeared pock-marked from the bits of black debris strewn from her head to her feet; in short she was a miserable sight, as though she had fallen from her marble pedestal. Ray was about to address his sympathy and aid when Ruby ejaculated:

"Well, don't just stand there, help me up from this cockeyed floor. Ain't you ever seen anyone keel over before? Hop To It! I sure wish my help around here could bring themselves to move as fast as they did this afternoon, maybe we'd do a little business around here for a change." She was laughing that embarrassed but good-hearted laugh, like a madam who had been overlooked by a drunken sailor for one of her more luscious girls. She slowly pulled in her various vanes and transformed her immobilized toy-form into her usual animated self.

Ruby was finally more like the uncontrollable spontaneity of a fireworks device, a pinwheel, that demanded the attention of all persons in the vicinity. Two firemen, who had everything under control, stood near the door as they whispered about how nicely her two globules of ass settled once she stood up. Their tongues hung out as though they expected more in pretending that one of her teats had fallen out of its restraining device, her 34-B cross-my-heart cup for her prideful

131

36-D's. About twice the number of truck-driving customers had assembled and many of them fussed over her and helped her to her feet. Her eyes, though, never left Ray during the entire ordeal. Again her neck seemed to twist off as they carried her to her back room, but Ray lip-synched that he was right behind her and not to worry. Ray thought, momentarily, of Masters and Johnson and how they might have evaluated a certain degree of secondary gain going on in Ruby's mind as to being handled by so many men who tended to apologize at every step: "Please excuse my hand beneath your armpit, it is necessary," or "Sorry about that" as another had to run his eighteen inch bicep between her legs for support; and still another stroked her forehead, casually allowing his fleshy inner forearm to pet her right, suspended nipple as though he were testing a baby's pabulum for the correct temperature. They were most encouraging and ever so concerned with her health; had the explosion done any damage that they might be unable to see? Had she been bruised when thrown to the floor? Would she like a drink of water or a damp paper towel pressed to her, to her temples (for each did seem to worship her in his own immoral manner)? Ruby had become, finally surpassed that childhood, Lilliputian-drawn head in Appearance versus Reality.

Meanwhile, there was a great commotion in the outer room as police tidied up, took eye-witness accounts, and insisted that those not actually involved should leave the premises immediately. There was unbaked dough stuck to the windows where a handful of greenish-black flies had enmeshed themselves. The acoustic tiles on the ceiling dripped more of the tacky dough as though a fire had melted the tiles—visions of the classic film "The House of Wax," cinematic cum complete with Vincent Price surveying the situation. Poor Emanuel, one of the lesser actors, a walk-on, sat in a corner to himself; he looked distraught, as though he could predict where the blame would fall. His white apron and paper hat were a mosaic of jams and jellies and one glazed donut ringed his left ear. He had lost a shoe and sock in the scuffle and the barebottom blackness, from going barefoot much of his life, stuck out from the larger penumbra of white arcs of leg and lap and apron and head and bonnet, with the lone circular donut finalizing the unsigned Picasso.

Once some semblance of order was established, once the bright red water-houses and the black-and-white dots with swirling blue lights evacuated the scene, once the regulars, the truckers dashed back to their horrendous buzzing hulks of radiator and aluminum in an attempt to make good their lost time, and once Ray instructed Emanuel exactly what he should do to close up the shop, then Ray retreated to Ruby Francis' living quarters to find her scanning the day's obituary column.

"Lucky, Ruby, not to find your name in there," Ray tried to joke.

But Ruby quickly took command of the conversation once she realized she had another male in the room. "I expected such a conflagration, Ray, for some months now. Even the Gas Company warned me that I simply couldn't continue operating on the volume that I have been and expect the same harmonious, safe working conditions." Ruby had propped her legs on a small desk: Ray thought of Yosemite and water running down hill, refreshing all in its path.

"I suppose you just laughed at them, like always," Ray ribbed her.

"Well I'll tell you one thing, this damned explosion sure put the fear of God in me; and I'll tell you another, Ray, I sure was glad to see you; I'm sure glad you're here now. It means the world to me."

Ray kissed her on the forehead. "Now I want you to promise me to sleep." Ray thought of how the multitudes had manipulated her in carrying her to safety. "I'll look in on you later." Ruby quickly fell to sleep after he lowered her legs and covered her with her yellow afghan. Ray let himself out the front door. He heard the Katydid humming on the neon light still itself on automatic timer and the venetian blinds banged against the glass and metal door knob. He thought HE saw some dentureless hag wink at him through her white plastic eyelashes. He thought he saw Etta-Mary Fordyce melt into a dissembler of a caryatid and then into a pile of powder upon the sidewalk.

133

16. CHANNEL-FEVER

IT WAS ONE OF THOSE rare Southern California evenings, one with hints of mock orange and jasmine and honeysuckle. Ray decided, four days after the flare up, to take his friend Ruby Francis for a promenade in Long Beach. The heated emotions of male-attendance after the shop's explosion, Ray's personal conflagration of emotions, constituted his version of a holocaust. He had "burst" himself some three times per day in the confines of his shower or kitchen or magazine reading, the ultimate burst being when he had awakened from a terrific time of it as he had donned Priapus' muscle and kept forcing it between the various Caryatides, scraping and chaffing it in his bold attempts, until he awoke shouting "Simmer Down," and had to take matters in hand—and that a revelation in itself. The waterfront of Long Beach seemed a likely locale to set the best atmosphere; a sea breeze, rosy lights, elderly couples leisurely walking their leashed dogs, and young couples escorting one another along the pier as they kicked an occasional sand-castle that had been left by the eager children earlier in the day. A Mexican child went skittering down the beach to alert his sleeping father that he had found a "sand peso! a sand peso!"

Ray made sure that Ruby had her sweater pulled over her shoulders. He joked that even the off-shore replicas of San Juan resort villages that disguised the oil rigs didn't do any harm to this evening. A few fire flies danced about her head and he thought her mascara pure bits of gold glitter mixing with the on-shore drilling plans of his rotating, gyrating, boyish urges.

Ray drove to an intimate spot not fifty yards from the entrance to the Queen Mary parking lot. It provided a spectacular view. He had, many times, sat on one of the huge boulders placed in the middle of the small tourist's garden off to the bow of the regal hulk ahead of them. He had walked along for a short distance, a doddering centipede. He had lunged his poison fangs in front of himself some three or four centimeters and then laboriously pulled his long, flat body with its 173 pairs of determined legs up to their grip. He was propelling himself by displacement of jellied mass, uncertain of a horizon before him. He had not put his arm on or around her since the drive earlier. He was unaware that she was near in the garden. He had kept to the path for fear of the larger insects and endless ribbon bush plants that might swoop down and envelope him. Ruby cooed softly that she had never been to view the Queen and that she found him especially handsome this evening. The lights from across the bay, the double Ferris wheel lights, the electricity of lonely centipedal rides across the sky upon a giant centipede cyclone runway made him mince further into the garden; his right side, the side to the nearly defunct amusement park, kept sidestepping to avoid the harmful glare, to avoid perpetual paralysis.

"Ray," she said, "what a lovely spot. Have you been here often? There are good smells here. It reminds me of my childhood and our mammoth family reunions at the city park. We children would be sent off to rollick in the wading pool, perhaps with an older cousin in charge, and soon we would get a whiff of shrimp boiling in diluted beer. I used to think, that's my family filtering through the park-night-air."

Ray rather liked this newly-discovered sensitivity; perhaps a touch of the poet in her fine physical form after all. "You must have had a fine family, Ruby-dubie (Ray withdrew his centipedal pairs of hairy legs; he neatly tucked the 346 legs within his trousers and vest pocket; he was like a folded umbrella, though, prepared to open at any moment). You look lovely with the carnival lights on your blonde hair, and with the smell of jasmine dancing at your ankles—your breasts alive with early evening harbor dew, dew that I would like to collect and loll on my tongue. Do you miss your family...I mean, I would like

to help ease the pain of absence if you'll only allow me to."

Ruby didn't answer with words. She knelt to the sandy lawn and found a patch worn bare by the tourists of the daytime. She was to carefully inscribe initials and blow them away with her fingertips. She traced a dwarf rose bud, bent to it as though she could appreciate its pent-up fragrance, then she puffed it away without looking to Ray. She was obviously recalling names, faces, carefree moments of traipsing off to the rock quarry at the edge of town in her teenage days, then she would as quickly smile away those minuscule images at her fingertips. Occasionally, the swirling lights of the gaudy Pike's Wild Mouse would shimmer across her fire-engine-red nail polish, and she was like a harpy moving in black light, or she would be Delilah dancing and tempting Ray with her voluptuous, massaging hands—red, heartshaped butterflies patting out a pneumatic rhythm across the sand. They once chanced most close to his kneecap; his temples boiled at 100 degrees centigrade. At any moment he feared that his insect segments might break forth and reveal themselves to her unprepared silence.

"Have you ever truly looked at this great Queen of the oceans?" she next astounded Ray with a shared keen observation. He rolled over on his back and elevated his chest and craned his neck, his arms stiffened behind him so that he might give Her Majesty every consideration. The huge vessel not far away rested in the cleft of Ruby's lowcut bosom; rosy nipples seemed to be indicators, brightly tipped straight pins placed into the bow and stern for schematic measurement. He chose to be a wise captain and listen to his subordinate. We always listen to those in our employ, so to speak. Ray discerned that if this were to be the nautical (and naughty) game of placement, then he could hardly wait for the incomparable moment of pin the tail on the donkey (he also flashed on her cherries jubilee upturned ass on the day of the explosion, spreading it all across the floor; he mused how uncanny that students of the chimp world phrase that marvelous period of female-in-heatedness, "Behold, Our Pink Lady").

"You see, Ray, she's a desperate lady, she is. She was part of something truly big once in the history of all ocean-voyaging nations. Her coming to this harbor was another monumental feat. We were all fortunate to be the recipient of such a grand lady. As a matter of fact, I was here that very day that regattas and tugs and airplanes and traffic congestion struck this fair Long Beach. I was rooming with my SDS friend at the time. He insisted that I join him for the viewing. We joined a few other couples who had a small apartment right on the beachfront. We got plastered on screwdrivers by 9:00 a.m. The droning of planes and cannons and novel, confettied noisemakers made it much like a New Year's Eve, but all celebrated at mid-day. It was terrific, the feeling of being so small and insignificant—I mean everything that approached her in any way. Everyone who lived or worked in Long Beach considered it a great day, believe me. But I say she's a 'desperate lady' because she isn't free any more. Sit up a moment, make a two-inch square frame with your two hands and play the photographer for a moment. I'll look over your shoulder. So. See, she is in fact land-locked. There is a 'wading pool', if you like, about her body. The boulders that create a breakwater were put in place after they had burrowed a resting place for her. Every time that her horns sound, why it is a farce, a mock-joy that echoes across the bay. The phantom crew, the deceived, delirious, sometimes drunken 'passengers' are attempting to vicariously feel an excitement that no longer excites..."

"Til human voices wake us, and we drown...."

At that moment, a strong gust of wind forced Ruby to shake and she fell into his rigid back. A small branch, half dead, half alive, was blown across her sand-tracings and it appeared that a high tide had effaced all of her efforts.

"What was that you said, Ray?"

"Oh, love, it's from a beautifully, sad poem by T.S. Eliot. It seems appropriate to your observation of sensing that something is missing in the grand ol' lady's restraint. Granted, we can't put our finger on society's problem, or Her's, or for that matter ours..."

"Ours? I don't see what you mean. These past few weeks have been more than I could have expected. But you do see what I mean about Her? Sometimes when I scan the obituaries looking for some sign of Gerry I think about the Queen. I pretend that I sneak down here some evening, take a shovel and tunnel out a channel that she might secretively slip away and become herself again. It's ridiculous, but most dreams are. Look at me; pretending that I'm getting somewhere in life and all along I just keep replacing one empty wire rack of donuts or coffeecakes with another. My goodies stay fresh a couple days—though my customers want nothing over twelve hours old—and then I have to throw any leftovers out the back door. It's revolting that, other than yourself, no one really knows that I exist. I'm just one of an ever-growing list of numbers who has a lease, a franchise to sell something invented, exploited, by someone else. Oh sure, I tried in the beginning to promote my 'Pastry of the Day' but the slobs I serve are such creatures of habit that the specials usually sat there and got harder and harder. So I gave in. I don't even plan ahead anymore. It has become a routine, I guess you would say. It's an income, something I can count on, but it's no great 'voyage,' believe me. I feel the stagnant waters seeping into my shackled ankles each night as I lock up. My smoke stacks are upfront and visible from all parts of the city, but they issue billowing gusts of impotent black smoke. The only fresh air that gets my way is when the door-bell tinkles and you've come for a chat. It's nice, you know what I mean. You never rush me; you don't try to change me: you're just you. It's nice. But about that sadness and the Queen, I know I am right. I've even asked guests of the shipboard hotel and they know it, too."

"Thank you, Ruby. Believe me, the feeling's mutual. I remember when I was a junior in high school, I ran around with a wonderful gal, her name was Julie. Her looks could range anywhere from a homely sort to that of a covergirl, overnight. It took me a long time to understand why, though. You see, she was a dedicated individual. She wanted to be like everyone else, and be liked, too; but her mom was a widow and that meant that a pretty huge void had to be replenished, daily. So, she elected to stay closer to home than to others her age. Occasionally, she and I would 'borrow' my dad's car late at night when everyone else was asleep, and we'd get someone to buy us a six pack, and then we'd drive out past Asylum Hill. We would lock the car door, turn down the windows and keep the radio dial constantly on music. She loved music, soft, rock, jazz; once we went to a horrible dance and she blew everyone's mind by pulling away from me and exercising her momentary freedom. She would back away from me, all across the room, poise like a track star, then swell up her breast, dart towards me and yell at the top of her lungs. I've never told any-

139

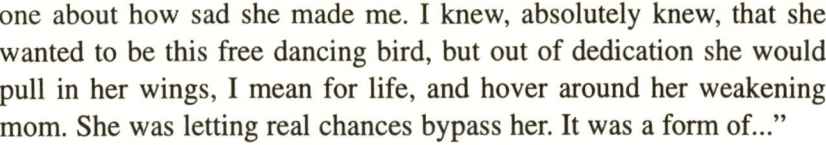

one about how sad she made me. I knew, absolutely knew, that she wanted to be this free dancing bird, but out of dedication she would pull in her wings, I mean for life, and hover around her weakening mom. She was letting real chances bypass her. It was a form of..."

Ruby chimed in, "Like a parasite, you mean?"

"No, I'm afraid it's a bit more complicated than that. You see, she, Julie, needed this, too, unfortunately. Some people are like that. We have a good term for it in the plant and animal kingdoms...it's 'symbiosis.' She was unaware of it at the time, and I certainly didn't understand. But now years later, it's more easily seen in others and it becomes a frightening prospect. I've lived to avoid such an existence. And I think that you've managed the same. It's something you can pride yourself in, this non-symbiotic freedom of yours. Why, I don't see you akin to the Queen's plight; purely and simply you represent just the opposite. How many other individuals, male or female, can say that they are as independent, as self-sustaining as you are? You pay your bills, you supply a commodity that society finds in great demand, you have an even head, and heart, and you don't have to answer to any one."

"Well, I suppose I have my grandmother to thank for that. Don't misunderstand; at this point in my life, I'm not exactly sure I want it this way, but at least you appreciate me for who I am, so I won't burden you with my less-confident moments. The nights when I lie in my darkened, glaze-ridden atmosphere, a lonely waterbed; a waitress on selfish men, my orange beanbag chair and its sunrises; Emanuel, god love him, clanging pan after pan like some metal-throated rooster chuckling to himself that he got to awaken me; I loathe his petty revenges."

The temperature dropped five degrees since their arrival. They huddled closer. Ray Landre felt that his body heat, his internal combustion, though, could douse any cold climate.

"You see, it sounds to me as though Julie wanted to protect her virginity. That may be a bit too simple an explanation, but I find that type of guardedness difficult to relate to. I had first been made by one of my high school teachers by the middle of my senior year. I couldn't tell my parents, why they would have killed him—tar and feathers the usual local method, ha ha. He and his wife had asked me over one evening for dinner; we ate; she excused herself to go bowling with the girls; he flipped out a book on loan from the University library, it was a huge volume of Greek gods, goddesses, and Greek history. I mean he could barely wait for her to slam the door and he locked it and drew the shades to the front of the house. I noticed how nervous he became, he sidled closer on the living room couch. The book resting on our laps didn't seem steady. He hadn't shown me more than five pages than he threw the book to the floor, undid my dress from the back, pulled my bra down, not off, tasted my nipples and called me some virgin-goddess, his little Persephone, as my breasts experienced another human touch for the first time. His tongue was like the texture of a cat's tongue. It stung a bit; I just rested back into the cushioned seat, I closed my eyes. When I did open my eyes, he had his other hand, the one not caressing my left breast to his protruding tongue, masturbating himself. I had never seen a penis before, my father had always kept himself covered when leaving the bathroom. My mom, now she had an entirely different philosophy about the birds and the bees. She would stop me cold by leaving the tub, dripping, and force me to walk past her, like two people on a congested bus trying to pass one another without falling down; our eyes darted across one another. Sometimes she would have me towel her off. Anyway, he finished his business and poured me another portion of wine. I drank it, but moments later he said I had best get dressed because his wife might soon return. He took me home, but along the street I felt my stomach churning and I asked him to stop. He did and I stepped outside only to throw up. Luckily, none of it touched my clothing or arms. He dropped me off and I swear to god, I haven't talked to him since; that's been some fifteen years."

"Didn't you ever hear from him again?"

"Well, sort of. You see, by then I had moved to the West Coast. Somehow he got my address, probably from my unsuspecting parents. I started getting these letters. Oh, by the time they would reach me, perhaps a month had passed. Needless to say, they didn't receive favorable reactions from my beaus at the time. But what was strange was, he would pledge his undying love to me and plead couldn't we please get together, that he would gladly fly out to see me. He always remembered what a good student I had been and he desperately wanted to continue our relationship. Well, despite my hero worship, his advances had totally blown any respect I had had for him. I simply ignored the letters. My parents never inquired as to his interest in me. But what was even stranger was, he started enclosing some self-taken Polaroid shots. Apparently, he would stand in front of a full-sized mirror and snap closeups of his pelvic area. He said that he had done something special for me just so that I would know he was thinking of me and that I was special. It was around Valentine's Day that year. He had shaved his pubic hair into the form of a gigantic 'V' Subsequent photos revealed more and more hair missing; eventually there was a small 'v', almost heart shaped, about his sometimes soft, sometimes hard penis, until, ultimately, he had mailed me a hairless, boyish peter and balls, surrounded by obese tissue, grafted onto a middle-aged abdomen. My boyfriend at the time began intercepting the mail, tear up the photos and give me the letters. He often threatened to write the guy and threaten his life but I would defend the poor dude and say Let Him Be; he was, after all, thousands of miles away and what harm could it do to me? It eventually blew over because I wasn't of course, answering the letters. Sad. Very sad.

"Anyway, as I started to tell you, Ray, my grandmother, lord rest her soul, was a very moral woman. She hadn't lost touch with anything in the real world up to her last and 86th year. She was completely independent, having been widowed some fifteen years earlier. She managed to attend church and tithe. She was simple. She meant and did well everywhere she went. She would drill me as to biblical accounts of avarice and adultery and the need for brotherly love. In short, she was all that my parents wanted me to be. Although I don't go to church today, Ray, I feel that none of my churchgoing days were wasted. I know that my god-fearing family and faith has helped me tolerate the obstacles set before me. I could even accept, though not understand, those feeble attempts at communication on the part of his letters and photographs. I'm sure that my family could never have accepted that. But grandmother instilled a 'live and let live' attitude in me. She once told me about her early courtships and how she had had to exercise great tolerance in her marriage. Apparently, my grandfather had been a great teetotaler and he often came up with hair-brained ideas for fly-by-night proposals. She said that, as a female, I must

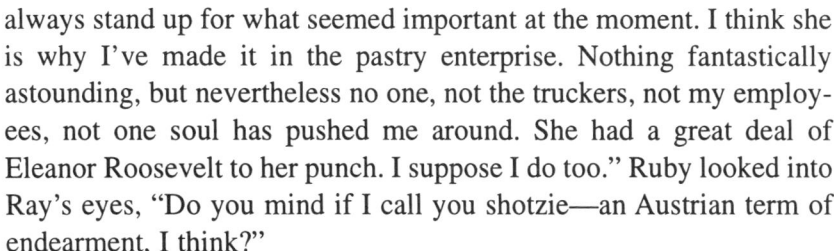

always stand up for what seemed important at the moment. I think she is why I've made it in the pastry enterprise. Nothing fantastically astounding, but nevertheless no one, not the truckers, not my employees, not one soul has pushed me around. She had a great deal of Eleanor Roosevelt to her punch. I suppose I do too." Ruby looked into Ray's eyes, "Do you mind if I call you shotzie—an Austrian term of endearment, I think?"

"No, I'm touched, and I'm going to say that I think your grandmother instilled more than a gentle nature within you. Courage. I believe she handed you a stiff shot of courage as well. I should tell you about..."

"Courage, Ray; you haven't heard anything yet. I learned that from my mom. You know that on one occasion we had gone on a picnic in the green Missouri countryside, and twister weather was upon us. My mother's wisdom had always compelled her, upon receiving dangerous weather reports, to collect her Bible, a hurricane lantern, and the family dog Ladybug, and hastily retreat to the basement for safety. Dad would stubbornly remain in his rocking chair beside his horseshoe-shaped Philco radio as he laughed at her precautions. She always assured him that she would, someday, have the last laugh. Anyway, that day of my childhood, we heard a terrific thunder in the near distance and looked up from our fried chicken and iced tea and melon slices to see a black funnel approaching. It was horrendous. Even dad's weaker side took control. We all cowered to the side of an old gnarled oak while the napkins and plastic knives and forks and styrofoam cups swirled across the tops of milkweed and up into the tree branches. But not mother! She ran to the car—now mind you, Ray, she, too, had respected and feared this wrathful locomotive, but on this occasion, since she had no basement for retreat, since she was face to face with it, she instinctively found only one course, retrieve the brownie box camera and capture the damned thing. She stood eye to eye and, as it bobbed across the uprooting, vulnerable terrain, she snapped a steady finger. Later, the local newspaper featured her photo with a two line credit on its front page. Few housewives would have had that sort of courage, I feel."

Ray agreed with Ruby, "True, I've always respected and retreated when in the face of such danger. I've often wondered if that's why I've chosen Southern California as my residence; at least, until recently, one has never known when his time is up, although seismologists are claiming more and more accuracy in prediction. I want to tell you about an incident in my childhood, it took courage but it wouldn't qualify as does your mom. I merely experienced and endured by clenching my teeth and walking straight ahead. You see, I was twelve, my parents had insisted that I must wait until that age before being baptized.

"I'll never forget that Sunday morning. My parents always hustled my brother and myself off to Sunday school and church; they worked long hours at the shoe factory and sorely needed Sunday to sleep in. The courage I needed was to enable me to walk the mile and a half to the church, undress, save my undershorts, don the white robe of immersion and ultimately entrust my shaking, heaving, believing bosom to the Baptist preacher. I kept sneezing and the awareness that the entire congregation's eyes were upon me caused a rushing sensation in my temples.

"When we waded into the small baptistery I could feel my teenage peter contract, shrivel to nothing more than a ball of rolled up flesh. It was as though the ceremony and God were stripping me of everything including my manhood. I assumed this constriction was consistent with Reverend Hands' words, 'And do you commit your all to the Lord's wishes and continued glory in the Christian kingdom?' But the humiliation wasn't to end there, Ruby-love. As I mentioned, I had been so shy about undressing that I had stupidly left on my underwear. I should have stripped for Christ, because I still had the long walk home. I felt some courage in seeing through the ordeal without the moral support of my parents. Maybe, like so many other times, they felt I had just been rambling and hadn't seriously planned on baptism. I felt embarrassed at the moment of immersion that they hadn't chosen to be present to smile and wink and be proud of my conversion. Anyway, the long walk down the local main street proved traumatic. As I consciously trekked along, every so often drops of water would dribble from my soggy undershorts. A patch of darker blue cloth soon encircled the crotch and seat of my light blue suit pants. I could feel tears of humiliation come to my red eyes.

"But as though I hadn't suffered enough or been adequately test-ed, an automobile eventually pulled beside me and the driver rolled down the window and offered a ride. Courage entered here, for I recognized the driver as a local resident, in his early twenties, who had a notorious reputation as the town queer. He kept insisting that I get in, that he would give me a lift home and no one need know. I kept shouting for him to leave me alone—perhaps he thought I was so afraid that I had pissed my pants—but he would idle along the sidewalk, his snail's pace parallel to my water-trailed steps. Finally, once he realized that I was not going to get in, he gave a command, at which some five or six teenagers surfaced from the front and back seats and they let out a blood-chilling peal of laughter. I was mortified. Apparently, he had pre-arranged my crucifixion. Fortunately, my reluctance to accept the ride was the only face-saving factor of the day. I had already lost the true intention of my immersion. I firmly believed that I had been abandoned by God, and now this Judas, this wicked helmsman was driving the spikes in further by unleashing my peers on my carcass to maim and devour proved too much. The car left a strip of rubber and I chased them down the street with curses, for which I still, half-believing, asked forgiveness of some-god whom I wasn't sure existed. Certainly not deserving. The laughter filled the village and I was left alone on the main street near lunch time when others had easily arrived home to sit to piping hot dinners and formal prayer and nice scents of freshly cut lilac centerpieces."

"My god, Ray, no one should be subjected to that. I think you were a very brave little man to walk along in that manner. I don't suppose you even told your parents?" Ruby leaned forward.

"No, Ruby. I think it's one of those incidents that has the capacity to irreversibly alter one's life yet you find the means to effectively lock it away and tell absolutely no one that it happened. I merely told my parents that the Reverend had conducted a nice service and how he had made everything so easy for me. And how many, past teachers and the butcher at Piggly Wiggleys and the owners of the five and dime, etc., had all come forward and shaken my hand. It was the Reverend's son who used to grope me during Wednesday night choir practice, but I never told them of that either." Ray's unburdening left him spent.

"Ray, before I forget it, I want to tell you one other incident regarding my mother. Here's the setting: a bitter, crisp morning, there

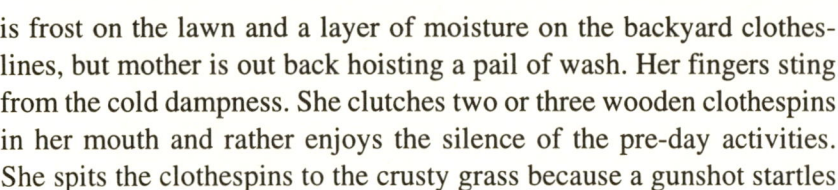

is frost on the lawn and a layer of moisture on the backyard clothes-lines, but mother is out back hoisting a pail of wash. Her fingers sting from the cold dampness. She clutches two or three wooden clothespins in her mouth and rather enjoys the silence of the pre-day activities. She spits the clothespins to the crusty grass because a gunshot startles her methodical fingers..."

"A gunshot?" Ray was bolted back to conversation.

"Yes, in our quiet little neighborhood. As mother later related it— she first saw a blue uniform, then a pistol anchored on a steady wrist, and a second bullet fired. She, frighteningly, was witnessing a death. The officer, actually a friend of my parents, had taken aim and killed some 'goddamned German Shepherd next door in Peck Cassel's flower garden.' As she told it, she hysterically ran over to the clump of mixed red and yellow cannas, she had crisp, half-frozen pillow cases and stockings and bras tangled about her in-motion ankles, and she saw, flopping, foaming, bleeding, a black and grey dog among the giant flowers.

"Mother wasn't afraid, she was devastated and feeling for the pain and tragedy of the animal. She had no control, as she put it. She start-ed beating the officer in the face and arms and chest. She called him foul names. She knocked his cap to the ground. She was rather noted for her individuality and as a young bride had been one of the first ladies to take her husband's hand-me-down suits and as a seamstress she would convert them to smart slacks and suits for herself; so, to question or challenge authority when she saw authority at fault did not cause her to waiver."

"What did the officer do, Ruby?"

"Do? What could he do? She had caught him red-handed at his arbitrary slaughter. Sure, he claimed that the dog had been roaming the neighborhood and presented a danger. She jeered that she didn't see any danger, and how could his wife sleep with him at night knowing the potentiality of his nature. She dissected his facade. She, in turn, used him for target practice; she spat on him. Later, she was to say that her madness caused her to look away from the dog and the officer for some hope, and she saw Peck's hollyhocks standing at attention. She irrationally hoped they would at least stir or contest all that their vigi-lance had witnessed, but nothing abated her stupefaction, the rusty phlegm in her eyes."

"What was the outcome?" Ray asked in an attempt to prod Ruby Francis past her obvious emotional state.

"The outcome was inevitable. Mother ran into her house and phoned the chief of police who immediately defended his officer's actions. He did implore her to simmer down and in turn phoned father to come home and console her."

"And what of the carcass?"

"It was all very expeditious. He tossed it in the trunk of his car, guiltlessly waddled back to Peck's yard, held the unnozzled hose to the spot and washed the bloodied soil into the clump of cannas. That was the end. Oh not for mother, it had sapped something, permanently, from her. She's told and retold the story. But she had the personal fortitude to stand up to the officer and speak her mind. Her example has, likewise, given me courage. She's a true lady to my mind. Unfortunately, she happened to be there. It blew over. I try to think of that incident from time to time. I never want to lose it. I guess she thought a lot about that morning, because many mornings afterwards, I would awaken and find her seated at the yellow formica kitchen table, nearly in the dark, having her coffee, and literally be in a daze while staring out the window at Peck's cannas. I would have to cough or flick on the light before she would snap out of it. She'd say she was fine, just thinking about how unfair it had been, how hopeless the bitch's fate had been and how despicable were mankind's actions. After two, maybe three months, she never mentioned it to me again— apparently only when she had a few beers around friends at fish fries, would she verbally assault him. It was father and myself who kept alive the story of the twister. Both incidents breeze through my mind, often, when I'm stationed at my little outpost counter, singularly serving good hot coffee and pastries. You'll have to excuse me, Ray, for being so—nostalgic."

Ray didn't have to answer; she had related to him such an honest, beautifully sad part of her existence that he felt more drawn to her.

* * *

Quite a wind had come up by now and lights across the bay started to blink off. First the Ferris wheel died, then the Wild Mouse came to a halt. Laughter funnelled out of the amusement park by handfuls. The master switch of the Hilton seemed to acknowledge some adult curfew in this city of old age. Ray Landre thought that as a couple they had reached an understanding of their understanding of one another. There was a kerplunk in the smooth water about the stern of the ship. Rivulets of miniature waves moved away from a lone rat as he had tried to scale the fake ratlines thinking that to stowaway might be an answer. He had, like all others, fallen to the stilled waters, not to drown, not to any sort of doom except that of floundering. Barely would his ears and nose be able to tread water endlessly while lights continued to bring on the dark night.

Ray began a squeak of his genesis: "Well, I know it's cold, and I think that we've accomplished a bit here tonight. I don't want to promise more than I am capable. I could offer, perhaps, to comfort you on cold nights like this, to build a fire for our safety and warmth. I would want to sponge your back as you idle your white form in a relaxing bathtub. I could stir up the mounds of suds for you, dribble in the bathbeads for you. I would want to stand next to your bent form by the basin and shampoo your lovely hair for you, as my parents have always done for one another. It's a dependency without being dependent. Do you see, Ruby? I think we have tidbits of life to offer one another, if we'll only allow it."

At that moment, a piercing blast made the rat quiver in his dog-paddling; Ruby and Ray both jumped for fear of the unknown noise. It was the closing blare of the Queen Mary making another symbolic voyage, a crossing that signified nothing, except that the restaurants and shoppes and bathrooms had closed for the evening. The tired tourists had turned in to pretend to sleep at sea. Ray and Ruby had not paid any boarding fee, any passage. They had no right to the terror of moving on, but that terror, nevertheless, lingered. They had reached out for a while, but Ray slowly started to release his legs once again: Ruby turned to her sweater for warmth. She argued about the absurdity of even discussing topics such as 'virginity and stagnancy and a future.' She frightened him with her facial distortions, all the while the Queen's foghorn roared and bleated as though She had been an industrial sacrifice, as though the rat's stirrings might be creating a drowning vortex, as though She would be sucked down some bathroom drain because the plug had been pulled.

It was a ringing confusion that attacked their ear drums. Ruby snarled, her teeth showed when Ray tried to take her arm. She escorted herself back to the car. It was time for Ray's centipedal self to retrace his steps home. He had munched and left small holes in the foliage. He had battled with an armored snail in the garden beneath the steel, land-locked vessel with a bold white stripe painted about her girdle. The Mary could know of no real danger; the rat could only scratch some graffiti, perhaps its initials, on her side with its teeth. It was, in fact, this insect-ridden pair that found themselves swirling about. Their edifice of ennui had swelled to a blood-drenched climax. It was time to rinse off the shampoo-suds which he had suggested. It took thirty-seven arms to force open the lock on the steel-belted carriage in the Queen Mary's parking lot. Ray's appendages neatly took up every square inch of steering wheel as he did wheelies up Long Beach Blvd. to her front door.

II.

Ray did his best to detain Ruby. The vacuous interior of the car made him want to lecture his captive audience, his dearheart.

Ray finally wove a story about a giant cactus tree he had once seen in Whittier. "I drove to the front door and asked the occupant if she knew about it. The legend is that the now deceased owner of the property had found it in the depths of Mexico and carted it to plant in California. It grew far taller than it should have, overshadowing his hacienda so that botanists came from all around the world to photograph it and take cuttings. It had many nicknames but the genus, the bottom line was a label of Euphorbia, Candelabrum."

"But why are you telling me this, Ray?" Ruby looked puzzled. "I don't even know what the plant, the word euphorbia means."

"I can give you more common examples, poinsettia or Crown of Thorns, they are succulents. They mimic cacti and have acrid, milky sap."

"Ooooo, I hate poinsettia. Aren't they the ones you have to put in dark places, like basements, so they'll bloom? So cruel!"

"Yes, Ruby, but back to my story; you see some of this milky substance is even poisonous in some species. Anyway, this Whittierite, he built his home as a love-present to his new bride, now we're talking 65 years ago, easily. And he planted this small cutting of the cactus tree in his front yard at the same time as a present to her. At the wedding party however he had a few too many brews and started embellishing his stories of adventure across the Mexican border during his bachelorhood to include the myth that if one mistakenly drank from the limbs of this particular tree then it would render him speechless. Many scoffed so he took the dare to partake of it with a large wager with one of his buddies."

"What happened?"

"Well, seems that after licking several white drops from the incision of a thorny branch, he fell to the ground in convulsions. Those at the party carried him to the second story master bedroom that he and his new bride were to have known for the first time that night. It seems the charm of the misleading beauty of the tree with its delicate yellow bracts had fooled him; the plant had lived up to its reputation."

"Then what happened; did he chop down the cactus tree?"

Ruby, ever the pragmatist, would have cut out the thorny source much as a seasoned dermatologist would remove an insignificant skin-cancer.

"No, no, as I told you, I saw it not a year ago, it's a mammoth raising its thorny, sword-shaped arms to the heavens. I'll take you to see it sometime. But their marriage was doomed for he was bed-ridden for two weeks before succumbing to the milkweed. And the tragedy during all that time is that he was unable to speak. He had been so busy with the construction of the house, with the landscaping of such vast acreage that he had not had the time to say the loving words he held for his dear bride. It proved to be a fine inability to speak on his part, for she kept vigil each of those fourteen nights, reading to him and speaking of her love for him but he was unable to reciprocate—his tongue remained a bluish glob of calf's liver. It was a flirtation with fate that he would never overcome."

"What a genuine tragedy, Ray. What a mistake to not believe those stories sometime; what's the old saw, Better Safe than Sorry?"

"Exactly," Ray paired off with his perchance bride.

* * *

150

The foregoing stroll had occurred on Tuesday. Thursday came and Ruby Francis admitted that she had thought a great deal before submitting the following as her first and only stab at a poem: however, she confessed that Ray's Euphoria (sic) story had moved her. The crinkled piece of paper held the following:

SUCCULENT - by Ruby Frangible

Mangy ole thing: looks like space-flower
too brazen for the garden
too gangly for a vase
too thick-skinned to be precious

Greedy ole thing
suckin up the moisture
shadin out the sweetpea
smellin up the patch of lawn

Shapeless ole thing
Ichabod arms
copycat sunflower faces
old exposed granny roots

Worthless ole thing
takin up space
crying to be moved
in need of a paint job

Kindred ole thing
just like me
fit for a garage sale
pin a 25¢ or Best Offer
into my liquidless neck
and get your hopes up.

17 GARDENING A NEW VENTURE: PRUNING TO SHAPE

RAY HAD PLACED A NOTICE in the local Long Beach newspaper that he, Ray Landre, was doing business as PRUNING TO SHAPE. It had only cost him five dollars and the mere exhilaration of seeing his declaration in print kept him company for several days. He assumed that if Ruby's peripheral vision had overshot the obits, then surely she might have seen his preoccupation.

One of Ray's earliest call backs had been to a Mrs. Fordyce who, in a somewhat broken British accent, had stated she needed his services. She needed weeding, watering and fine pruning of her wee Japanese Display Area, her "JDA," as she hastily described it. He had carefully deliberated his business' name and it was proving to solicit an esoteric clientele, or that was his intention. If they had bonsai he could do that; if they specialized in orchids or ferns he could accommodate. Even California grasses were not beyond his expertise. Since this Mrs. Fordyce turned out to be Etta-Mary of the New World Pharmacy environ fame, Ray condescended to step around the damp dog turdies for she had lovingly referred to her "JDA" as her pride and joy. He did, however, feel that such minimal pay did not require he soil his ex-teaching hands so. He was doubly burdened as he felt, sensed that she was watching, clocking his toil from her elevated window.

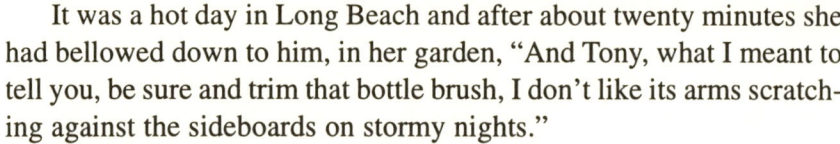

It was a hot day in Long Beach and after about twenty minutes she had bellowed down to him, in her garden, "And Tony, what I meant to tell you, be sure and trim that bottle brush, I don't like its arms scratching against the sideboards on stormy nights."

"But Mrs. Fordyce, my name's Ray not Tony..."

But Ray internalized that people like Etta-Mary did pay his bills and she was advanced into her horticultural tirade. He acknowledged that he needed accounts like Etta-Mary's and was now fettered to such pathetic demands. She was, for example, on a fixed income and he had outbid other gardeners for the job and he had to live up to his newly professed reputation. He had even cinched the job, endeared her by offering a senior citizen discount as well as a close-proximity reduction whereas he lived close by. She expressed that she liked that and he had been able to finalize the deal on the spot of the estimate. He liked that expeditious nature about his newly chosen field. And if so uncanny, unexplained fancy, a kinky fantasy called "Tony" and it worked for her—then so be it.

As Ray proceeded to dig in her backyard space (for Long Beach real estate had drastically contained such space), his shovel pinged against metal—although nothing surprised Ray-as-gardener, coffee cans, animal bones, old shoes, doll parts, veined marbles, they all greeted his blunted shovel tip, but since he had such a small area to work, he chose to scrutinize his find: not volunteer tree roots, not a half-decayed log, but metal, a shape that resembled a bank's safe deposit box. About then a yellow cat jumped across Ray's band of vision; it startled and momentarily distracted his attention, sort of like an archeologist who might have been opening, for the first time, an Egyptian tomb and noted in his journal the appearance of a specter. The five gallon ceanothus waited its planting as he questioned the box's contents. Etta-Mary shouted from the window, "Don't worry, lad, you'll find loads of treasures back there, but no gold' Just plant the lilac, it should do well there." If there was anything Ray disliked in his new venture, it was the customer telling him about plants. Right plant, right place; he had written that book long before its publication.

Ray's new philosophy kicked in, though: please the customer. His newly established days were, after all, blocked into fluid divisions of time. He still allowed himself to be preoccupied with Faulkner and

Rilke and Sartre, and yes, Ruby Frangible, as he bored into clods of rich, steer-manure enhanced granules of soil but conversely comparative literature had been, realistically, chucked out the window like that same clod of dirt, so it all was basically an echo of remembrance spent in the classroom, the Roberta Markmanns, the Dr. Bones at U.C.L.A. just sort of swirled on Ray's periphery, for now he had to shovel shit for a living, that paid the bills, that was his reality. And it was all self-chosen. He liked that. About then he tossed aside an expensive staghorn fern which Mrs. Fordyce had commissioned him to select and he would later, time, yes time permitting, position it on the shaded entry gate to her little Edenic world.

Ray took as gospel his father's old saw 'The Customer's Always Right'. After two hours of pleasurable labor, Ray's next audible connection to the Widow, old Rhino Snout, proved an invitation inside for a tumbler of iced tea. He accepted. It was then, as he luxuriated in her cushiony sofa, disregarding his soiled bib overalls, that he spied a collection of odd black wooden boxes, music box size, arranged across her lacquered black baby grand piano. As she served him his tea, to exit she had had to mince through a forest of strategically placed figurines of rhinoceros. He asked her about the piano-boxes.

"The boxes, yes, the boxes—that's what I'm known for, or hadn't you heard? I'm famous for my dogs, my cats, but I have a secret, I outlive them, just as I did my husband Arnie. They need to be put to sleep, and I have them cremated; it's somewhat costly but they're worth it. Once they are returned to me, usually by pre-arranged cab rides, I station them on the piano top. Most people have never met me but they've heard about the crazy old lady with the boxes atop her piano. Word gets back to me, especially around the pharmacy where I get my prescriptions filled, you know. Some find me eccentric but that's just as I am. Far from morbid, I'm just a concerned citizen; I'm a female Bartleby with my fixed concerns—you see, I care not." Her silhouette in the kitchen doorway was hermaphroditic and that was a turn-on to Ray.

"No problem-o, mon." Ray soon heard her mynah in the kitchen where it was caged. It was true to its species, loquacious, but for most of its repertoire, he heard "Stow it, matey; papa's home soon; bury it in the south forty." Ray knew better than to ask any questions. Soon

155

enough, though, Etta-Mary sat opposite Ray and her robe, though unintentional, parted. Amid the mynah squalking and a distant ringing of a telephone unanswered, he took advantage of an invitation for tea and forced himself upon her. Something about an older woman had summoned more want than he had felt for Ruby Francis or any blind date. It was not an action in any way premeditated, just one he chose to enter into. An orange and black monarch forced its way between the rusted screening and the window sill of Etta-Mary's upper living room window and nervously hovered above the bed before flapping out into the darkened apartment hallway. The last thing that Ray remembered before loading into the cramped space of his VW truck one shovel, one rake, one hand lawn mower, one weeding utensil and an empty plastic bag of soil was an uncanny replica of a human voice that said "Naughty boy, daddy spank; naughty boy, momma gonna git you" and the fluttering of some clipped black wings.

18 KEW GARDENS AND OTHER XERISCAPES

Ruby's comments about the influence of her grandmother had served to touch off many nostalgic thoughts of Ray's grandmother in the days that followed. She had worked much of her life in the employ of one of the original state hospitals of the nation; it was one caught in the bite of shrill transition from the traditional, firm-handed approach of treating the inmates to that of the more modern methods of imbecilic dotage and permissiveness. It had been a location where gloating camera crews from neighboring television stations could parade about and come upon concrete examples of supposedly "secret tunnels" beneath the grounds where one might still see manacles affixed to the dank eroded stone walls. It was preserved as a carcass from a by-gone era of professional confusion, mistreatment and of a humanity with dark efforts to rehabilitate; one inadequate to see past its own clouded *pince nez.* And always a photo of the old fart Freud as some canonized saint on the walls, Freud the collector of crumbled souls among the human bric-a-brac.

Ruby, too, had been a great collector of things. She had indexed these "things" as she described to Ray her early childhood and familial relationships. She had been taken with postage stamp collecting—she would borrow money, accept stamps from the stamp firm's loan-system and then not pay for them, she would steal her peers blind when they were sealing away a new philatelic treasure and not looking; in short, she had enthusiastically acquired a sizeable heap of stamps. Then she had placed that binder on a forgotten shelf and turned to coins. Her austere background had precluded any great strides forward in this venture, but unlike her stamp collecting, this preoccupation had stuck with her all these years. Ray didn't find this objectionable, in fact, he felt this a rather universal propensity for collectibles, be it a housewife saving redemption stamps or coupons, or the suburban husband who must have on exhibition, in his front yard and driveway, a camper complete with loaded rifle rack; a boat-out-of-water, covered with plastic; two or three automobiles, enough toys discarded by his bored children to supply a Mattel warehouse; an assortment of bicycles, skates, rakes, shovels, post-hole diggers, a hoist for removing car engines, power mowers, piles of untouched lumber that will serve as firewood should he ever buy that cabin in the mountains. Collectibles; worth little, other than to prove his virile existence. All these material things to reinstate his niche in society as he daily leaves the house to create purchasing power for more dust-collectors.

Now Ray's understanding of fetishes proves another consideration. He had once held down a job at said institution of "declared insanity", during which he was placed in charge of two patients from the previous era—when all hope had been abandoned and those individuals lucky enough to have endured the system, or to have escaped the newer, permissive atmosphere, whichever, Ray came across a collector of collectors. His job humbled him a great deal. His partners on the work force were named Gibson and Coffee. Gibson or Gibby would be up and ready to work for the state and "the boss" at the crack of dawn. His sidekick Joe Coffee would sit in his catatonic stupor unless one of those entrusted with his keep kicked him in the seat of his pants to "get a move on." But Gibby's fetish was a fondness for small metal pieces: screws, bolts, straight pins, clasps from purses and old zippers that he had scavengered from the Asylum Hill trash barrels. When he wasn't kept busy enough, he would take one of the small, shiny objects from his biboveralls pocket (no matter how many were taken away from him he could always produce one more once he was left alone; he apparently had found the means of hiding a back-up supply in his privates which occasionally required a strip search).

Gibby's eyes would light up as he fondled it; he was momentarily lost to another more sensual world, one that had obviously perplexed his psychiatrists and family for some three decades. He had been neglected in this hell above ground because it had been easier, besides cheap labor was badly needed to make the institution "work." There were clothing and food supplies to be delivered to the maze of wards, to the youth hostel for teenagers, and even for younger children who were from broken homes; the geriatrics complex; the building of double-fenced security for the criminally insane. There was the marvelous inmate Master Mustang who would proposition and "take" any ass he could climb on. He had been so frequently placed in isolation, and assigned to work details because of his superlative degree of strength, that it had become a reward instead of a punishment over the years. To tease poor Gibby, other patients as well as employees would shake him down, kick him, demand that he empty his pockets for the mere pleasure of humiliating him. His squat, 240-pound bolt of Levi that represented him comprised of his work cap of blue Levi down to his ridiculously long-legged Levi pants that cascaded over his work boots, the hems always tattered and covered with tobacco juice, and watermelon seeds, and caked coffee grounds from his rummaging through the patient cafeteria after his comrades had walked their death-daze back to the wards, corralled along like fatted cattle.

Gibson was a collector; his collection harmed no one, yet no one was willing to tolerate his idiosyncrasy. He suffered every day of his life for his small desire to do what others on the outside did as an escape, he gorged himself on the fruits of life. How his digestive mechanisms managed to work baffled all of the doctors. Overall, though, Gibby had assimilated far too adequately so that this grown man had become childlike in his willingness to be lead about and forfeit his identity.

Once when Ruby had asked Ray about any hobbies he might have, he told her about his attempt at writing a three-act play that would utilize these strange, warm characters whom he had been fortunate enough to meet. Ray's apology that served as an introduction explained that this writing more than likely had served as therapy for himself, something too sad, too small to share with friends or colleagues. He eventually gave in to Ruby's request, though. He shared his crude beginnings, for he never completed the work past act one, with her over coffee and one of her blueberry long-johns one evening before closing time. The original idea for the play had been snatched from some insignificant dialog by Emerson: "Henry, what are you doing in there (jail)?" Thoreau replied sternly, "What are you doing out there?" It seemed so appropriate to Ray's sadness for others at that point in his life. Today, though, Ray had experienced changes, he could walk past a derelict wallowing in the gutter or past some crone as she bellows a hymn from her syphilitic lisping throat along Long Beach Boulevard without any remorse. He could look towards the ocean, the other direction. But he had gone through his idealistic period, it had all been very important then. Samples:

THE OCEAN

The ocean. The ocean...
His favorite recollection from one of his father's
rare letters form the Midwest to Southern California
had been a rejection to come for a visit.
He said, "Why would he need to come all the way
to California to see a sunset over the ocean
when he had thousands of them in Missouri?"
The argument: "Dad, it isn't the same."
Midwestern dads seldom give in though, and quipped.
"We have sunsets here, too, you know."
I no longer came home.

OUT THERE - a one-act play by Ray Landre

Scene: the supply room of one of the state mental institutions in the Midwest. The three men have just returned from the daily milk delivery and Eli is seen kicking and cursing from behind the first patient, a pathetic, thin man of sixty years. Both wear bib overalls and blue denim shirts with billed caps. The second patient is a gluttonous fool. He sashays about the stage with a strange grin and twinkle in his eyes. He singles out individuals in audience, winks, feigns masturbation. The two keep their distance from Eli.

ELI: I told you I would kick your ass (and he does, with
an unexplained venom in his stare) when we got back
Now stack up those milk racks like you're supposed to.
I saw you flirting (exhibiting much disgust on his face
as he derides his inferior) with those crazy gals from
Ward D–how many times have I warned you? Deliver
your milk and hightail it back to this truck–and you be
waiting there for me!

(At this point, Gibby sidles to a corner rubbing his cor-
pulent ass. He cowers there, pulls out a clumsily
wrapped newspaper that quickly draws flies; it contains
a coffee filter full of reused coffee grounds; he hastily
lifts over-running handfuls to his mouth, sucks on the
juice, then slides the grounds down his throat. He burps
loudly. He repeats this until Eli gives Gibby permission
to continue his feast; he pulls out some wilted cabbage
leaves that disappear as though a worm had methodical-
ly erased them, a tooth-bite at a time).

ELI: Just keep eating, but tell us about your girl friend.
I know you spend what little money we give you on her.
You get her a pair of anklets, or some cheap perfume,
don't you? (Eli sadistically taunts G; tickles G under his
fat rib cage) Tell us about what you two do when you
meet at the Canteen. Do you get a feel in? (Again, Eli
twists G's arm behind and up until G pleads that it hurts
and he'll tell him anything he wants to hear—there is
silence as Eli towers over the wet-pup. G is forced to
empty his pockets, and hair-pins, tin tops of lipstick
capsules, a thimble, and four miniature dress-snaps
click to the concrete floor. G looks extremely embarrassed. He has only to wait for Eli's second, and harder,
kick in the kidneys)...

"Well, that's as much as I had written." Ray could sense that Ruby
was disappointed. She stressed that he should someday finish the play.
Ray personally liked its idea, too. Ray told her that his head literally
swam with other equally colorful characters to progress the action of

161

the play and this excited Ruby Francis about the prospects. He had tentatively titled the work-in-progress "Fragmented Fetishes and other Collectibles." Truthfully, though, Ray became depressed in realizing that he was fictionalizing that which the public could accept only as fiction. They would see themselves, perhaps too vividly, in the task-master Eli, or else in one of the two all-encompassing characters of the manic-depressive Coffee or gluttonous Gibby. Ray wanted to deny any kernel of cruelty within himself that proposed to shove such a night of theatre down the throat of conscientious, paying patrons of the arts. Thus Ray questioned that he should ever finish it, but Ruby didn't need to know of his lack of plans. It had brought them closer together. Ruby's pasty-eyes that had iced endless racks of donuts and the fact she had given in to so many men amazed Ray in their conception, their compassion.

Such blurs of talkathons allowed the friendship to continue amicably and Ray's hours spent on his new business, Pruning to Shape, kept him occupied. That which needed to be kept secret remained so; he had not anticipated any complications with Mrs. Fordyce. She simply was not the type of individual to report the incident. She had even mailed him the full amount reflected on the invoice that Ray had left her for his gardening services. As to him and Ruby, though, the most difficult aspect to accept in the days that had followed the Queen Mary discussion was Where Are We Headed? Ray continued his frugality, his sure-one-day, not-sure-the-next preoccupation. He conversely appreciated her honesty. He still longed to hold her again. He wanted to follow-through on the shampoo, the domestic proposition; yet, the reality of his knowledge of the inn-keeper and inmate relationship of caring and hating, nursing and destroying had been enough to douse the flame. Often, working in clients' gardens, his mind would drift as some horticultural defense mechanism when there seemed no answers for him.

Besides the time spent at Ephesus and a week's cruise of the Agean that terminated with a second week in Athens, he had also spent a lonely week in London. Ray had defied anyone to interrupt his pilgrimage to Kew Gardens. The rich history, botanically and dynastically, had served to magnetize his visit to the area of the Thames. He had taken the tube to Kew on a misty morning. He exited at the Turnham

Green Station. Bewilderingly, several ladies, elders of the neighborhood, invited him to join them in a stuffy, V-shaped breakfast house for scrambled eggs and a muffin. They prepared Ray, as much as possible, for what he would see in the few short blocks of walking. The lovely mysterious quality of Kew is supplied as a fitting accompaniment to Ray's preoccupation as to the future of his ever-growing affection for Ruby. Would she stay on at Winchells? Would he work alongside her, would he work for her? Would he scrub the floors? Would she cuckold him as she positioned him, like an Emanuel, at the window while she winked some stiff-pricked trucker back to her drape-drawn room? Would they close their eyes together and see the orange explosion of her knowing-beanbag sunrise? It pained Ray's temples to conjure up a visual confusion like that of a mad child who released the lid from a gallon mason jar that is filled with bolts, and screws, and faucet tap nuts and straight pins and bits of chain as it falls in metal confetti across the garage floor; except his confusion about her comes in myriads of cake-donuts whirling about him, orange and red and lavender bits of flesh, he reaches to catch and taste one, but he cannot. She has greased them and her price keeps changing and he wails; the neighbors in his reverie think they hear a caterwaul from behind Ray's apartment. There are cordons of "wills" and "ifs" and "pleases" and "perchances" erected all about him until he cannot get outside himself.

* * *

Journal entry while enroute to Kew Gardens: A Parable

The brown-shaggy haired youth stepped from the
District Line at the Turnham Green Station. He exited
laboriously as he placed most of his handsome weight on
the bent, wooden cane. On rarer days he continued to
Kew Gardens but not this day, not after overhearing the
conversation between two Catholic nuns. He never listened to, considered religious people, but something
about the vivacity, the eyes, compelled him to catch snippets of what they said to one another. "Well, I think the
highlight for Spain was the Bullfights...." She had
paused, as though anticipating enthusiastic agreement
from her sister, but the other had merely frowned a silent

frown. "Well, for me: I mean, Rome—St. Peters;
Florence—David; and Spain, the Bullfights, for me, anyway."

My God, the lad thought, how could a nun say that!? He
thought religion of any sort just so much poppycock, but,
after all, she had chosen—oh so many things, a Bride of
Christ. She even mentioned being so mad recently, that
she yanked the cloth from her head. He thought again,
What are things coming to if even the religious aren't
devout. Even he believed in commitments, vows, loyal-
ties—that is, he had until two years ago, around his twentieth birthday, when it had happened. The Cane often preoccupied his gaze. And riding on the tube, he would think:
cane/pain: the filigree of curtains in my second story bed-
room/pleasure of isolation, of masturbation. And this
phrase played hide and seek in matching the clickety-clack
of the tube's metal wheels meeting the rails from Turnham
Green to London to Turnham Green.

...But that nun, that takes some gall. She probably enjoyed
Ken Russell's film The Devils, too. He started to ask her.
Best to debark. Best to return home and masturbate. That
was his world—almost as sweet as entering the world of
Kew Gardens. He fondly remembered going there for the
first time on his twelfth birthday. His parents were still
alive then and, after much ale and his timid father's drunk-
en attempt at singing bars of "My Wild Irish Rose", they
argued, so on both good legs in those days, he ran to the
Garden. He had had to ask directions from a pleasant
chap, keeper of an antique shop just outside the KG station. The chap eyed him, almost for too long a period, but
finally he smiled and directed the boy to retrace his steps
in through the station, and that, once he exited the other
side, he might even smell the flowers of the Garden some
eight blocks away. That lovely ringing phrase, "You might
even smell the flowers," accompanied him. Sure enough,
he did. Leaving his parents, the tube, and even the
stranger. But that was then, when he knew rare honeysuckle and primrose and...he could feel, and he looked only for

pleasure in life, not the pain.

He could no longer smell the flowers. And visually, they were only a blur of that first visit. They had become a burnt ash of a Monet Lily canvas. Now he even noticed the dead leaves along the gray sidewalk in the middle of summer. Early August and the leaves already dead. Early August and he was near death. He thought, if only the passengers on the tube knew his secret. Each evening he would retire to his room and light candles and shut the windows and disrobe and lie back to masturbate with the right hand while pinching his bad leg with his left hand as painfully as possible. Matter of factly, the pain of today was far greater than that of two years ago. He had read of T.E. Lawrence and other biographies of people self-conditioning themselves to pain, but he could not discern exactly where he had learned the secret, the plea-sure/pain principle. And it was funny how the chamomile and bellflower, the rose and jasmine accompanied his cli-max. They stayed outside his room until the moment his senses screamed at the touch of the fingernail and the ejaculation began for unknown hours. He had tried with-out the pain. It just never came anymore, without the pain. He was not bitter anymore, and now he might even kill that ridiculous excuse for a nun in his next reverie. But nothing to labor over, for tomorrow he would again leave Turnham Green Station and return and again the pain would come. Again he would assassinate one of the cloth, as the beads fell off stolen KG rose petals resting on the oak bureau top.

The End

* * *

Ray Landre felt that it wasn't as though he couldn't continue to exist without such thoughts, such fabrications. It was Ruby Francis that he worried about, though. But Ray had to admit to himself that what would be labeled fantasy for some was too often reality for him: he was enraptured with his hospital days and his mystical hankerings of his other selves to walk away from himself and board a tram that he knows will crash, or wander onto an elevated rail to Kew Gardens to be caught in the rain, yet commune with a brown squirrel as it chases its shadow through the piles of leaves for survival of the grounds man's machete. For he cannot meet a character who is without potential to become a character. They are becoming and at once are nucleolus and plasma membrane. They are allowed perversions beyond comprehension or they are sweet just like his Ruby, who is, after all, his prime concern. She should have so very much to compromise, to accept, to become. She cannot go on collecting men in all varying sizes and shapes, or so Ray Landre is wont to hope. Ray has convinced himself that he is not willing to let her continue feeding her days and draining her nights like a gluttonous Gibson or an insatiable masticating oscar like his pet Waldo. Eventually, the obituary column must reflect her demise. Ray also did not want to wake up someday to discover that he had over-looked her beauty. To counter, he kept telling himself that she is as creviced and unseeing as the weather beaten and smogged up sentries of the Acropolis: he could choose to say that she is unworthy of one like himself, that she should be thrown to the "dogs" in her backstreet pastry salon (for he could as easily transport, make a beeline himself to the other side of town where numerous brothels cluster about the freeway exit like whitewashed bee hives dotting the ancient hillside of Golgotha); but Ray perceived himself as one who has established a line of responsibility; he had borne a faith that she has in him.

Ray contemplated that surely he had learned something from all of this human-consumption, from this simulated baby-sitting with the insane and his cold, lone trips to the market of nights with their posh offerings like forgetfulness and resentment. He grimaced at the thought he may have effected a forgery, this existence that states "I do arise during each day and filch about the agora of western civilization to clasp an alabaster set of balls and phallus cast about an ancient image that never breathed air or felt the surge of red corpuscles about the tense head?

Ray held up to the light the genuine veneer of Ruby's recent request that he join her in her business venture; try living together for a while. No strings, no hassles, new promises. It sounded plausible. If he had endured those rainy nights with a snaggle-toothed lady some thirty years his senior while hopping about the English landscape of Eton and Sandwich, plugging her in the damp, nude air for fear that he might not wake the next morning to daydream of the reputed Charles Dickens' residence across the bay, then he had no right to continue his existence without a willingness to make a stab with it with younger, lovely Ruby Francis. He would fold his mania into a newspaper and toss it behind, in his alley. He would shuffle a refreshed real estate of prospects by admitting, to Ruby, that he did wish to be hers. Yet, he knew he was dealing with, propositioning an amoral lady who had, a matter of hours ago, confessed that she had recently run out of white thread in mending a ripped armpit in her only clean uniform, and she had rushed to the nearby Woolworth's, and, no sooner had she purchased a replacement spool, she had made eye-contact with a handsome young man who stood nervously thumping a wrinkled dollar bill at the candy counter. They exited the dime store together and he asked her if she had come there for "variety" as the sign stated. He also asked if she lived in Bellflower and he cleverly pushed the conversation to casually mention that she might step outside and view the interior of his newly purchased Winnebago. Ruby described it as immaculately decorated and cleaner than her own living quarters. The camper was parked on Bellflower Blvd., and he offered her a drink of vodka and asked if she needed to use the restroom. He eagerly wanted her to see each compartment, including the pulldown bed. She laughed that he clumsily dropped a tube of Vaseline from one of the storage shelves in pulling open various paneled doors. He was most forward and commanded her to take off her blouse. She said it was out of the question, right in broad daylight, on the main street of the town in which she lived. She expressed fear that a nosy policeman might at any moment come poking his eyes and handcuffs into the miniature house. She kept pushing shut the part in the matching yellow drapes.

But as always, in Ray's mind, she had given in; she watched him undress first; he kept his dark socks on, and she could hardly believe the size of the third member in the hot stuffy air of the afternoon coach. He assured her that the police would not interrupt their fun and if they should he held a most influential position in state government and, as he snapped his finger, the incident would be discarded–just like that. She told Ray that she was impressed with his self-confidence and his finesse. He proved most versatile and she was pleased that it was daytime because his overpowering, towering technique in screwing her, in night time, would most assuredly cast a mean, suggestive silhouette to carlights passing the area. He whispered to her that he didn't get out often and that he would soon come inside her. He also insisted that he not use a rubber. She admitted to Ray that she seldom allowed that but he had gotten her so hot that she gave in easily. He climaxed in her by saying he would ride her like a pony. A good-humor music box of "Comin' through the Rye" played outside. She figured that they were in that hot box on wheels in front of the little housewives browsing and bargain-hunting in the variety store some two hours. She wondered, though didn't really worry, whether anyone seeing her step down from the modern street-gypsy wagon would recognize her. After all, what could any local banker or saleslady or beautician remark? "Why, isn't that Ruby Frangible? She must be purchasing flour and sugar and dehydrated apple pieces and chocolate and dragée for her donut shop. I wonder if he's a new salesman in the area?" (for as Ruby described it to Ray, if they noticed his crotch at all, its pant-creasing ability, they would realize he was new on the block; this she tooted, soft or hard, it was gargantuan.)

Ruby told Ray that she had made it back in time to take over the evening shift, after finishing her sewing. This may have been a mending for her own enjoyment but it rather turned Ray off. The confusion, the jealousy, her being oblivious to Ray's feelings, were starting to crash in upon him. He also was cable of projecting the tale to a future date, when he might be the clerk waiting for the boss's relief and the fabrications she might thrust at him. He thought of sending her flowers in appreciation of their stroll at the Queen Mary but couldn't actually bring himself to do so–sending roses to a lady who had confessed such promiscuity, such blatant betrayal of his interests? Ludicrous. A dozen long stems aren't to be suffocated by cigarette butts and smelly armpits of truckers. The flowers sitting in her back room or at the shop counter would be like wiring flowers to some bull dike working at an automobile assembly line. The dike wouldn't appreciate the incongruity, her co-workers would scoff, the boss might fire her or make her the butt of daily jokes. Ray rationalized away the sweet thought even though the gift of flowers would have been easier than to reprimand or put her down just for being herself. A nomadic whore traveling in a brothel-on-wheels, or more like a touring lunatic asylum, and he was falling hopelessly more in love with its mistress, its turnkey.

All of this was forcing Ray into a corner, one where decisions had to be made. But if one were to strip away the props, the Cane, the mynah bird, the blatant sexual abuses, the joblessness, then the core of Ray Landre might be tapped. He was a sweet person on the outside; his outer self did not reveal the inner maladies. Ruby's infatuation could not know his infirmities, could not see Eli the task-master within, the hard-coeur dissembler who called at her door. One who had pinged defenseless wet mutts upon their heads and flung them down the deserted boardwalks. She might guess it was his poetry that pacified him, that kept him in check when such decisions needed to be made. But sadly, this was not so.

II.

Upon walking into Ruby's back room that same day of revelation, his eyes bugged at her change. She was actually sitting up, drooped in her devouring orange bean-bag chair and he noticed her panties and bra blown across the edge of the unmade, white bedspread. He quickly propositioned her. He told her that he had not worked out the details but union was the intent of his coming to her. She had no reluctance. He noticed she was reading a different black list; she was busying herself with a Gideon Bible. She suggested that he enter into a partnership with her. She knew a lawyer and she felt confident that she could arrange for the change or addition of the legal franchise. She proposed that Ray could immediately move into an apartment complex that sat adjacent to her building. Ray sat on the edge of the bed as he toyed with her lace-trimmed undies. She lay the opened Bible next to Ray so that she might better use her hands to figuratively build their future house-solid-on-the-rock picture. But Ray was made to think she may have played architect in this manner too many times before. He sensed the move she proposed, the imminent reluctance showed; he was angered. The rise that the underwear had begun, began to falter. His house plants and his prized oscar Waldo with his controlled environment flashed, swam through Ray's retinas. It suddenly sounded so good.

Ray tried to change the subject. He would be ready for the loony-bin if she continued her apologetic-bitch-of-a-self. He tossed the Bible up and down in his one free hand like a circus juggler while the other wrist supported his reclining form.

A stranger's bed had never felt so good nor so repulsive. He could smell the moist glandular drippings of her tossing night of sleep. The hot glaze from out front started to permeate the room and the gap between his ears. His arteries pumped gallons of gooey dough and tried to force it through his kidneys, his lungs; his heart felt it would burst because the propelling apple fritter had got caught in the aortal opening. He must have gone crimson for she, too, tried to change the subject. Ray's singular problem was that he had never known a character like her. He had to decide as quickly as possible how to handle her.

"Where did you pick this up?" (Ray immediately regretted his casual, premeditated question because it had probably been one of her few momentoes of the nights before he had met her, from her so-called Christian charitable servicing of souls and bodies combined as they partook of her whip-cream-topped breasts. Communion after communion after communion, conducted so willingly and sincerely by her naiveté: Let's see what passage of dissemblers you've chosen to occupy your off-duty hours.)

Ruby Francis began her assault: "Ray Landre, why have you come with roses in one hand, and pruning shears in the other? Can't we retrace our moonlight walk through the Queen Mary Garden and just be Ruby and Ray...need and reward...gentle and compact? As to the source of this wonderful book, I answered a knock at my back door a couple of days ago and a teenage girl with much free time on her hands, what with summer and no school, was selling those unbound nuisances that preach of after-life and doom."

She gave the Bible to me because she said I was sweet and reminded her a great deal of her older sister. Her sister had run off from home two years ago and joined one of those Hari Krishna cults. It had devastated their mother; she had gone insane and now she was an outpatient. The clinic had apparently made her whole again; she had, quite simply, disowned the older daughter. Her psychiatrist had counseled her that that would ease the pain. She was cured! I'm rereading the Sermon on the Mount. It always refreshes me. I am growing each day of my life, for though I am not perfect...(Ray nearly choked on his bearclaw nuts) I strive to approach a working understanding of perfectibility. The Lord said: 'Blessed are the meek, for they shall inherit the earth. And 'Blessed are the pure in heart: for they shall see God;' and finally, 'Love your enemies, bless them that curse you, pray for them which despitefully use you, and persecute you; That ye may be the children of your Father which is in heaven: for he maketh his sun to rise on the evil and on the good, and sendeth rain on the just and on the unjust.' The idea of tolerance, understanding, rain is all so reassuring, so comforting. I think at times I can make it."

Ray thought, Poor dear, hara-kiri of the soul.

Ray yelled to her, "You know you have nothing to be ashamed of; you live your life as best you can. You simply must cease living in fear and remorse. Enjoy the beauty that you give others. The loss of virginity is no great travesty. Look at Queen Elizabeth (Bess's) concern with this lock and key game. You needn't wake up some day to discover that it all slipped away while you were keeping it behind the counter and pushing caffeine and butter rolls. We've got to take a stab at it sometimes. Now is as good a time as any. I fail to understand your sudden piety. I can appreciate self-respect, old or newly found, but not this 'holier than thou' shit. I'm not buying it. You stand here rejecting my offer to share something undreamed of while I slither beneath the waves? Afterall, Rube, you remember I once quoted for you T.S. Eliot:

> I have heard the mermaids singing, each to each
> I do not think they will sing to me."

"But Ray, I once knew, once lived with a well-meaning hunk. He would get on his knees some nights and actually cry that he loved me so much. He begged me to please never leave him for I meant everything in the universe to him. To make a long story shorter, and to hopefully make my point of self-concern, or survival, he had been getting plenty on the side yet professing complete faithfulness; he had drunk with another lover of his, on one of his orgiastic nights, champagne that I had been refrigerating for one of our special upcoming occasions; he had scrawled our initials and endearing phrases in four inch high characters on the kitchen wall with a tube of my lipstick, and it wouldn't come off. He wrote I was his slave and belonged to only him in fourteen inch scarlet letters. I knew the landlord, once he saw it, would file a law suit. He ran off to Tucson with some other broad. He had the audacity to send me a post card. He was very sadistic, as time proved. He used to tie me to the bedpost, once upside down, and he would try to scare me with dildos; he would throw my teddy bear (a present that he had made much ado over after giving to me for a birthday present) across the room right when I was ready to climax. He hated my cooking. Said it wasn't fit for a dog. Luckily, it all ended with his going away 'For Artistic Freedom.' I never acknowledged the card; of course, I've wondered a lot as to his whereabouts, his sanity. But you see, that's why I can't just up and say, sure, Ray, move in. I need you and know it can work. You have your mental patients that storm through your mental attic nightly and plants that chafe your underside as you care for them; and I, well I have my penance—I have my shop, my men, Emanuel and bills to pay. I'm lucky if I break even each month; but I have my dignity, my sense of toeing the line. I can read of biblical times and promises and characters who no longer walk the earth, just over-seers who walk the land and sprinkle ashes for those of us no longer capable of seeing the daylight. Who are you, how could you attempt to wake up here each morning in my womb only to discover that I will not let the sun rise, I will not open the drapes. I have signed this agreement, you see, with myself; and as badly as I would like to tear it up and sail with you a while, never theless I cannot. That bastard I was telling you about, he was into double-save coupons at this one massage parlor he frequented. For Christ's sake, can you imagine. He was such a cheap, or uncertain bastard, he had to have something to take home with him because the orgasm was too ephemeral. He apparently would insert his minute penis only to find he had climaxed. He was a baby. I traced down the origin of his credit card carbons and he was getting off at the local 'Touchie-feelie' hot spot. I threw him out. He, one other time, wrote me a letter. I read it because it was sealed and I can't stand not knowing the contents.

"Now a post card, I can glance down the margins and know that I'm not missing something, but a letter, well, you would not have believed how raunchy it was. Since moving to the desert he wrote that he mainly just rode around in his jeep looking for snakes or lizards to shoot. I'm not surprised. He never knew why he had moved to the desert in the first place. He said that one afternoon in July he had been out by himself looking for mesquite wood along the dirt roadway. He eventually came to a dry creekbottom. He saw some good-sized branches lying in the center of the rock bed so he walked out to retrieve them for firewood. He said that he had no sooner reached mid-stream than he heard a thunder up the way; he had walked directly into a flash flood in the desert. He said he had finished a sixpack of beer and that his reactions were slower than usual. There was a strange electricity and dryness to the air. Before he knew What was happening, the flood was upon him. He had little time to think and had to whisk us up to the shores. We were both dripping wet. He forced my face into the mud and ordered me to undress. He brought some rope from his jeep and tied me, facedown, between two tree trunks. He whipped my ass with his worry-beads-keychain, but not too hard, and proceded to screw me. The only lubricant was rain. He wrote that it had been the best ever with me or with anyone else and that just as he was about to climax he handed me a single-edged razor blade and ordered me to ever so lightly cut his abdomen: Draw Blood! He claims I did. P.S., clothespin-bruised nipples. "My point is, he says that he had this fantasy with my memory. He had the audacity to have the same or similar fantasies with other broads and then to get caught with the double coupons.'

"You see, Ray, I just can't take the chance of such a lie again. I mean he says that he loves me. Of course, he doesn't, but he doesn't know it. We even did it once in the back seat of a Greyhound bus on our way to Las Vegas. Only the bus driver showed any signs of recognition as to what was going on and he certainly didn't say anything, just a big old Cheshire cat grin when we got off but he never saw me again. Hell, it's like my dime store afternooner: he probably has a lovely wife and two kids, and for all I know, he just puts his camper in neutral and rolls down to the next block to save gas, and buys more peanut clusters and screws someone else and whispers, while climaxing, that she's the best fuck. But this other creep keeps 'seeing' me and writes me about it, and I don't feel he has that right. I just can't let it happen again. I'd rather die in the desert, without food or water."

Ray mustered up his cruel streak, he assaulted, "You know, you remind me of a playmate I had when I was young. We would sneak off during the late summer months and hide above my grandfather's garage. He had grown some choice grapevines; we would break off stalks of grapevine about the size of a thin cigarette and smoke them until we would become very sick. But he was never satisfied with that; once I was down, usually green to the eyes, he would hold my hands behind me and blow smoke into my reddened eyes; he would even take a pinch of tobacco from his pockets and plug it in my nose and eyes. Yet he wanted to be with me and I likewise needed his friendship. He even seemed to prefer to befriend me, he seemed to prefer to hurt me instead of others. But then I've told you about him. So, I must leave." Ray was able to exit, though, with a handful of new poems floating in his head not to mention several good landscaping ideas for a new pet project due soon in his city college night course.

Ruby Francis was left in her crucible, flushing her toilet, watching the swirling mass of nothing dropping down. She kept telling herself that she must be here on Planet Earth for some purpose.

Ray turned the ignition key in his bug and the mechanism seemed to stick; he was accelerating with gear stuck in neutral. He would think twice before returning for another sitting with Ruby. As he exited, he could faintly hear her telephone ringing. He knew she wouldn't answer it. The blade cut her fingertips, the mental umbra of such diverse xeriscapes drew blood from each participant. The ruttish wails continued tearing down the erectile night.

* * *

Once home, Ray ignored his pets and pet project to doodle in his journal. That afternoon he had delivered half a cord of cherry wood for a customer. They often found odd jobs which, though vaguely related to gardening, always proved a welcome sound to the strained wallet since having left the secure field of teaching. It oozed forth in spurts onto the page:

CORD OF WOOD
(for R.F.F.)

The last cord of the fall
was purchased with silly pride:
we compared it to the earlier greenwood
and boasted of our rare find
(something about birch vs. oak).
We took charge of the situation
and we perpetuate the ageing process
by "letting" it set, crack, brown
split. We marched along the aisles
like a brigadier general surveying
the costly thing as a whole—
merely with our eyes we tackle,
assault, weaken (all to make Love
in vain; IT still towers over us).

Sometimes we discover we are cheated:
we consume haphazardly
as though we must, we even pay for
greenwood of running sap and willowlike.
Yes, we hoard—often never to use
while others actively burn and beget
in their logarithmic relationships.
So, all comes to naught, merely
chords of woulds, ifs, maybes
and platitudinal qualifiers
like those daily dissemblers at drill;
the more we think we take from
or contribute to,
the more it becomes fixed
in the inner woodbin.

PARTY-LINE
(POLICE REPORT)

"HELLO; DO YOU HAVE your instrument out? Is your cunt ready for this special-order vibrator that Dillinger would be jealous of? Let me hear your golden throat beg for mercy, baby. Come on, I said get down on your knees..."

CLICK. Although not surprising, but unknown to Ray, Ruby had been receiving these obscene phone calls in the middle of her sequestered sleep since way before the explosion at her shop. This was one secret she had kept from Ray. On the other hand, Ray had had no idea as to how complex, how inadequate she felt to be in their relationship. Via fallacious process of elimination, she had narrowed her list of assailants down to one—Ray Landre. Ray had no way to discern whether this was a form of personal revenge or she had "evidence" of such questionable betrayal. Frankly, the fact that there might be another culprit out there stimulated Ray, excepting the mental hardship it caused his Ruby-sweetheart. There were other maniacs out there steeped in autoeroticism, though this must be a misnomer: for Ray and some telephonic significant other gravitated toward Ruby. Ray was made to think of Warhol's study of an autoerotic, the marvelous documentary staged for his <u>Chelsea Girls</u>; the young, long-haired lad exposing his vulnerability to the red-tinted filter of the camera. His soliloquy (for what else can one caught up in this common affliction turn to), his analogy of visualizing himself a bead of perspiration secreted at the top of his scalp, slowly moving down the back of the neck, gaining momentum, caressing his shoulders; swishing his thick brown hair tips back and forth across his shoulders, admitting the sensuousness of the self-inflicted moment. Warhol accomplished the ultimate in audience participation. The viewer nearly felt a transference of the sordid molecule of water from his timeless physique–the male counterpart of the unblimished caryatid sans amputation and pock-mark features. The viewer who stuck his foot out in the aisle to trip the droplet, to entice it to come his way, yet he would no sooner reach out to accept the penetrating beam of electricity than it had evaporated (for the viewer, not for the boy on the mesmerizing screen). Mission accomplished. There are countless others doing penance for existence across the face of the earth, but Warhol's allegorical boy-man rests in a shelved can of celluloid until the need for this red-image resurfaces. There are marvels, celluloid secrets, pure sexual encounters; better these porns in UCLA's film vaults.

What followed was unforgivable in Ray's mind's eye. Ruby had erroneously identified the voice on the phone as none other than Ray Landre. Ruby's assumption in itself was devastating to Ray, but that he was the holder of the mysterious, battery operated dildo, when in fact he had never seen one let alone owned one mortified him (the only near-object he had known was his unpredictable jolly green giant beneath her donut shop table top). Ruby raised many eyebrows the next morning when she had waltzed into the Bellflower police station and asked to speak, in confidence, to one of their officers. Since visiting hours had ceased between Ray and Ruby, he could only surmise the goings on: the precinct protocol, the concern for sonority, the fatherly type wishing to extend his guidance and warm touch to such an innocent young flower, this victim of desert rape should those details ever surface. Ray Landre was soon to see he had been had: age and maleness was definitely at a disadvantage when it came to combat with youthfulness and wishful-virginity. There ensued a great deal of flourish and typing of forms in triplicate. The only reluctance to aid, the only upturned brow of skepticism emanated from the widowed secretary with hair stretched behind her ears as she officiously typed and tugged away at the manual Olivetti carriage; she synchronized her gum chewing to the exact characters per line and managed petite bubble and pops at each carriage return. She might have found some secondary gain in reading and retyping the alleged words of the caller. After all, she saw no damage done to this, this:

"FRANGIBLE, RUBY FRANCIS, SINGLE, LIVES alone at 7,000 DESCENDING DRIVE (cross streets Long Bch. Blvd. & Crescent.) STATEMENT: While relaxing and reading at night the above received an anonymous phone call. She reports that it began with heavy, uneven breathing; he asked if she were listening carefully; he continued 'Hello; do you have your instrument out. Is your cunt ready for this special-order vibrator that (not clearly understood) would be jealous of? Let me hear your golden throat beg for mercy, baby. Come on, I said, get down on your knees...I've seen your boobs hanging out the window like over-filled cream-puffs with hot glaze collecting at the nipples...CLICK.'"

That concluded the report, signed Officer Gonzales. Such a report must have heated up the police station.

Ruby reported, when pressured to do so, that such figurative language could be that of none other than her current boyfriend Ray. Had she been totally honest, she would have realized that the caller was more than likely a client at her shop who, daily, grew fatter and fatter because he wasn't actually getting what he had so arduously stood in line for.

Some days after she had given the report to include Ray's full name and address, Ray was abiding his regained autonomy while relaxing on a bench in Cerritos Park. He had given his attention to two small brown squirrels that were fussing at one another about something (Ray's facetiousness presumed which had the biggest nuts) and he found himself taking sides. They would stand on their hind legs and spar, their claws clutching for any loose fur so they might more easily throw the opponent off balance. Although they seemed to be about equal in size, the one to Ray's left was most dominant. He had two or three bare spots about his ears and head as though a cat or dog might have swatted or teethed on him. Eventually, Ray saw that they were arguing over what appeared an acorn or bit of organic food the size of

179

a marble. "Lefty" took a final staunch stand and bit into his opponent's side; yelps of pain pierced the night air and the other scurried off to safety in a nearby tree branch. They had a manner of keeping their eyes on one another without actually looking in that direction, much like the times Ray had often sat for hours at a time and watched his pet oscar Waldo as he fed on two or three miniature feeder gold fish. Ray was an outsider viewing the microcosm sailing through space. One second Waldo could be 'sleeping' at the other end of the tank, none of his fins erect for movement, yet the next he could be upon them with force and violence and survival; the water would become a swirling cloudy mass of severed gold gills and small intestinal tubes. He would rub his tummy with his grin and retreat to his corner until next feeding time. It goes on this cycle. W.H. Auden was reportedly attacked by New York youngsters; his swim across the Atlantic in hopes of escaping the devouring jaws; Oh, For a Respite Before the Requiem is Sung! Ray was about to laugh, for fear of crying for the loser's pain and empty belly perched up on the limb above his head, when a human hand touched his shoulder. Someone was behind him, behind the bench. The hand kept its grip; the grip tightened. Ray could only see the well-manicured fingers and a ring, a ruby-setting in a college class-ring on the right hand. Oh yes, he saw an Acutron wristwatch, one of those expensive ones.

The reigning squirrel, the dominant Jerry Quarry of the boxing rodent set, took to his tree: Waldo kept torpedoing into the sides of Ray's cranium; he was caught; Ray was caught, trapped like the Queen Mary set in virtual concrete. His headache grew with his confusion. His meditation in the gardens had been interrupted. Ray felt that he had disturbed no one. He let Waldo swim away, he collected himself. He folded his hands across his lap, but the fellow's nails in his shoulder blade kept hurting as they burrowed deeper. A second police officer walked around and stood his vantage ground. At that point, Ray could think clearly about two things: his name and the melody to Dvorak's New World Symphony. He could not deny the first and verified his home address, there was no escape, and as to the second, he had been listening to it that afternoon and it complimented the serenity of the park, the trees, the squirrels, the fondness he had known in Ruby Francis. It took courage to take up residency on a public park bench alone these days. There were so many ogres tucked into the

foliage as they looked down on Ray Landre.

Perfunctorily, the officer before Ray asked if he were "Landre, Raymond;" did he know one Frangible, Ruby Francis? Had he talked to her in the past week? Ray responded Yes to the three questions. The first officer, asking the questions, kept slapping his black leather hand-cuff-case. The second officer had sidled more to Ray's side and he kept levering the butt end of his night stick, levering it forward and backward like the slow movement of an emergency brake. His eyes seemed to squint as the stick would reach its farthest point, then he would be a slowpoke in returning it to his belt. Their conversation was very businesslike, but their actions were a bit clumsy, a bit expeditious; they were a bit irrational for Ray.

In a servile tone, Ray asked, "Please loosen your grip, sir," to which he responded, "We have ways to deal with your kind, you pervert. We'll slap a 502 or serve a yellow notice or whatever it takes to get you out of Bellflower. Got it!" For the next twenty minutes Ray was held in place by one officer while the other used him for his private punching bag. His nose fell to the left side of his face, his chin was forced in the opposite direction. His cheeks bled and grew in size. His eyebrows filled with matted dandruff and dried bloody flakes. He became the male counterpart to the Athenian Caryatid who chases him always in his dreams down Long Beach Blvd. He received a shiner to outshine the blackness of the park. No one was around, no witnesses. It made it easy. The dominant squirrel watched while the other fled from the scene. There was a distant chord from the symphony that helped ease Ray through the ordeal, it was the upsurge of a near-Negro spiritual that maintained his faith, faith that Ruby would know, someday, that he had not made the calls, that she had irrevocably wronged him, she had bit the vulnerable fleshy part beneath his armpits, she had drawn blood like all the others.

Ray could compromise that she had needed someone to blame for her infirmity, for listening to her vicious lover over the wires. He would have to take the punches. He would have to admit his guilt for the moment. He had wanted to screw her, he had wanted to draw blood but in a different manner. Not this; not this humiliation. His suffering at the hands of the community inn-keepers for sins that he condemned rather than condoned. She had irreverently betrayed and turned her back to her most ardent disciple. Where was the reward for his devotion?

Their frolicsome justice had ended with a bitter threat that Ray was, within the next five days, to move out of the area or they would make it rough, "Very Rough" on him. This had been a mere taste of what hung from the other side of their two inch wide leather belts. They left when they had finished with him. Only then did the first officer's fingernails leave his shoulder. There was something missing, a bit of flesh. Only then did the first squirrel drop his throbbing tail from its erect position and rush off into the night, a churlish laughter filtering away from Ray. Such skulduggery to remove such small tufts of fur. The officer, the squirrel, had seen what there was to see: his sad hunched shoulders, his pathetic bald spot. They had already labeled him the proverbial glob of so much chopped liver to be thrown out to the dogs.

II.

Once Ray let himself into his dark, toothless apartment, where even the seeming amplified gurgling of Waldo's air filter shocked him, he took out his journal and began writing. A trickle of blood reopened the scab inside his right nostril and it rushed to eat into the journal page as though in combat with the moist ring from his sweating glass of scotch: the marks reminded Ray of the television commercial where two leading paper towels vie for proof of absorption and strength. Ray managed to drop a few disjointed black words onto the white and red and watermarked paper. He reversed roles with Ruby Francis and scribbled additions to his on-going poem:

PARTY LINE

(A journal of things to say to the bitch who awakens
me in the middle of the night with her obscene
phone calls—if and when I see her)

First, there is a smack, smack in the receiver;
then, I tell myself I'll chew out the O-operator;
these obscene calls must halt,
I'm no impotent listee in some age-old yellowed

pages
of lonely hearts out in the country,
a two or three digit hardship case;

it is a she-voice smacking double-bubble
and she is deaf and she doesn't know how
annoying is her amplified saliva;
why, in a room, at a party,
every head would jerk, find her out,
she is a wild woman with frizzy, over-done
spaghetti hair
and someone who wanted her cherry throat
once whizzened her
into believing she could speak
(gutteral, monosyllabic beauty).

I think I'll dial O
and punch her right
in the kisser: she shouldn't
connect that with me:
I'm busy nights
beating off my poetry,
working out trig,
and the water's boiling
in my semanticized apartment.
I'll rip the damned thing out
before I'll bare my balls
to any deaf mute's smacking
like her out there!

At the bottom of the page, the drop of blood formed the dot to the first "I" in his scrawled "to be finished later." He flashed on Ruby's proverbial quip: "Well, that puts a period at the end of that sentence."

Once Ray finished the entry, he couldn't bare his loneliness and ability to confront Ruby. Even the spotless varnished hard wood floors blinded him, and eyes without heads blinked up at him. The cleanliness reminded him of his mother's upper realm dream and the perfection of her floor-plan. So he finished the fifth of scotch and walked, in the opposite direction of Winchells, to an old haunt called

Larry's Viking Room. Ray had neglected, in the past, rapping with the owner, but it was a slow night. It was well-known in Long Beach that the man had been most successful in his establishment and that was a good topic for openers; however, he soon became morose. The proprietor sincerely exposed his vulnerability as man and father in saying, "I know, you hear that I own that three story chalet on the tip of Lake Arrowhead, and that my wife comes in here, nightly, boasting of our travels to Tahiti and St. Thomas. Some nights I swear that's the only reason she insists on being our hostess. You see the sleek black Continental out front and like others scoff at my fifteen dollar price on the lobster. Etc. Etc. It disgusts me, you wanna know the truth. Money is nothing, Ray. I'm unhappy, goddam it. I worked my entire life to make a decent income and future, for what? For my daughter, right? And what happens? She goes sour on me. I know, people walk in here and say 'God, I wish I had that man's problems.' It's nothing, Ray, nothing. Hell, the only decent moment of my day, now, is when I walk into this dark place, smell the fresh, undisturbed, costly pine scent from the urinals and tip my first highball in the darkness here, alone. That's all there is now. Oh, and I occasionally rinky-tink out a Joplin tune, but no one to listen in the darkness. How did good ol' Eliot put it? 'I have heard the mermaids singing each to each. I do not think they sing to me.'"

Because Ray was a bit perplexed, the man elaborated. It seemed that his teenage daughter had been suicidal since the age of ten. She hadn't finished high school. Since business had been excellent over the years, money had been no object in seeking professional advice, but nothing nor anyone proved helpful. Her method was one of driving down the coast, say Capistrano or San Diego, and stuffing herself with reds or booze or both, and then phoning at the last minute before the stupor took control. Daddy would, of course, make the drive or appropriate calls each time and her life would be spared. She had been attending weekly meetings at a local church called Back to Calvary where young group leaders preached of the innate evil of individuals and the inevitable doom to destroy the world for its wickedness. All biblical interpretations and forecasts were negative and therefore a dark shadow hung over the entire meeting. They all walked away from the building as though Black Beauties had been offered for communion. His daughter had become more and more disturbed and he felt that marijuana was compounding the problem. The girl, when at home, would sit around, do nothing. She would often receive phone calls from her friends at the church who continuously kept her under their control, according to Larry. He said that he and other parents in the area had had such disturbing reports about young people involved at this church that he felt maybe he or some of them should investigate the operation. Ray encouraged him to do so. Ray brought up, simply to make related conversation, the excellent movie <u>The Manchurian Candidate</u>, and they explored their layman's concept of brain washing. Ray stressed that if he were a parent, and having been an ex-high-school teacher, he would be down there in the front row for the next service. He reminded Larry of the political and personal threat of the "moonies." Ray's drinking kicked into high gear and he confided in Larry that he had a secret plan to assassinate the Reverend Moon in the near future. He nodded in agreement. The daughter would sit around and go on long crying jags to spout her crazy alcohol-talk, and it was all bringing the entire family down.

Ray and Larry took a breather. They escorted one another into the men's room. It was a small box with little room to turn around. They unzipped their pants and pulled them out. Larry asked Ray if he had seen that one before as his eyes motioned towards a bit of graffiti on the chalk board: "Edith Head Gives Good Wardrobe." They both smiled. He looked at Ray's penis, some fifteen years younger; Ray looked at his like a mesmerized six-year-old might stand and stare in discovery. Larry's started to firm (Ray was reminded of his poem-in-progress called "Sign Language," of the maleness, the feigned sexual curiosity) just a bit, then he noticed the cut over Ray's left eye and a drop of blood reformed on the tip of his sore nose. They zipped up and while washing their hands together under the same warm tap, Ray retold his experience in the park that afternoon. "All over a broad, too." Larry proved empathetic. His eyebrows raised and he wanted to kill the fuckers. He declared they had no right and he was influential in the community when it came to such matters. Ray assured him it would pass. Not to make an issue of it. It was the alcohol talking. Ray was really thinking of protecting Ruby, though.

Before they left the restroom, Larry gave Ray a sort of fatherly bear hug. Ray was momentarily weak in his arms but pushed him on out the door. Ray identified somewhat with his Waldo: he had observed the fish wants to come close to him when he's near the tank but he generally swims to the fartherest corner and cowers once Ray tapped the glass. The men tried a few shots of 100 proof Russian vodka, but both realized that they had exhausted the topic of fatherhood and disappointment and general ennui. He kept mumbling that everyone just looks, just assumes that some guys have it really smooth and fail to realize what inner hell ferments. He added that, some fifteen years earlier, he and his wife had lost their only other child at birth. It had been devastating. He confessed that he often worried whether someone might be inadvertently walking on the infant's grave; that there was such little respect these days. He told Ray a story about an elderly aunt of his who had her purse stolen from her parked auto while placing flowers on her deceased husband's grave. Ray felt uncomfortable. The beaten man stared a long time at his empty shot glass, as though he saw an untainted other child/embryo floating in a jar of formaldehyde, in it, one that had been whole and made it, and effaced his suffering at the hands of his surviving daughter.

As Ray walked out, he felt a tinge of guilt to leave Larry alone in the room that reeked of alcohol and cigarette smoke. Ray, barely audible, ineffectively soothed him with words, "I'm sure it will all be fine, Larry. These things have a way of working themselves out; I'm glad we had the talk, I'll be seeing you soon. Take care now!" Ray knew, as the fake green clutch-door swung shut, that he wouldn't be seeing him again in remembering the policeman's absolutism; and he also knew the probable working-out of the daughter's problem—she would not have the courage, one lonelier night, to pick up the phone and he would probably receive word of her senseless death while taking a leak at the iced-down drain of his $1500.00 urinal. Ray's heart went out to the man, and Ray's inadequacy in offering him anything concrete, any abatement, overwhelmed him. Ray lit up a cigarette in the damp night to exhale his hurt from his lungs. He flashed upon the sergeant's pathetic announcement back in boot camp days: "Smoke 'em if you got 'em." Yet ironically Ray missed that comradery and discipline. Perhaps with it he might not be in the predicament he now found himself. He wished he could cuddle up behind Mauer on the

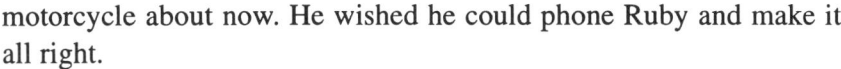

motorcycle about now. He wished he could phone Ruby and make it all right.

About then a squirrel jetted down the cracked pavement in front of Ray as he walked back home. He kicked a shiny, empty aluminum beer can at him. It fell to the gutter beside cigarette butts and an old faceless woman's shoe. Ray spat. The vodka tasted terrible–he knew he should have stuck with the Tankarays.

III.

Once home, the vodka induced a nightmare: Ray was condemned to be a professor of composition. Above him hung a rheostated chandelier that housed an over-sized tarantula with hundreds of hairy legs that kept slipping over the edge of the light fixture to drop on Ray below. Mechanical wrist bands and manacles came out of the fiber of the recliner and anchored him there as victim. His hair turned instantaneously white which forced him to jump from his dream and run into the bathroom. Looking into the mirror and seeing his hair had actually turned grey in places, he soon realized that his experience with Larry at the bar, their rapport had triggered the various in and out-of-dream personae like Mauer and tentacle-possessed beings like the spider. The idea of gardener Ray being made a professor amused him. But the desert floor of boot camp, the pink bathroom, the wounds, the spider seemed only a prelude to things that Ray truly didn't want to discover.

> Dreams, though some Jungian and simplistic,
> others drastically nighmarish, can inspire
> a half-way decent poem
> (poem-in-progress by Ray L.).

SIGN LANGUAGE
by Ray L.

He had those good mechanic hands
dime a dozen yet seldom seen
mid-Missouri-veined, poolhall taut

187

I wanted to touch
those overworked hands:
"Seventeen! Seven–teen yearrrs
I worked those Nashes.
They don't build 'em nowadays..."

a break filled with crankshaft oil

"What's wrong with your car? starter?

It was the starter
and too much need
and her waiting at home
(he on a daily excursion from his
and me on my last lap home to mine)
and I'd rather just talk to his hands.

20 "FIRE AND ICE"

"SEVEN DOLLARS, PLEASE. That includes tax."

Ray handed the pock-faced lady his fare. Her penciled-on eyebrows didn't even match, they were a harsh reddish brown that reminded him of those well-endowed miniature birds tattooed over a man's chest seen at the beach as though they were flying in opposite directions. Ray had slept and stayed in his apartment for two days before he could even begin to consider whether he had any recourse. It was a sticky situation; very unpleasant for everyone involved. He might further embarrass her (or maybe she would consent to marry him and that would set everything straight with the police force); or it would degrade the law enforcement's image, or the donut shop might fold; his landlord might evict him; the phone company might refuse to service any request spelled "Landre." He wouldn't be able to face anyone.

"Would you turn loose of the bill, please, so I can give you your change?" She enunciated loose and change as if she might have uttered them a thousand times. Her ruby, wax-filled lips didn't change their glamorous shape and they didn't go with anything else that she had "added" to her face. Her red hair hung over her forehead and ears like pasta dripping with tomato paste. She had a blue ribbon tied in a bow over her right ear; it was ludicrous. Ray had hoped that she would turn out to be one of those amusement park, mechanical fortune tellers that sat there in a glass case for centuries on end—a charming gypsy; but this one lit a cigarette and disproved that theory. Her only words,

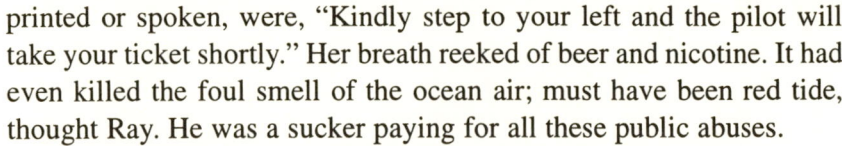

printed or spoken, were, "Kindly step to your left and the pilot will take your ticket shortly." Her breath reeked of beer and nicotine. It had even killed the foul smell of the ocean air; must have been red tide, thought Ray. He was a sucker paying for all these public abuses.

A middle-aged man with a Dodger ballcap unfastened a small chain across Ray's path and took his cheaply-printed ticket. The ticket had no indication of what he had paid, no bold, colorful letters to remind him at a later date of his last visitation to the city and girl that he loved and detested. Such momentoes were becoming harder and harder to come by. It might have been a ticket stub to some sleezy theatre along Ocean Avenue, or a circus ride, or admittance to the underworld. Ray hoped to at least run into another lost soul, a poet, a film-maker, someone that cared that he had come this way. He did not want to be shuffled along without consideration. The man rattled off some emergency instructions should something go amiss (but Ray was already mentally aloft, looking down on the fair Queen of the Seas from his purchased branch where the wind and coastal fog would part his mustache, and the grotesque black hairs in and around his earlobe would tickle him, would irritate him, distract his vision, his last look at the once-roller-coaster below him. Ray decided that the ballplayer was a kind man. He cautioned Ray to take his time, for business had been slow the past month and there would be more time, more leisurely viewing. Although Ray scarcely heard his words, he detected something gentle about the man. He felt comfortable with another human being for the first time in many days. The employee knew that Ray wasn't exactly old, but that he might need some special attention. He refastened the turnstile chain. It was final and nice. Ray gave himself to the gentleman's expertise in flight. Ray felt smug that the lady in the cage was being left behind. He assumed that they were not husband and wife, but if so, he hoped the man would be glad, in spite of her.

As they ran towards the whirly-bird, it lay in dormancy like a sleeping, yellow grasshopper, a young man in overalls escaped from the chamber, he had started the rotary blades and rushed back to a shed where he lay back on the ground, but he kept his eyes turned towards Ray and the pilot. Ray was just preparing to board through the flimsy door to the chopper when incessant winds, a Santa Ana, blew off his toupee. It was like being decapitated and he instinctively knew to reach upward and grasp it. Humiliation swirled throughout the air, gulls were keeping their distance although their cries of hunger and search joined the drone of the blades. The pilot helped Ray jump up into the cockpit and he motioned for Ray to slide over to the far side.

Ray soon felt himself neatly enveloped in a warm, clean bubble much like Waldo's 86+ degrees watered world (Ray's subconscious kicked in and he feared he might have to bury Waldo in the backyard, Etta-Mary style, and leave behind an aquarium with the filter and water pump system still operating; but he couldn't stand the thought of the fish going hungry). Ray was gazing out from the bubble as though it was all beginning, and nothing could crack the shell. There was no time to actually think about what had happened, nor to worry whether his pilot would laugh or empathize over his "accident". Ray sat rigidly, at first, and clutched it in his lap like a flop-eared Pekingese. Both hands folded over it in an attempt to cover it, yet Ray knew it would be too full to hide. He felt like a cheap whore who was feigning shyness by placing her hands in front of her hairy clit, in cleaning up on the bidet while her customer walks in on her. He got a peek of himself in the bubble. He was a stranger, a nondescript tourist, ready for a flight over Long Beach but beyond that point all was uncertain.

The pilot jumped aboard as though he had not noticed Ray's disguise. He roughed up the various knobs and levers and started to help Ray engage his seatbelt, but there seemed to be too much commotion, too much growth about his pubic area so he withdrew his hands and Ray watched him for instructions. Rotely, the pilot said that they would begin by making a wide sweep west of town as far as the San Pedro area and Ray might see the Ports 'O Call village and the Port of Entry for the Los Angeles harbor. Ray recalled shopping in the tobacco shop there some years prior and sitting in the Ports 'O Call restaurant pretending to see off a friend as the Bon Voyage was announced over the loud speaker system.

Ray often imbibed too much there, because the bartender always remembered him and would serve doubles for half the price. He was introduced to other clientele, other revelers. Ray was busy, in his head, saying good-byes to a myriad of strange faces and names; he was forever confusing characters. Once he had been mugged and rolled as he

closed the bar and unknowingly walked to the parking lot.

"To your right, there, is Fort McArthur; that's their firing range. And that tower way up the coast, that's Marineland (Ray thought he vaguely made out Waldo floating on his side in the huge outdoor Oceanarium, he was gasping for air. A guardian standing on the concrete bank was waiting for him to die so he might cut him up and use him for feed for the larger sharks).

"To the north there," Ray noticed how the pilot squinted forward, nearly breathing steam onto the bubble, like an explorer intently surveying ahead, "you see that glint of sunlight bouncing off the Palos Verdes peninsula? Somedays it almost blinds me: luckily we don't venture closer. It's Frank Lloyd Wright's chapel, Wayfarers Chapel (Ray heard no more of the spiel: he focused on more loving days, when he had driven Ruby Francis over the corrugated macadam of expensive real estate that annually resettled itself in increments of inches to accommodate the land displacement of southern California. They had just missed a wedding as the party poured out the glass chapel and Ray had turned to Ruby as if to say that will be us. He had nearly run off the roller-coaster road that others blindly commuted daily. Wayfarer struck Ray as a most fitting moniker for him as of late).

"Now, we'll head back to the metropolitan area. There is The Pike, well, Queen's Park to you youngsters. (Ray wanted to shout that he be quiet, but how could the innocent man know about the HMS, how could he understand?) Undoubtedly, you've ridden the Ferris wheel or had a tattoo at one of the world-famous tattoo parlors? (A swarm of honeybees attacked Ray's groin. He doubled over in pain). There she is! (He had intended for Ray to look out his left, but Ray was straining to see past the pilot's fists on the steering lever, trying to glimpse a block of buildings several neighborhoods north of them, to her shop and line-up of rigs and, sure enough, he could detect its approximate location, and puffs of diesel rose to the otherwise blue sky. Peterbilts pierced his dehydrated abdomen). Yep, you know we're all very proud of Her. You see that Old English village they've added to the grounds recently, and Her stacks; ah, She's quite a sight, ain't She?"

Ray turned to him with a nod; he pursed his lips so the pilot might know he was truly with him, that he wasn't only daydreaming. Ray tucked his hair into the crevice of his lap a bit more, like a boy sitting quietly in a movie house, and having removed his baseball cap, he nervously continues to tuck it into his crotch; however, Ray was not having that much luck. It would not disappear. Ray found himself staring at it occasionally, when the running commentary would cease. The man spouted monetary figures of Her cost, Her renovation, Her assets, Her deficits. Ray couldn't absorb figures of thirty, sixty million when he was preoccupied with the amount of city blocks from the shore to the billowing black bursts, like someone down there blowing smoke-rings, maybe getting a feel in the back room, maybe belching and scoring. Winnebagos winding down Bellflower Blvd. Obituaries fulfilling their quota flashing through his head.

"Yep, the British were pound-foolish when they let Her go! Our hotel and tourist influx has tripled. I use to have to rely on a handful of investors and oil men here to keep going, but now I have flights daily. Are there any questions I can answer for you?"

Ray only hoped that that Wanda-witch on the ground, in the booth, wasn't part of the pilot's life. Ray was happy to see that he was a happy man as he soared up in the blue air. He knew his business, his territory, and he liked his work, that was obvious. Ray just hoped that he was able to leave her behind in the cage at night when he closed up the operation. It would, undoubtedly, be intolerable otherwise. In circling above the three infamous red stacks, Ray could see maybe fifty or seventy-five bodies strolling about the top deck. Children of the tourists would wander away and discover some secret doorway, then they would be flushed out by some guide or pseudo deck-hand. The parents would again be pleased to grab their hands and wander further toward the end of the tour. Ray snickered to himself, the Cousteau exhibit would unquestionably disappoint many children as they kept high their expectations to see live fish swimming about the inside of the museum walls. There would be much explaining and apologizing. There would be much for each child to adapt to, to accept. They were lucky to still have their imaginations.

The international flags whipped in the breeze like the whirling excitement of a car rally. Ray expected Popeye to shinny up a ratline at any moment, perhaps returning from some debauch. Olive Oil would box him on the cheek and then kiss him, ever so gently, as the ropes were thrown to the crew from shore and they could move on. But it's insane. This vessel doesn't move anymore! Ruby-dubie had articulated that predicament. His eyes quickly traced the tidewater wall of rocks strategically placed about the skeleton. She wouldn't be going anywhere, ever. He had seen enough.

"Now, we're coming to another port: I'm backtracking, because as I said, I'm not that busy today, so I get to sightsee a little myself." The pilot gave a hearty laugh; Ray wondered if the man weren't more akin to the sea than the air. Melville had synthesized such a personality in Billy Budd: Handsome is as handsome does. Ray felt that he loved both. "Below you, see those pink buildings, is the grandeur of the old Hollywood days. And that over-sized Golden Bear you see there on the blue and white stack of that vessel is the one and only Mariposa. Movie stars used to flood the hotels along the berth-entrance as they crossed and recrossed the oceans; as they greeted and saw-off their friends. My uncle once got Mae West's autograph over there."

Ray craned his neck. He could faintly hear a dixieland band playing "When the Saints Go Marching In" and thought it was a reenactment of Mardi Gras below. Pink and Green and Blue and Yellow pennant flags danced above the deck and lines of them were tied from the boat to the pink building along the berth. The band was suspended on some scaffolding that bridged the two. A few wheelchairs, occupied, were rolled up to the edge of the deck. A swimming pool sat undisturbed, like lime jello, nearby. The invalids were watching two or three younger couples as they danced to the music. Paper cups had been thrown upon the deck as the frenzy of dixieland and drinking raced on.

"Financial reports say this is a dying business. The bands, the crew, the food, the services just can't keep up with air travel." Ray was made to feel that he was peering down on the last adventurers of the twentieth century. Ray could only scan, register, sort out the details of the Bon Voyage for later. The pilot asked, "Hey, bub, you feel alright, or would you like to return to Control Center?" Ray conceded that perhaps it best that he return to the ground.

The pilot glanced at Ray's lap. "I don't know what to do with the damned thing," Ray confessed. The pilot laughed but not unsympathetically. As they descended, the only concrete image before Ray, as a result of being aloft, was an imagined line-up outside the Winchells location. Ray duplicated a photographic sculpture in his mind not unlike an article he had read years ago in *Time* magazine. There were two elegantly slim silver-gilt angels holding a ruby and emerald studded casket of the late 16th Century: what they held in the air with their extended arms—which blew Ray's atheistic mind—was a reliquary of Christ's circumcision. It intrigued him, and Ray recalled showing the clipping to Ruby Francis; the "Holy Foreskin" had been stolen, and manhandled by crude hands, from the sanctum sanctorum of Rome in 1527 and now rests in Calcata, north of Rome. "Devout guardians" are credited with preserving it for posterity. Ray wondered what they looked like, who they were, how they managed to get their hands on it. He wondered if his ex-dentist had any inside dope. Ray felt envious; he chanted a quatrain to a puff of cloud out the helicopter window:

> We know the flesh-guardians
> must have gummed it to
> insure against conterfeitism:
> I go down on mortals in remembrance.

Ray's mental duplicate was of two bare-chested truckers, outside Ruby Francis' window at Winchell's, holding up a five hundred pound golden image of her nude form; it, the seductress of Thomas Hart Benton's bare-chested Persephone, rested on a severed ball from each of the men and they, the truckers, had halos and wings. They were able to fly up in the atmosphere and deposit their burden to the other mortals waiting below. Shop never closed. Cheers were deafening.

Ray next remembered the donut shop explosion. With his luck, he would probably next be accused of causing that. He nearly passed out before the helicopter landing. He saw a jeweled casket suspended over the Pacific and its contents, in ash, dumped to the waters. Ray recalled a time in his childhood. While his parents did their piece-work at the shoe factory, he would sneak away from the house. He would get permission to peer into the incubators at Griffith's Hatchery. He would see thousands of yellow baby chicks struggling, writhing to avoid being stepped on. His forehead used to get warm from holding it too close to the tiny windows. They always looked so fresh. They all liked to look at his two huge eyes wondering about their yellow future. That same time he would wander some three blocks away, past the icehouse where he could pick up chips of ice that had fallen to the dirt road off of the delivery truck. He would suck their coolness and scan the warped wooden laths wondering what inside made such mysterious, mammoth blocks of calm. Ultimately, he would wander to the local slaughter house. He would jump on a wooden fence rail and strain his neck over the corral. He would see five or more cows being forced along their path until, one by one, they reached a destination. The gate would swing shut behind them and old man McGilicuty would step from his shaded lean-to, lower his rifle, pull the trigger and the bulk would try to fall to the ground, but the confines were too close. It would just hang there until someone released the latched sides. Ray had heard his father and older boys talk about how marvelous it was to watch this. When his mother thought too heavily about life she would quote impossibly lengthy passages from Faulkner's "The Bear;" she loved old Boon. She would plop down on the living room floor and cry over ol' Boon. So, Ray had tried, time and again, to sense this great adult wonderment. He would try to cheer and applaud, for he knew the slaughterhouse men were watching. He just usually jumped back down, turned his back to them and walked away. He had cried the first time, but after that it wasn't too different from the baby chicks as they watered and fed themselves; and some just got trampled to death.

"Well, hey old bub, here we are' And yes sir'ee, I want to thank you. I think you got a special tour today. No rush you know. I wouldn't care if I didn't have another customer today...something real satisfying about being up there, you know. Now, you don't take no mind to your hair. Tilly says I've been losing it for some ten years now. You just have to take the kidding sometimes. The women, they'll always come back anyway."

Ray knew that she wouldn't, though. He knew Ruby Francis would hold her grudge, or prefer her promiscuity, or pacify herself in counting her coin, her profits. Ray knew that the pilot meant well but he just didn't know a damned thing about Ray's convoluted life.

"Yes sir'ee, that ticket-taker there, Tilly, she's been lovin' it and me for years now; and h'ain't none better."

God, Ray thought inwardly, if he just hadn't said that.

Ray meandered to the commercial stalls. He bought two post cards. One was an aerial view of the Queen Mary, and the other showed the Queens Park at night—the Ferris wheel divided the card in half, visually, and some superimposed letters read "Greetings from Long Beach, California." He couldn't find any that read more appropriately "Bon Voyage." He returned to his apartment and used scrap paper to figure out exactly what he wanted to say to her. No matter how he deleted, he found that it would take both cards, and the message would need to be typed in order to squeeze all that needed to be said onto the blank surface. He began his message on one card and finished it at the very bottom of the second. He then scotch-taped them together and folded them so that her name and address showed. He haphazardly grinned..."I can't stand not knowing the contents." This guided his efforts. He placed staples around the perimeter of the cards and set "it" by the door for mailing.

* * *

Ray's focus on the cordial pilot and his at-peace demeanor helped him decide that he would complete one final gardening job before moving on. The McGinnises, an elderly retired couple, always greeted him warmly as he unloaded the tools of his trade. They had asked him not to use the gas-driven blower for clean-ups whereas it disturbed the neighbors with its grating noise; otherwise he had carte blanch in his alterations upon their small patch of soil. He had made a diagram of the minor changes he would effect: transplant the magnolia to a sunnier location, the opposite side of the backyard, and relocate the willowy white astilbe for more shade and they would be able to see them more easily from the kitchen window. A small border of dark blue Crystal Palace lobelia and some golden marigold for accent. Also there was some peach curl to artfully be removed to complete the pruning of their prize satsuma plum tree. Then a quick mow and blow (well, since the last visit, why not use the blower to affirm his having been there). And they had wanted him to check a damaged irrigation head. Petulant 'til the end.

Ray's strategy was interrupted, though, as the answering machine moaned in the other room with an angered female voice: "And don't

197

think I don't know what you did, you bastard. She's in her seventies, for Christ's sake. That nice Mrs. Fordyce was in yesterday and she was asking a shit-load of questions about my knowledge of some young man who did gardening around the area, did I...." Ray reddened in the face as he caught that other side of Ruby, that person he needed to fly away from. He left the machine recording its tirade, as he hastily ran out the apartment after unthinkingly picking up the bundle of communication. He did say a mental farewell to the sweet McGinnises, picturing them over the kitchen counter bickering at one another about which flower, escalating prices, who would cook, and kissing good-bye that same shampoo-swapping scenario he had proffered Ruby Frangible so many light years ago.

21 RED LIGHT/ GREEN LIGHT

A BIT, THOUGH, like the children aboard ship, Ray Landre had an imagination. He posted the cards without thought of content. He could imagine Ruby driving past the Bellflower Mortuary. She flashed on the resident corpses that viewed pink and pastel yellow gladiolas and wreaths of May Our Dear Sister Rest in Peace, etc., from their black morsel of a porthole. She merely missed a red light because she fondly remembered one other crossing to reach that deserter of her love life who had taken up residence in the Arizona desert with scorpions, some tarantulas, and a pussycat named Schroeder that was capable of running the rented house beneath Silver Back Mountain. Upon arriving in the middle of the night in her faded green Toyota, Ruby had been hassled by the local cop and he assured her that his questions—and looking up her sheer nyloned legs—were routine, for there had, indeed, been a murder in the locale recently. Everyone was out looking for what he could find, he assured her with his words and eyes and nightstick down his leg and walking in front of her dims in checking out the license plate number from out of state.

The next day he and Ruby took a drive in her sun-roofed car. It was a sunny day in the desert clime. He insisted on driving her car and rolling back the sun roof. They weren't five miles outside the burg when he pulled her head over to his crotch. She had not encouraged such foreplay with his cock before and found it an insane act to commit on a desert, county road where who knew who could happen onto them. He was nearly dead while keeping his eyes on the road when a throbbing, swirling, sucking motion presented itself overhead. Cruising at ten miles per hour could surely cause no hazard, she assured, yet they were being scrutinized from a Highway helicopter overhead. Her oral fantasies painted a surrealistic canvas in her head of some Dirty Green Apple scalped at the top with two green-puss-oozing worms emerging from the hinged, opened top while a manually operated egg-beater churned overhead and Warhol neon-light-stars flicked on and off above mesquite and decapitated heads of Bob Dylans, maybe three hundred reproduced on the canvas in her mind as she blazed along a dirt road giving mediocre head to a frump who hadn't known any better head.

The Red Light changed to Green and the cacophony of auto horns behind her forced her to accelerate past the house of death that was so neatly tucked astride a street of macadam lined with permanent foliage that was already covered with auto exhaust. You know, that almost green, plastic shit...sad, sad. The simulated plastic dieffenbachia and sun-bleached, squalid, squawkless heads of birds-of-paradise belched at her as she, paranoiac, rolled up her window and cranked shut her sunroof, respective misnomers in themselves. Why didn't they call it what it was: an escape for Camel cigarette smoke from that young lover's prematuring yellowed teeth and lungs; a vantage peep-hole for the whirleybirds; a way for death to sneak into her daily drives of escape from the donut factory. Why didn't they call it a necessary evil, this death, this voyeurism, this contracting-lung machine on the traffic arteries of So.Cal.

Or what if she weren't driving around Bellflower, driving in circles on streets that she had already explored and taken in for her insatiable, pulsating winnebago-womb. Of course, all of the independence bothered Ray. And if she weren't cruising around in limbo she would be doing something equally as meaningless; she might be idling her time, like the huge bulks of rigs idling outside her incensed-parlor or reading some inane work by a Jacqueline Susann, or scanning the L.A. obits, or masturbating with her tiny white bikini briefs pulled down on her thighs, or draining a rack of ordinary glazed donuts. She, too, had an active imagination; she might be placing a person-to-person call to her sleepy parents and lying that she adored her occupation. She might be placing a tracer on her police-complaint, but that was unlikely. Her assassination had surely made her guilt-ridden.

For all Ray Landre cared, she could rot.

Ruby's push past the mortuary was appropriate in Ray's mind it had come out in their sittings that she was fond of hanging around the elaborate miniature golf courses of Southern California with their uniquely manicured landscapes of mock windmills and chlorined waterfalls, with gigantic clown-lips that could swallow the carefully putted balls. She liked lolling along the elevated and inclined runways and sandtraps and walkways where all could see. Or she would frequent the combination pizza / penny arcades. She loved pinball machines and Pac-Man and could easily beat most challengers as Ray early-on found out. Her favorite pinball had been one that was thematically centered around the career of Elton John. She could make out the reflection of her first bee-of-the-tattoo in the glass of the machine. She liked places like Moskatels, too, because it smelled good around Christmas time. She liked touching the choppers outside the Pig Pen—a well-equipped motorcycle shop in Bellflower. She was probably there. Wasted. Ray felt it was tragic that he had reached a stage in their relationship where he knew exactly the spots to check if she were absent. It had come to that. He hadn't imagined all this; he had attempted, though, to repress all that she had once served him with her lemon-coconut tart.

II.

The red and green interplay of oversized mechanical lights further forced Ray's preparation to take in the crisp desert air: he recalled his dishonesty with others over the years. He drummed up an image of gossipy old Etta-Mary's professor Yolander. "Yo" they had called him on campus behind his back. Ray had once had a run-in with him (Ray had never admitted this acquaintance to Ruby). Ray had, one summer, submitted a brief lesson plan for a proposed Philosophy in Literature elective. Yo had hastily perused it, grunted, "Excellent, excellent," and scrawled his approval. Ray had enthusiastically endorsed his choice of Hesse's *Narcissus and Goldmund,* and as Ray's colleagues often teased him, Ray could do no wrong in Yo's sight, teased that he, Ray,

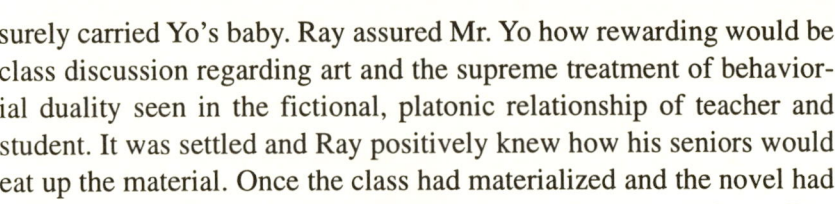

surely carried Yo's baby. Ray assured Mr. Yo how rewarding would be class discussion regarding art and the supreme treatment of behaviorial duality seen in the fictional, platonic relationship of teacher and student. It was settled and Ray positively knew how his seniors would eat up the material. Once the class had materialized and the novel had made its predictable mark upon the literature-hungry students, Ray was summoned to Yo's inner sanctum.

"How could you subject students and this English department's reputation to such filth–I got around to reading your Hesse–such unprofessional choice for impressionable high school students. My God, Landre, this could land us all in hot oil—what were you thinking of? Why, every third page they're jumping in the sack; and three-ways!"

In spite of Ray's assuring Yo that the discussion never focused upon sex, Yo threatened a written reprimand in Ray's permanent record. Not Necessary! Ray guaranteed his resignation at the end of the semester. Ironically, months later, upon Yo's return from Cambridge where he had chaired as one of the three national graders in English composition for college board exams, he admitted surprise when opening the envelope to the unannounced topics to include Hesse's novel. Ray had become nauseous at Yo's ex-Marine handshake of thankfulness, seemingly forgetting the hell that he had put Ray through. Although Ray gloated at Yo's having to eat crow, he nevertheless was never able to transcend the affront to his professionalism and accepted the uncanny happenings to him throughout his life to effect such developments, such synchronicity. And his resignation? Now unimportant history. He discerned that the traffic light changed to green and he ultimately would have the desert to face. He coaxed Midnight onto the deserted boulevard with a dog bone.

22 ARCOLOGY FOR THE EPICYCLE

ONE LAST STIMULATING yet gruesome detail remained to gnaw away at Ray. In Ruby's hallway to the john, she had framed a note from that desert charmer that she couldn't refuse displaying its diminutive scrawl of artwork. This letter he had sent her, without provocation, could be studied on the wall, side by side, with the mischievous-looking male lion—an ink drawing in permanent black ink. He was sketched at the top of the piece of bond, lying on all fours, his tail swirled to the left, his right fore-paw tilted up to his grinning chin while his head rested on the other paw. There was a freehand style zigzag effect beneath him as though he were lying in a pool of black semen.

The wall-piece, the hanging read: Baby Ruby!

> I ain't li'on! I just been thinking of you and want to tell you
> so. Wish we could be together. I'd strap you down on the
> Bed so you couldn't figet back—you'd be helpless and my
> slave. I can't wait to use my big leather belt across your bare
> ass. I'll wear a black leather jacket and bring a club to cram
> up your tight little ass. Getting fucked by my rod is an expe-
> rience you'll never forget. Forcing that big cock, harder and
> deeper. You waiting anxiously, panting like a wild animal for
> that big throbbing cock. I'll give a lunge that you'll always
> remember; driving that hard prick with force enough to tear

open your asshole. Rhythmical fucking every inch of this long cock, driving, passionately overpowering your weak helplessness.

Take it now, you cocksucker! Take my load—a real man's load of hot juicy come right up your fucking ass. Oh, Baby Ruby, I love it. You're going to get your ass plugged often with my big prick. You love it. Work your tight ass on my cock and draw out the last drops. Your ass is tight on my cock and so hot. You felt the delightful sensation deep inside as the hot come jetted in—your mind blank to everything except the sheer ecstasy of the moment.

P.S. (After reading this letter I found it necessary to come while fantasizing of our adventures in the back room of your donut house. I miss you and need to see you–we will get together soon–

Love,

T.

And this was part of her interior decorating: a woman's touch. (Not exactly fit for an English Department dinner.) She expressed her real concern that he would never sign his name to any of his correspondence. Ray assured her that he could understand the man's reluctance to incriminate himself. She had felt a need to share these letters with someone and although Ray had listened with interest, he remained perplexed at the prospects of their future in light of such erotica in literary experience.

Another missal read Ruby-Dearheart:

Enjoyed talking to you on phone; getting so sexually aroused I had to jack-off thinking of golden moments of ecstasy we will share. Putting my big hard cock in your tight clit will excite and stimulate hard thrusts. I can't wait to pound you. You, panting furiously in eat/eager anticipation, spread your hot quivering cheeks wider and wider as incentive to work more and more my thick cock inside your hungry box. The thrust of my prick, being hard and deep, will be buried forever in your upturned box as a delicious cry of joy and pain makes you draw to the edge of the bed, your quivering flesh pleading for more darkness. In and further in it continues—until you gag from its length and head. Your entire body feeling crammed full of cock, and without mercy, the rod bores further until balls collide and you let out pent-up breath. I hold you in muscular grasp and begin to fuck in long, slow deep thrusts, far into your aching body, driving, grinding my hard rod in pounding thrusts long and deep as your legs quiver and ass bounces back from every jab. Fucking you is more enjoyable than any other woman's cunt. Our excitement grows as our husky purpose pumps and pounds. Two beings in heaven, engulfed in tender embrace.

Fuck. I feel the tenseness of your muscular ass waiting for that hot load and continue to ram my prick until your upturned hot ass is wide open and I feel that hot come ready to pour forth like slick white iceing being smeared across twelve donuts at once. You groan as I give the final rams of that even harder cock and shoot in hot thick come-iceing (like lava filling your hole). I am greedy with new hunger for your body and unrelenting sex. See you Tuesday, when I will jab-fuck you.

Love, T.

There had been a "dear-Ruby" letter as well. She framed it behind the "li'on-letter" for posterity, Ray had to suppose.

Back in time, when Ray had been shown these letters, he felt the chances lessen for any real relationship with Ruby: there could be no measuring, comparing, coming up to such sensual promise. He remembered once when they had been lying in bed, enveloped in sheets of after-glow, and she had concluded her baffled women's lib braggadocio with a dazed, absent look to the cow's skull that had been tilted over her bedsted by the last tremor on the Richter scale (his braying bravo still clawed from within during those days): "Would you believe, he even dropped post cards in the mail to me" (she continued assassinating Ray's burrow brown furry anima). "I mean the landlady could even read what he was 'thinking' if she bothered. I never found out or cared if she did. She was German and used to sneak in and tidy up without my permission. Things like, on the card I mean, 'Ruby, thanks for the really neat note. I really think of you often and continue to go to bed alone, frustrated. It would surely be great to share an evening with you soon—if I can get out. Let's get it on; I miss being with you. Sincerely, T.' "

Sincerely, T. He probably can't forget the sex in the pool, or the self-portrait-tiger he drew, or the cops watching him be blown in the desert oral Santa-Ana condition, or, or, who knows what is in his demented mind? Sometimes Ruby confided in Ray that she would just like to be an old maid, earn her keep at the donut shop, shuffle to the back room at night when everything is cleaned, the counter, the floors, the heavy stainless steel and aluminum pans, the char-lined ovens; the paper napkin holders replenished, and the coins counted out neatly in piles and rolled. Maybe read some Keats, or Rod McKuen, or just turn on the tv, you know. Ray agreed that he couldn't imagine sending such revealing cards through the mail, but that it seemed that almost anything went these days.

Ray, at the time, had felt it must have taken real courage to divulge such letters, yet she had seemed unconscious of their potential danger to them. She seemed to be sleeping in a rose-scented, candle-lit niche of the Bellflower mortuary. Her dark hair accented by the white satin binding beneath her head in the sun-roofed backroom black casket just breezing along untainted—that was the ink drawing he saw of her. She was just breezing along thinking to herself, in a collected manner, hadn't there been some controversy about the plastic plants lining the boulevard in the L.A. Times? Hadn't housewives paraded along with placards refusing to allow such mediocrity in such a rich state of sunshine as was California? She seemed to be in the midst of some degree of self-flagellation outside and beyond the mortuary in her anathema of autoeroticism.

II.

Ray had no choice but to exit via Bellflower Boulevard. The black mortuary turned up its nose at him and someone turned off a light near the entrance. He thought he saw a red light in his rearview mirror although the bird cage and plants suspended for his exodus from the clothes hooks had fooled him. Waldo's half-emptied, feces-lined gravel sloshed in his aquarium on the floorboard. One of his eyes, for he had lost all color and turned on his side, focused on Ray like a peacoat button, huge and detached. A bird's nest fern spilt its dry potting soil into the tops of his shoes. It seemed uncanny that he hit no red lights although it was late and they were generally timed for something he never quite understood. A railroad crossing black-and-white bar fell before him. A potato-eater man in his crusty, too large black suit and oily baseball cap swung his dim red lantern before Ray's fog lights. Once he was cleared to pass, he glanced to the wrinkled mass beneath the cap's bill; it was his omnipresent, caryatidal friend from Long Beach. She was off-duty. He bit his lower lip in the chrome frame of the visor as T.'s oratorical powers reduced Ray to a new impotence. He thought of the eternal pot of coffee that had been "on" all night and her politeness. He thought of the sweet-smelling gladiola afghan over her eternally disheveled bedcovers, its yellow and orange variations on his loaned-life of walking in and out of her shop room. He thought of the mail delivery tomorrow and her note-comparing of cards and contents. She would have no guess work, there would be no T., no initial, only Ray's "X" that she had diminished to limpness. He would think of her articulate cheesecake-ways. Perhaps tomorrow, in the promised Loving City of the desert, Arcosanti, he would resort to skeet shooting (and find his skete; he noticed the early morning headlines tucked in the corner squawker's fist—he kept running back and forth from his banded stack of papers to the railroad crossing like the quick-change artist he was—JFK ASSASSINATED: then HOWARD HUGHES DEAD AT LAST, then PAN AM CRASH KILLS—one headline and its impact effacing the next, throw away pop-culture) and pay his dues away from the rigs that rolled past to a rendezvous of her awaiting delicacies. For Ray Landre it had become Ruby this and Ruby that; she was the headlines!

Ray could see the proverbial writing on the wall: all that was left was mobility. Walk. Run. Little seemed to matter. He had been unleashed, a mummy set free from the Long Beach arena. He would soon need his seconal and mescal, his nepenthe. He would be a resuscitated-corpse Tijuana-two-stepping about. Enraged and pacified on quaaludes. The departure of the Bellflower city proved to be the funest ride ever encountered. He chewed gum for an inward rehearsal, a Canticle for Ruby Francis or Variation on a Poem for Ruby. The dust and mold whistles up his shins and enfolds his unused, acrid genitals. He feels the pithy shaft in his swollen hands and brushes away the encasement, perhaps, by flexing it against, scrunching himself against the lower blades of a century plant; or makes love to it as a coached-John Wayne might. And there are to be rain showers and scorchers to weather in this futuristic city. The paranoia of the C.onstable O.f P.eace snaps manacles, metal sun-hot, about Ray's gonads, or worse clasps them about his brain, all-encompassing. There was to be no key, except the master key locked away in Bellflower; to release it, squirrels nibble at the cacti needle embedded in his scrotum.

The desert heat causes Ray Landre to remember that Ruby once told him that as a child she would take her grandmother's dimes and visit the Gym Theatre. She adored the Saturday matinees of the Tarzan serials. She was able to leave all outside the movie theatre. She would fidget in her seat as she became the fine ladies on the mammoth screen. One jungle film she described holds great significance in retrospect for Ray. She recalled screaming with pain when the white intruders would be captured by the natives. As a device of torture they would somehow innoculate a hive of wasps and weave them into grass mats much like the technique and appearance of a fan of popsickle sticks. Then they would tie the white man to a tree and hold the soon-to-revive wasp mat to his bare chest. The pain of the actor was excruciating. Ray concluded that she may have, symbolically/unconsciously, wanted to similarly torture him. Ray had read of the tarantula wasps of Arizona that most audaciously crawl into the crevice of their natural enemy and then drag the victim out where he is repeatedly stung, but not killed. After flailing it over the desert floor to insure that it is adequately doped, the wasp returns to its hole and deposits its egg on the stored-food. Ray now felt he was being saved for a colossal wasp matt to be drug across his bare chest. They are seen tearing at his flesh and he cannot see the hands that hold the mat. He thinks he sees bright red finger nail polish of the feminine fingers dab a styptic pencil that smarts yet heals. But as though the suffering is not enough, she drags Ray to his pre-arranged absorbing well where only dyastole and systole function. She had once admitted to having no female friends because of a sense of competition and their failure to meet the standards and qualities of her mother and grandmother, while she additionally knew no male friends because she had now reduced Ray to a sightless heart implanted in a desert trap with only electrodes, sun-driven, pumping, pumping, and aging some eight hundred years while the sands blow overhead. Remembering her 24 hour theory of aging, the baths, salts, creams, exercise, Ray felt then he must be aging every 24 seconds and that he would soon be the grain of sand to be cat-apulted into the side of large desert boulders to pock-mark and alter— to at least effect something. The yellow larkspur would again bloom.

Ray thought how far-fetched all of this would sound to Ruby. Or to his ex-landlord, or his family. Instead of becoming the movie actor, he placed a toll-free call to Arcosanti. The unisexed desk clerk assured that accommodations could be had in, say, six to eight months, and that the service was excellent, to be topped by none in the world. Walk. Run. Police. Nepenthe rushed him. The transfer to voice-mail concluded the salesman's pitch with promise of fine weather, a relaxed atmosphere, and that the pastries were superb. It all meant so little except that Ray now had a place to run to. His motor-movements would take approximately that long to dip into the dry valleys ahead as neon-lit cities dropped off the edge of the world behind him like mayflies endlessly dying.

Mayflies. Ray put one last question, one last wish to the service representative who had come back on the line: would there be a cycloramatic-television screen and video-taping equipment to allow one indelible fantasy for his incarceration? The scenario is precise: the Queen Mary, shuttled by huge ropes across the desert outside the bedroom window, booms a flat and elongated note to shatter the love-making in progress between Ray and Ruby (or what remains of her). A lady below the window is massacring a newly sprouted pep-per tree, "a living being." Ruby Francis keeps sobbing, because it drops leaves on her patio and is a nuisance. A piano on the turntable whispers a Beethoven concerto, but this is soon replaced by a pulsat-ing jungle rhythm of drums, drums. There is some smoking, some meditation, some fucking while standing before a mirror in the spare bedroom amidst African masks and headdresses of antelope and intense skin-stretched skulls with black natural hair and grasses for manes and beards. Fetishes and spool-dolls stand sentry on glass shelves. They find the camel-like head and massage teaspoonfuls of Crisco into it; they fondle it with baby oil. There is a slight slap on a bare white ass in the gentle night. Something about the mummy in Ray feels at home with this primeval fantasy as he will incessantly loll in his futuristic bedroom and munch on larkspur leaves (merely a matter of conditioning; small doses at first builds up miraculous immunities to poison and hurt). The Vivaldi Concerti for Diverse Instruments bring Ray down properly in Arcosanti. The tastefully designed wall-paper in his room is patterned with flourishs of R.F.'s and petrified insect and Ray is thankful for this one last fantasy as he is reminded of the AB on the Unicorn Tapistries as they flap against The Cloisters' walls, century after century after century.

III.

Ray IS IN THE DESERT NOW. The fever caused by the sun reminds him of two things. Ben Franklin, in his eighties, compared the ephemeral quality of the mayfly to that of human life and he longed for a lady friend. Ray wouldn't care to find himself wingless to drop into a tarn and dissolve to nothing. Nothing. And secondly, once in his youth, Ray had sent his father a series of snapshots. They captured various stages of a splendid setting sun over the Pacific Ocean taken from a high vantage point near Santa Monica. His reply, his put down was that the sun also set in his midwestern state. But he missed the point; the point was that he had never in his entire lifetime seen an ocean, a body of water any bigger than the Lake of the Ozarks. Ray pitied him. Ray had long since decided he would not die with such lack of initiative. So Ray chose to come to the desert and he has a plan. He feels an inherent need to disprove Celine's statement, "The truth of this world is to die," or at least a need to amend it, to die, yes, but to feel the death in all of its utter splendor.

Take this Paolo Soleri, he's considered by many to be a visionary architect. His plan is to burrow into the desert, to take hold, to survive in spite of death. Ray thinks that perhaps he is evolving to his own Arcosanti of the mind. He would prefer to find his harmony in becom-ing a pebble of sand, half or fully baked by the sun, and be kicked about a few millennia, not lost in the deterioration and evaporation of the mayfly wing. It is a logical extension of the swift kicks already delivered. Ruby's pointed toe in one buttock, the policeman's boot in the other (Waldo's hunger and suffocation somewhere in between). Ray recalled with chagrin his buddy Cleveland's evaluation: "Landre, you just can't allow yourself to reach out and love someone...Oh, sure, a Waldo, a fish in a tank, but not a kitten, or God forbid, another human being." Christ, Ray winced, no wonder he nonplused Ruby when it came to romance. T.E. Lawrence best professed the fruition of the pleasure-pain principal and the desert proves the ideal environment. He was right; Ray could count on the winds, the chafing, the fidelity of the succulents and wail of camel in the distance. No women to betray him, no mortician to scoff at him. Yes, the desert might well be the answer.

As that petulant wayfarer, he could be tortured with dignity.

- THE END -

EPILOGUE

CLOUDS

I cannot see it
out there on a chilling cloud
no directions to ever get there again

As science is, this too a mighty
image that dissipates like
a child almost touching cotton candy.

It is out there but I can't see it
ruminating, sexually active
ruining my first night performance

Applause for nothing resounds through
the distance up to the clouds
fondling me with cactus-like understanding.

I just can't see it...

SEASONAL

Ever notice Lily of the Nile
in Fall without its blue
or ever fear the spark's return
into the Winter's flue?

As Spring approaches I sometimes drew
fair portraits of your white face
then painted on sprightly blush of pink
for nature's lack of grace.

No cradle's rock nor call of geese
can match the turn of soil
the way you mount the ladder's rung
will benefit love's toil.

The meal you eat is square as mine
and rain the drink we crave
fizz of hummerwings the song we've sung
but 'til Summer quench
my tragic he-man's thirst
I keep you for my brew

and post delicate fleur-de-lis
scrawls to another land
dub them Winter-valentines
from a muse like sad me
till you rejuvenate my seasonless room
and recapture that which lost its bloom.

ISTANBUL

(For Bette Orbach, she who is full of life, a great sense of
adventure and, yes, Love)

I fear the slouching turtle has overlooked something
here in this land of anklebobs and tinkling dusty bells
and bitter black dots of eyes flashing a hidden femininity

this international airconditioned rosescented
vortex of three hills plunging into the Bosporus
suspended by the golden horn of donkeys and dirty feet

the populace daily congregates before the walls of
the bazaar and wash their male hands before entering
the mosque to pray/they fall prostrate in the earthen street

their starved limbs create a *vesica piscia* for
Christian tourists to walk on with their snapshot fingers
a bath is not a bath in the brisk unhurried dry treetops

I think ants could not penetrate the July crust
of barren soil; I think the splashes of water from the rite
do not even reach the parched soil; the soil dies as it thinks

up to caress, devour but never make contact

And as Ruby always said, "Well, my dear, that puts a period at the end of THAT sentence."

ACKNOWLEDGMENTS:

Lines from "Touch Your Solitude to Mine" from When Elephants Last in the Dooryard Bloomed, Alfred A. Knopf, 1973, reprinted with the kind permission of Mr. Ray Bradbury.

Lines from "The Love Song of J. Alfred Prufrock" in Collected Poems 1909-1962 by T.S. Eliot, copyright 1936 by Harcourt Brace Jovanovich, Inc.; copyright 1963, 1964 by T.S. Eliot. Reprinted by permission of the publisher.

Lines from Cannibals and Christians reprinted by permission of Norman Mailer and the author's agents, Scott Meredith Literary Agency, Inc., 845 Third Avenue, New York, New York 10022.

Lines from Collected Novellas reprinted by permission of Gabriel Garcia Marquez and publisher Harper Collins, New York.

Epigraph from "Oh, for a poet..." in The Children of the Night by Edwin Arlington Robinson, is reprinted with the permission of Charles Scribner's Sons.

Reprinted from An Artist in America by Thomas Hart Benton, by permission of the University of Missouri Press. Copyright 1968 by the author.

Mr. Herring's book title That Fine Inability to Speak permission for lines from Arthur Miller's short story "Fritter's Night" from his collection I Don't Need You Any More, Viking Press, New York, 1967.

Lines of verse on pages 89/90 of Mr. Herring's book of verse Pruning to Shape, Robert D. Reed Publishers, San Francisco, California.

From ESSAYS, SPEECHES & PUBLIC LETTERS BY WILLIAM FAULKNER by William Faulkner. Copyright (c) 1965 by Random House, Inc. Reprinted by permission of Random House, Inc.